Table of Contents

Level 1

Basic Facts Workshops

Level 2

Basic Facts Workshops

Level 3

Basic Facts Workshops

Level 4

Basic Facts Workshops

Level 5

Basic Skills Workshops

Level 6

Basic Skills Workshops

Just the Facts

A Systematic Practice Plan for Basic Facts and Skills

Knowledge of basic facts and development of computational skills is essential to all areas of mathematics. Facts and skills do for math what phonics and decoding do for reading: They build fluency. Just the Facts, used with Houghton Mifflin *Math Central* or independently, gives students at Level 1 through Level 6 opportunities throughout the school year to learn, to practice, and to master basic facts for addition, subtraction, multiplication, and division, as well as computational skills for whole numbers, fractions, and decimals.

Just the Facts is organized simply and is easy to use. Basic Facts Strategies outlines each strategy for every operation for easy teacher reference. The Houghton Mifflin Mathematics Correlation assists teachers who use this program in applying activities from Just the Facts. At each level, workshops with accompanying practice worksheets give students opportunities to master basic facts and skills. These are followed by Cumulative Practice pages, Answers, and Support Masters.

Basic Facts Strategies

This section is comprised of 13 charts—4 addition, 4 subtraction, and 5 multiplication—that define and illustrate the strategies students most often use to learn basic facts. These pages familiarize teachers with the strategies that are referenced throughout the workshops. At a glance, teachers are provided with an orientation to each of the strategies and corresponding facts.

Workshops and Worksheets

Teacher-directed workshops systematically develop strategies that build understanding and facilitate recall of basic facts and development of computational skills. With the workshops, teachers can review previously-taught operations. Developmentally appropriate workshops gradually foster students' self-confidence in using basic facts strategies. The two worksheets that accompany each workshop are reproducible. They provide both independent and cooperative opportunities to practice a particular skill and can be used in class or as homework.

Just the Facts *(continued)*

Basic Facts Workshops, Level 1 through Level 4

Workshops cover basic facts for addition, subtraction, multiplication, and division. These workshops use number patterns, visual models, and prior knowledge to introduce and to develop the strategy for learning a specific group of facts.

Students create manipulatives such as flash cards and spinners to practice basic facts independently or with a partner. Once students create and build a personal collection of flash cards for each group of facts, they can then use their own set of cards to cumulatively review and practice facts at school and at home. The Practice Minutes Records pages facilitate at-home practice of basic facts and promote family involvement in documenting student progress. As a result, students earn a Practice Award for their diligent efforts.

Basic Skills Workshops, Levels 5 and 6

The workshops approach a given topic using number sense. Individually, in pairs, or in small groups, students engage in activities designed to explore the topic and to practice and review the algorithm. Students at Levels 5 and 6 who need more practice or maintenance of basic facts can review workshops at Level 2 through Level 4.

As students progress through Basic Skills Workshops, they can use the My Math Handbook Support Master to create a journal that describes in their own words what they have learned. Students can use this later as a reference or to reflect on mathematics.

Cumulative Practice

Cumulative Practice pages can assist in basic facts practice, serve as a tool for review, or provide assessment. One way to use Cumulative Practice is to have students circle facts that belong to a specific strategy or strategies they have been studying and then have them answer only those facts. As students work toward mastery of basic facts, they can use Cumulative Practice for self-assessment. The teacher can also opt to administer the Cumulative Practice after students have demonstrated an understanding of strategies for learning basic facts.

Answers

Answers to worksheets at all levels and to the Cumulative Practice pages provide the teacher with a quick scoring reference.

Support Masters

Just the Facts Support Masters includes workmats, spinners, templates, grids, recording sheets, certificates, and the My Math Handbook page. Easily reproducible as transparencies or for multiple copies, the Support Masters are referenced by number in the workshops under Materials.

Basic Facts Strategies
Addition

Zero in Addition										
+	**0**	**1**	**2**	**3**	**4**	**5**	**6**	**7**	**8**	**9**
0	0+0	0+1	0+2	0+3	0+4	0+5	0+6	0+7	0+8	0+9
1	1+0									
2	2+0									
3	3+0									
4	4+0									
5	5+0									
6	6+0									
7	7+0									
8	8+0									
9	9+0									

When you add zero to a number, you get that number. When you add a number to zero, you get that number.

Counting on 1, 2, 3										
+	**0**	**1**	**2**	**3**	**4**	**5**	**6**	**7**	**8**	**9**
0										
1		1+1	1+2	1+3	1+4	1+5	1+6	1+7	1+8	1+9
2		2+1	2+2	2+3	2+4	2+5	2+6	2+7	2+8	2+9
3		3+1	3+2	3+3	3+4	3+5	3+6	3+7	3+8	3+9
4		4+1	4+2	4+3						
5		5+1	5+2	5+3						
6		6+1	6+2	6+3						
7		7+1	7+2	7+3						
8		8+1	8+2	8+3						
9		9+1	9+2	9+3						

Put the greater number in your head— count on from there the number that the lesser number indicates. For example: 8 + 2 . . . put 8 in your head and count on . . . 9, 10.

Doubles, Near Doubles

+	0	1	2	3	4	5	6	7	8	9
0										
1										
2										
3										
4					4+4	4+5	4+6			
5					5+4	5+5	5+6	5+7		
6					6+4	6+5	6+6	6+7	6+8	
7						7+5	7+6	7+7	7+8	7+9
8							8+6	8+7	8+8	8+9
9								9+7	9+8	9+9

Memorize doubles, then use them to figure out the near doubles. For example: "I know that 6 + 6 = 12, so 6 + 5 must be one less, or 11, and 6 + 7 must be one more, or 13."

Making a Ten

+	0	1	2	3	4	5	6	7	8	9
0										
1										
2										
3										
4								4+7	4+8	4+9
5									5+8	5+9
6										6+9
7					7+4					
8					8+4	8+5				
9					9+4	9+5	9+6			

9 + 5
One more makes ten
and 4 more makes 14. ➡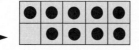

Basic Facts Strategies
Subtraction

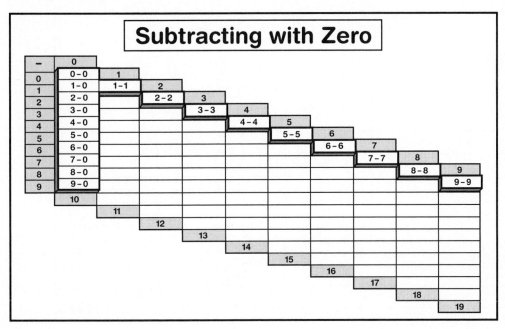

When you subtract zero from any number, you get the same number. When you subtract any number from itself you get zero.

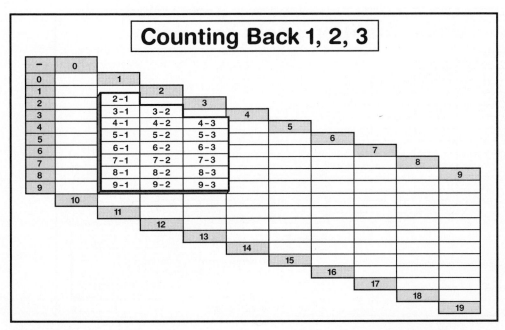

Put the greater number in your head. Count back the number of places indicated by the lesser number. For example: 6 — 2 . . . put 6 in your head and count back . . . 5, 4.

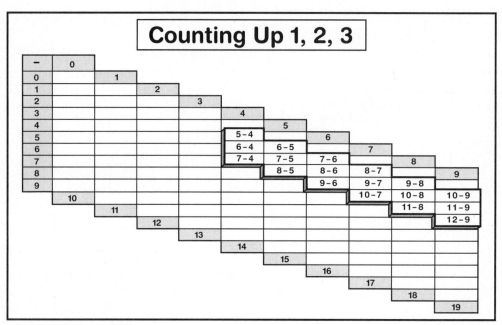

For example: 7 – 5. Start with the lesser number and keep track of how many numbers you count to get the greater number. Put 5 in you head, count . . . 6, 7– it took two numbers to get from 5 to 7 so the answer is 2.

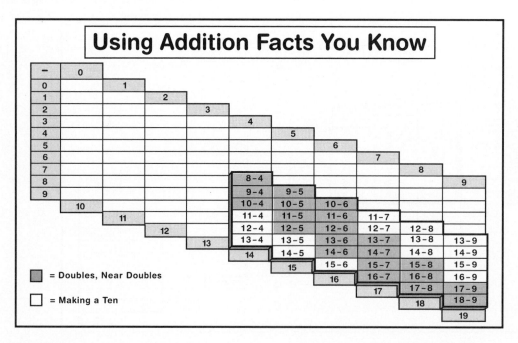

Use Doubles, Near Doubles and Making a Ten addition strategies to find these facts.

Basic Facts Strategies
Multiplication

Properties (0's, 1's)

x	0	1	2	3	4	5	6	7	8	9
0	0x0	0x1	0x2	0x3	0x4	0x5	0x6	0x7	0x8	0x9
1	1x0	1x1	1x2	1x3	1x4	1x5	1x6	1x7	1x8	1x9
2	2x0	2x1								
3	3x0	3x1								
4	4x0	4x1								
5	5x0	5x1								
6	6x0	6x1								
7	7x0	7x1								
8	8x0	8x1								
9	9x0	9x1								

Any fact in which zero is a factor results in a product of zero. The product of one times any factor is that factor.

Skip Counting (3's, 5's)

x	0	1	2	3	4	5	6	7	8	9
0										
1										
2						2x5				
3				3x3	3x4	3x5	3x6	3x7	3x8	3x9
4				4x3		4x5				
5			5x2	5x3	5x4	5x5	5x6	5x7	5x8	5x9
6				6x3		6x5				
7				7x3		7x5				
8				8x3		8x5				
9				9x3		9x5				

Skip-count by 3's and by 5's to find these facts.

Doubles (2's, 4's)

x	0	1	2	3	4	5	6	7	8	9
0										
1										
2			2x2	2x3	2x4		2x6	2x7	2x8	2x9
3			3x2							
4			4x2		4x4		4x6	4x7	4x8	4x9
5										
6			6x2		6x4					
7			7x2		7x4					
8			8x2		8x4					
9			9x2		9x4					

In this strategy, relate learning the 2's to learning the 4's. For example, since $2 \times 3 = 6$, then 4×3 is double 6, or 12.

Using Tens (9's)

x	0	1	2	3	4	5	6	7	8	9
0										
1										
2										2x9
3										3x9
4										4x9
5										5x9
6										6x9
7										7x9
8										8x9
9			9x2	9x3	9x4	9x5	9x6	9x7	9x8	9x9

Use multiplying by 10 to multiply by 9. For example, to find 7×9 think $7 \times 10 = 70$. Subtract the 7, the factor that is not a multiple of 10, from the product ($70 - 7 = 63$).

Use What You Know (6's, 7's, 8's)

x	0	1	2	3	4	5	6	7	8	9
0										
1										
2										
3										
4										
5										
6							6x6	6x7	6x8	6x9
7							7x6	7x7	7x8	7x9
8							8x6	8x7	8x8	8x9
9							9x6	9x7	9x8	9x9

Previous strategies have introduced facts for 6, 7, and 8 multiplied by 1, 2, 3, 4, 5, and 9. The remaining facts to be learned are 6 × 6, 6 × 7, 6 × 8, 7 × 7, 7 × 8, and 8 × 8. Use patterns from other facts.

Basic Facts Strategies
Division

Students can master most division facts from previously–learned multiplication facts. There are two uses of 1 in division.

Dividing by 1
Any number divided by 1 is that number.
Example: 7 ÷ 1 = 7

Dividing by All
Any number divided by itself is 1.
Example: 7 ÷ 7 = 1

HMM Correlation

Level 4

Workshop	Suggested use:
1. Fact Families	Module 1, use anytime
2. Multiplying and Dividing by 2	Module 1, after Section A
3. Multiplying and Dividing by 4	Module 1, after Section B
4. Multiplying and Dividing by 5	Module 2, after Section A
5. Multiplying and Dividing by 1	Module 2, after Section C
6. Multiplying and Dividing by 3	Module 3, after Section A
7. Reviewing 1's-5's and 0's	Module 3, after Section C
8. Multiplying and Dividing by 9	Module 4, after Section A
9. Multiplying and Dividing by 6	Module 4, after Section C
10. Multiplying and Dividing by 7	Module 5; use anytime
11. Multiplying and Dividing by 8	Module 6; use anytime
12. Review 6, 7, 8, and 9	Module 7; use anytime
13. Review Multiplication and Division Facts	Module 8; use anytime

Level 5

Workshop	Suggested use:
1. Addition and Subtraction: Mental Math Strategies	Module 1, use anytime
2. Multiplication and Division: Mental Math Strategies	Module 2, after Section B
3. Adding 2- and 3-Digit Whole Numbers	Module 1, after Section B
4. Subtracting 2- and 3-Digit Whole Numbers	Module 2, after Section A
5. Multiplying 2-Digit Numbers	Module 2, after Section B
6. Dividing by 1-Digit Divisors	Module 2, after Section D
7. Fractions: Comparing and Ordering	Module 4, after Section C
8. Fractions: Greatest Common Factors and Simplifying	Module 4, after Section B
9. Adding and Subtracting Fractions with Like Denominators	Module 4, after Section D
10. Adding Fractions with Unlike Denominators	Module 4, after Section D
11. Subtracting Fractions with Unlike Denominators	Module 4, after Section D
12. Decimals: Comparing and Ordering	Module 5, after Section A
13. Adding and Subtracting Decimals	Module 5, after Section C

Level 6

Workshop	Suggested use:
1. Adding and Subtracting 2- and 3-Digit Numbers	Module 1, after Section A
2. Multiplying 2- and 3-Digit Numbers	Module 1, after Section C
3. Dividing by 1-Digit Divisors	Module 3, after Section D
4. Dividing by 2-Digit Divisors	Module 3, after Section D
5. Fractions: Greatest Common Factors and Simplifying	Module 6, after Section A
6. Adding and Subtracting Fractions	Module 2, after Section C
7. Multiplying Fractions	Module 4, after Section B
8. Dividing Fractions	Module 1, after Section B
9. Decimals: Comparing and Ordering	Module 1, after Section B
10. Adding and Subtracting Decimals	Module 2, after Section A
11. Multiplying Decimals	Module 3, after Section B
12. Dividing Decimals	Module 3, after Section D
13. Ratio and Percent	Module 6, after Section B

Basic Facts Workshop 1

Readiness: Counting

Introduce It!

20 minutes

Counting Names

Management whole class
Materials name card per child, one set of number cards 1–10

- Hold up each child's name card individually and have the child read it. Ask the class to count the number of letters in the name. Then have the child retrieve the name card.

- When all cards have been distributed, hold up a number card. Ask all of the children with that many letters in their name to stand up. Then have them sit down. Have classmates help one another to decide

when to stand. Repeat with other numbers until every child has had a turn to get up.

- Ask, Which number of letters in a name is the largest group in our class? Which number of letters is the smallest group in our class? How can we be sure? **Count the members of each group.**

Tips

You may want to count children as they stand and record the number of children in each group.

Develop It!

25 minutes

Putting Names Together

Management whole class
Materials name card per child

- Ask a pair of children to stand up with their name cards. Have classmates count how many letters are in both names together. Repeat several times with different pairs of children.

- Have children form two lines so each child has a partner. Have each pair, in turn, hold up their name cards and tell how many letters are in their two names together.

- After each pair reports their combined name count, ask the front child in one line to go to the back of that line. Have everyone else in that line step forward to find a new partner.

- New partners may find the total number of letters in their combined names and report to the class. Continue the activity by asking the front child in the same line to step to the back of that line.

Tips

If children know how many letters are in their names, they may count on their partner's letters for a total.

Make It!

15 minutes

Name Chart

Management individuals
Materials chart paper, adding machine tape or grid strips, construction paper

- Cut and distribute lengths of adding machine tape (which has been pre-divided into squares) or grid strips to each child. Ask them how many squares they need to write the letters of their first name.

- Have children print their first names on the strips, glue the strips to construction paper, and write the number of letters.

- The children place their names on the chart according to the number of letters in them. They can paste their names in place on the chart for a class record.

Tips

Remind children to write each letter of their name in a separate square on the strip.

Basic Facts Workshop 2

Readiness: The Ten-Frame Model

Introduce It!

15 minutes

Organizing Numbers

Management whole class

Materials overhead projector, transparency of ten frame, counters

- Place ten counters randomly on the overhead projector. Quickly turn the projector on and off. Ask children how many counters they saw.

- Turn the projector back on and count the number of counters together, touching a counter as each number is said.

- Explain that it would be easier to tell how many there are if the counters were organized. Show the ten-frame transparency on the overhead.

- Why do you think this is called a ten frame? **There are ten boxes.** If I put one counter in each box, how many counters will I use? **10** Place counters in the top row of the ten frame from left to right, then in the bottom row as children count with you.

- Ask volunteers to show other numbers on the ten frame. Have the class identify how many counters are shown, and tell how many more are needed to make a ten.

Develop It!

15 minutes

Count, Write, and Switch

Management pairs

Materials overhead projector, transparency of ten frame, counters

- Have children work with a partner.

- Using the overhead projector, put counters on the ten frame to show a number from 1 to 10.

- One child writes the numeral that tells how many counters they see. The partner checks for accuracy. Children then switch roles.

- Repeat the activity several times so each partner will have an opportunity to write most numerals from 1–10.

Tips

This is another opportunity to check on the progress of children's numeral-writing skills.

Make It!

Ten-Frame Practice

 20 minutes

Management pairs
Materials 12 index cards, counters, ten frames

- Distribute 12 index cards to pairs of children. Have them write the numerals 1-12, one on each card.

- Distribute a ten frame and 12 counters to each pair.

- Ask pairs to mix their number cards and place them face-down. As one child turns over a card, the partner shows that number with counters on the ten frame. Children can check their results, then switch roles.

Tips

Have children retain their ten frames for future use.

Basic Facts Workshop 3

Readiness: Part-Part-Whole Model

Introduce It!

15 minutes

Introducing Parts and Whole

Management whole class

Materials overhead projector, teacher-made transparency of part-part-whole mat (Just the Facts Support Master 2), 6 counters

- Show six counters on the projector. Place them at the top of the part-part-whole transparency. Ask children how many they see. **6**

- Pick up the six counters and drop them on the projector so they fall on both sides of the line. Ask, How many counters are on this side? That's one part of six. How many are on the other side? That's the other part of six.

- Remind children that this shows two parts (e.g. two and four) that make up the whole, six. We can show other parts that make up the whole, six.

- Repeat several times by shaking and dropping the counters to show a variety of part-part-whole relationships for six.

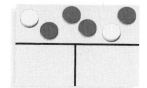

Tips

Have children state each relationship.

Develop It!

15 minutes

Parts of 5

Management individuals

Materials chart paper, 5 counters per child

- Have each child take five counters and shake them in both hands. Then tell children to open their hands with some counters in each.

- Ask children to describe how the counters in their hands show five. For example, three counters and two counters make five counters in all. Draw two hands on chart paper or on the board, and write the numeral 5 above them. Below the hands, record each combination of five as children report it. (3 and 2, 1 and 4, 0 and 5, etc.)

- Have children shake their counters again, and then open their hands and describe the new configuration. Repeat several times and continue recording.

Tips

Have children describe all the possible ways to show five.

Hands Mat

15 minutes

Management pairs

Materials file folders, construction paper, scissors, glue, 6 two-sided counters per child

- Have each child make a hands mat. Children should work in pairs to trace each other's hands on construction paper.

- Children can glue cut-out hands to construction paper or file folders, which can be used later for storing children's work.

- Distribute six counters to each child. The child shakes the counters in both hands, drops them and puts all of one color on one construction paper hand, the rest on the other one. Then the child reports, "I have three red and three white, I have six in all," for example.

- This activity may be used repeatedly over time to give children experience with the part-part-whole model. Use different numbers of counters each time, and show children how to record as they become ready.

- Collect and save hands mats to use in future workshops.

Tips

Show children who are ready, how to print numerals to record the whole and the two parts on paper. Save hands mats for future workshops.

Basic Facts Workshop 4

Readiness: Part-Part-Whole Model

Introduce It!

20 minutes

Parts of 10

Management whole class

Materials overhead projector, teacher-made transparency of part-part-whole mat (Just the Facts Support Master 2), 10 overhead pennies

- Place ten pennies on the "whole" section of the part-part-whole transparency. Ask children how many they see. **ten** Remove the pennies and write the number 10.

- Place six pennies on one part of the mat. Ask, How many pennies do you see? **six** If there are ten pennies in all and one part is six, how many are in the other part? **four**

- Place four pennies in the other part. Move both parts into the whole section and count to verify a total of ten. Remove the pennies. Record the parts on the transparency as you say, 6 and 4 make 10. Ask a volunteer to record the matching number sentence. **6 + 4 = 10**

- Repeat with other names for ten.

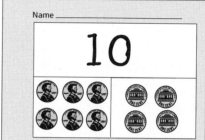

Develop It!

15 minutes

Heads and Tails

Management pairs

Materials hands mats (from Workshop 3: two hands traced on paper), 10 pennies per pair

- Provide each pair of children with ten pennies and a hands mat. Children take turns shaking ten pennies and placing them on the mat, separating the coins into heads and tails.

- Ask children to "read" their mats, naming the two parts and the whole (e.g., I have 3 heads and 7 tails. That's 10 in all.) Record responses on the board under the number 10.

- Repeat using nine coins, having children "read" their mats, and recording combinations on the chalkboard under the number 9.

- Repeat using eight coins.

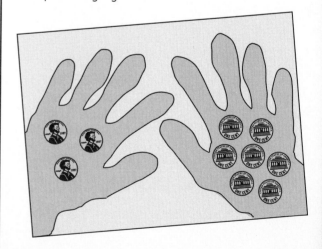

20 minutes

Heads and Tails Charts

Management small groups

Materials 10 pennies and one hands mat per group, 6 sheets of chart paper with headings

- Divide the class into six groups. Each group will be responsible for making a chart for a different number from five to ten.

- Distribute one chart to each group. Pre-record headings on charts with one of the numbers 5, 6, 7, 8, 9, or 10 at the top. Under the number, write the headings *Heads* and *Tails*.

- Each group uses the number of pennies shown at the top of their chart. They take turns shaking and separating heads and tails, and recording all of the different combinations.

- When finished, groups may report combinations they found to the class.

	8	
Heads		**Tails**
8		0
5		3
4		4
2		6
7		1
3		5
6		2

Tips

For further practice, have each group repeat the activity with a different number, then compare their chart with the previously made chart for that number. Did they find any new combinations?

Basic Facts Workshop 5

Readiness: Exploring Zero

Introduce It!

15 minutes

Zeros in Addition

Management whole class
Materials overhead projector and marker, blank transparency, ten counters

- Show four counters on a blank transparency on the projector. Ask children how many they see. **four** Tell children you're going to add counters while they close their eyes. Do not add any counters. Ask children to open their eyes and identify how many counters you added. **none** What number tells how many I added? **zero** Write 4 + 0 = 4.

- Next show five counters on the transparency. Follow the same procedure as above but when children close their eyes, move the five counters around into a new configuration. Ask, How many are there in all? **five** What number tells how many I added? **zero** Write 5 + 0 = 5.

- Repeat with children taking turns showing from 1–9 counters and adding zero. Record the appropriate number sentence each time.

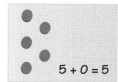

5 + 0 = 5

Tips

If children seem ready, ask them to write the number sentences.

Develop It!

15 minutes

Zeros in Subtraction

Management whole class
Materials overhead projector and marker, blank transparency, ten counters

- Show five counters on a blank transparency on the projector. Ask children how many they see. **five** Remove all five counters. Ask children how many you took away. **five** Ask children what number tells how many counters are left. **zero** Write 5 − 5 = 0.

- Repeat with a few numbers 1–9, removing all counters each time and recording the number sentences.

- Show three counters. Ask how many children see. **three** Tell children you are going to take some away while they close their eyes. Do not remove any counters. Ask children how many counters are left and what number tells how many you took away. **three, zero** Write 3 − 0 = 3. Repeat with other numbers.

Tips

Ask a volunteer to come up and "take away" zero from a number of counters.

Make It!

30 minutes

Make a Zero Spinner

Management pairs

Materials 3-part spinner (Just the Facts Support Master 5, paper clip, and ten counters per pair

- Distribute a 3-part spinner, a paper clip, and 10 counters to each pair of children. Have them write +0, −0, and − in the three spinner sections.

- Show children how to use a paper clip and a pencil to create a spinner.

- One partner selects any number of counters and places them on the table. The other partner spins the spinner to determine and carry out an action (add 0, subtract 0, or subtract all counters.)

- The first partner records the number sentence.

- Repeat, with partners taking turns.

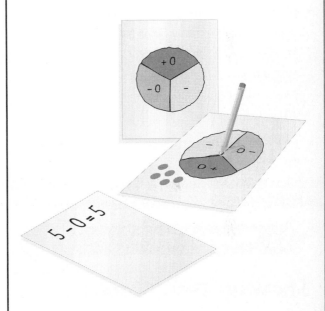

Tips

Initially, monitor groups to make sure they are carrying out the appropriate action and recording the number sentences.

Basic Facts Workshop 6

Readiness: Double Ten-Frames

Introduce It!

15 minutes

Ten and More

Management whole class

Materials overhead projector, teacher-made double ten-frame transparency (Just the Facts Support Master 3), 20 overhead counters in 2 colors (10 each)

- Fill the top ten frame on a double ten-frame transparency. Ask children how many counters they see. **10**

- Place three counters of a second color on the bottom frame. Ask children how many they see. **3** Write 10 + 3.

- How many counters are there in all? Write the sum. **13**

- Clear all counters from the ten frames.

- Write 15. Ask the class how to show that number on the ten frames. **10 on the top, 5 on the bottom** Write 10 + 5 = 15

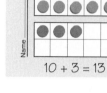

$10 + 3 = 13$

- Repeat with 14, 16, and 17.

Tips

This is a good opportunity to ask children whether they notice a pattern in the number sentences. Encourage them to describe patterns.

Develop It!

15 minutes

Showing Teen Numbers

Management pairs

Materials each pair needs: double ten-frame workmat (Just the Facts Support Master 3), 19 counters

- Distribute a double ten-frame workmat and 19 counters to each pair.

- Write 14. Ask pairs to show 14 on their workmats. **10 on the top frame, 4 on the bottom**

- Write 17 and say, Now show me 17.

- Repeat, having pairs show 18, 15, 13, 12, and 16.

- Watch for pairs who remove or add counters without

clearing the mats and starting over. Ask these pairs to share their strategy. **All of the teen numbers have 10 and some more, so it saves time to leave the top frame filled.**

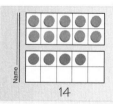

14

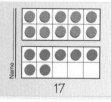

17

Tips

Suggest that as children work in pairs, they take turns showing answers so that both children have an opportunity to participate.

Spin and Show

20 minutes

> **Management** pairs
>
> **Materials** each pair needs: 20 counters, paper clip, pencil, double ten-frame workmat and 6-section spinner (Just the Facts Support Masters 3 and 6)

- Distribute spinners and have children label the sections 12, 13, 14, 16, 17, and 18.

- Remind children how to use a pencil and paper clip to create an arrow that attaches to the spinner.

- Distribute a double ten-frame workmat and counters to each pair.

- One partner spins to select a teen number, and the other partner models the number on the double ten-frame workmat and records (for example, 10 + 2 = 12).

- Partners switch roles. Each partner should have at least ten turns.

Tips

Note which pairs continue to use the strategy of leaving ten counters on the top frame and adding to the bottom frame only.

Basic Facts Workshop 7

Readiness: Order Property

Introduce It!

15 minutes

Front and Back

Management whole class
Materials none

- Have five children stand in a row with the first two facing the class and the other three facing away. Ask, What part of the group is facing you? **2** What part is not facing you? **3** What addition sentence can we write about this group? **2 + 3 = 5**

- Have the group link arms and turn so 3 children are facing the class and 2 are facing away. Ask, What addition sentence can we write about the group now? **3 + 2 = 5**

- Ask children what they notice about these addition sentences. **The numbers are in different order, but there are still five in all.**

- Repeat the activity with other groups of children to model 4 + 3 = 7 and 3 + 4 = 7; 1 + 2 = 3 and 2 + 1 = 3; and 5 + 3 = 8 and 3 + 5 = 8.

Tips

If some children have difficulty understanding the order property, review the concept of joining sets.

Develop It!

15 minutes

Flip and Record

Management whole class
Materials connecting cubes in two colors

- Show the class a cube train with two cubes of one color and four cubes of another color.

- Ask a volunteer to write a number sentence on the board to name the train. **2 + 4 = 6**

- Flip the cube train over and ask the volunteer to write the new number sentence. **4 + 2 = 6**

- Repeat the activity with cube trains for 8 + 2 and 2 + 8; 3 + 4 and 4 + 3; 5 + 1 and 1 + 5; and 4 + 5 and 5 + 4.

$2+4=6$ $4+2=6$

Tips

Children may benefit from additional practice by working with a partner to make their own cube trains and writing the corresponding number sentences.

Make It!

Practice Recording Order

20 minutes

Management whole class
Materials index cards, large paper clips

- Distribute one index card and some paper clips to each child.

- Each child should model one addition sentence by attaching paper clips to opposite edges of the card.

- Have one child show a card to the class. Each child writes the appropriate number sentence. Then, the child flips the card over and the class writes a second number sentence.

- Each child shares his or her card, then flips it, and the class writes both number sentences.

Tips

Extend practicing the order property with classroom objects.

Basic Facts Workshop 8

Strategy: Counting On to Add

Introduce It!

15 minutes

Counting on 1, 2, 3

Management whole class
Materials 10 counters, paper bag

- Hold up a set of five counters. Ask the class how many they see. Write 5 on the board. Put the counters in a paper bag one at a time as you count up to five.

- Hold up two more counters. Ask children how they can count on to find how many counters there are in all. Say, Put the five in your head, count on. . .five, six, seven. Put the last two counters in the bag as you count on. Write 5 + 2 = 7.

- Repeat the activity, having children count on to find 6 + 3, 4 + 1, 7 + 3, 5 + 2, and 8 + 1.

Tips

Help make connections to children's own lives by asking them to name situations when they might count on to add.

Develop It!

25 minutes

Spin and Count On

Management pairs
Materials each pair needs: 3-section spinner and 6-section spinner (Just the Facts Support Masters 5 and 6), 2 paper clips, and 2 pencils

- Distribute the 3-section and 6-section spinners to each pair.

- Have them write 4, 5, 6, 7, 8, 9 on the 6-section spinner and +1, +2, +3 on the 3-section spinner.

- Distribute paper clips and pencils for children to make a pointer-arrow for each of the two spinners.

- One partner spins both spinners. The other partner records an addition sentence. (Example: 6 + 3 = 9)

- Partners switch roles. Repeat until each partner has had at least ten turns.

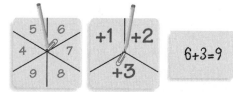

Tips

A common error children make is not beginning with the greater addend. Help them to see that it is easier to count on from the greater addend.

Make It!

Make Counting On Flash Cards

30 minutes

Management individuals

Materials for each child: 45 white index cards, envelope or plastic bag, practice minutes record and certificate (Just the Facts Support Masters 9 and 13)

- Have children make flash cards as shown.

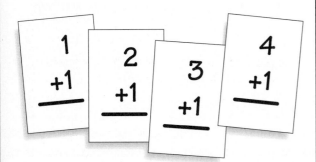

$$
\begin{array}{ccccccccc}
5 & 6 & 7 & 8 & 9 & 1 & 1 & 1 & 1 \\
+1 & +1 & +1 & +1 & +1 & +2 & +3 & +4 & +5 \\
\end{array}
$$

$$
\begin{array}{ccccccccc}
1 & 1 & 1 & 1 & 2 & 3 & 4 & 5 & 6 \\
+6 & +7 & +8 & +9 & +2 & +2 & +2 & +2 & +2 \\
\end{array}
$$

$$
\begin{array}{ccccccccc}
7 & 8 & 9 & 2 & 2 & 2 & 2 & 2 & 2 \\
+2 & +2 & +2 & +3 & +4 & +5 & +6 & +7 & +8 \\
\end{array}
$$

$$
\begin{array}{ccccccccc}
2 & 3 & 3 & 3 & 3 & 3 & 3 & 3 & 4 \\
+9 & +3 & +4 & +5 & +6 & +7 & +8 & +9 & +3 \\
\end{array}
$$

$$
\begin{array}{ccccc}
5 & 6 & 7 & 8 & 9 \\
+3 & +3 & +3 & +3 & +3 \\
\end{array}
$$

- When finished, children can work with a partner to use their flash cards to practice counting on to add.

- Children may continue to practice at home, recording practice minutes.

- The completed practice minutes record may be exchanged for a certificate.

Tips

Remind children to initial their flash cards so they do not become mixed up with classmates' cards.

Basic Facts Workshop 9

Strategy: Counting Back to Subtract

Introduce It!

20 minutes

Counting Back 1, 2, 3

Management whole class

Materials overhead projector, 10 counters, large index card

- Place seven counters on the projector and cover them with a card. Tell the class you have covered seven counters.

- Move two counters into view.

- Ask, How many counters did I cover? **7** How many counters did I show? **2** To find how many are still covered, start at 7 and count back 2. Think 7. . . count 6, 5.

- Remove the card to show the answer. Write $7 - 2 = 5$.

- Repeat the activity to model $5 - 1$, $8 - 2$, $7 - 3$, $9 - 2$, $6 - 1$, and $9 - 3$.

Tips

Remind children to start with the number they are subtracting from and count back the number being subtracted.

Develop It!

20 minutes

Spin and Count Back

Management pairs

Materials each pair needs: 2 paper clips and two pencils, 3-section spinner and 6-section spinner (Just the Facts Support Masters 5 and 6)

- Distribute a 3-section and a 6-section spinner to each pair.

- Have children write -1, -2, -3 on the 3-section spinner, and 12, 11, 10, 9, 8, 7 on the 6-section spinner.

- Distribute paper clips and pencils for children to make a pointer for each of the spinners.

- One partner spins each spinner. The other partner records a number sentence using the two numbers.

- Partners switch roles. Each partner should have at least ten turns.

12-3=9

Tips

Children who need additional support may want to use counters to act out the number sentences.

Make It!

Make Counting Back Flash Cards

20 minutes

Management individuals or pairs

Materials 21 white index cards for each child, practice minutes record and certificate (Just the Facts Support Masters 10 and 14)

- Have children make flash cards as shown below.

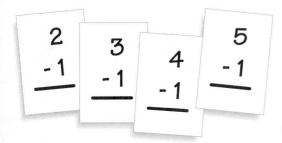

$$
\begin{array}{cccccccc}
2 & 3 & 4 & 5 & 6 & 7 & 8 & 9 \\
-1 & -1 & -1 & -1 & -1 & -1 & -1 & -1 \\
\hline
\end{array}
$$

$$
\begin{array}{ccccccc}
3 & 4 & 5 & 6 & 7 & 8 & 9 \\
-2 & -2 & -2 & -2 & -2 & -2 & -2 \\
\hline
\end{array}
$$

$$
\begin{array}{cccccc}
4 & 5 & 6 & 7 & 8 & 9 \\
-3 & -3 & -3 & -3 & -3 & -3 \\
\hline
\end{array}
$$

- When finished, children should find a partner and use their flash cards to practice subtracting by counting back.

- Children may combine these flash cards with the previously made flash cards and continue practice at home, recording practice minutes.

- Completed practice records may be returned to school to be exchanged for a certificate.

Tips

Remind children to write their initials or names on the back of each card.

Basic Facts Workshop 10

Strategy: Counting Up to Subtract

Introduce It!

15 minutes

Count Up If It's Close

Management whole class

Materials overhead projector, teacher-made part-part-whole transparency (Just the Facts Support Master 2), 12 counters

- Show nine counters on the whole section of the transparency. Ask children how many they see. Write 9.

- Cover the transparency with a sheet of paper. Slide seven counters to one part of the mat and two counters to the other part.

- Reveal the seven counters and have children count them. Remind them you started with 9 and they know one part is 7.

- Ask, How many counters are in the other part? One way to find out is to count up. Start with 7, think 8, 9. How many did you count up? **2** Reveal the two counters and then write $9-7=2$.

- Repeat the activity for $7-4$, $8-6$, $6-5$, and $7-5$.

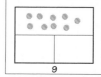
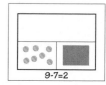

Tips

To check whether children understand the part-part-whole concept, ask volunteers to name and discuss the parts and the whole of each number sentence.

Develop It!

20 minutes

Count Up Trains

Management whole class

Materials 12 connecting cubes

- Show the class a train of nine cubes, then put it behind your back.

- Keep three cubes behind your back and show children the train of six cubes. Remind children you started with nine and broke off six.

- Ask, How many are hiding behind my back? **3** Have children explain how they knew the answer. **Possible answer: I started with 6, then counted 7, 8, 9. That is 3 more.**

- Ask a volunteer to write a number sentence showing the whole, the part he or she knew, and the part that was determined. $9 - 6 = 3$.

- Repeat the activity for $12-9$, $8-6$, $11-9$, $7-4$, and $8-7$.

Tips

By asking children to explain the strategy they used, you can assess how well children use the counting up strategy as well as other strategies.

Make Count Up Flash Cards

30 minutes

Management individuals

Materials for each child: 18 orange index cards, practice minutes record and certificate (Just the Facts Support Masters 9 and 13)

- Distribute index cards. Have children make flash cards for the facts shown here.

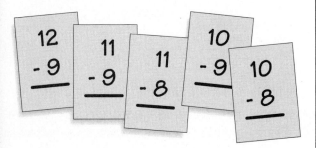

$$\begin{array}{ccccccc} 10 & 9 & 9 & 9 & 8 & 8 & 8 \\ -7 & -8 & -7 & -6 & -7 & -6 & -5 \end{array}$$

$$\begin{array}{cccccc} 7 & 7 & 7 & 6 & 6 & 5 \\ -6 & -5 & -4 & -5 & -4 & -4 \end{array}$$

- When finished, children should find a partner and use their flash cards to practice subtraction by counting up.

- After practicing at school, children may continue practicing at home, recording practice minutes and returning the record to school to be exchanged for a certificate.

Tips

Store flash cards in numbered plastic bags. If children are assigned one number for the year, they can quickly retrieve their numbered bag. Use for other manipulatives as well.

Basic Facts Workshop 11

Strategy: Using Doubles to Add

Introduce It!

15 minutes

Unfolding Doubles

Management whole class
Materials construction paper, hole puncher

- Fold a piece of construction paper in half and punch six holes. Ask children to count the number of holes in the paper.

- Ask the class how many holes the paper will have when it is opened. **12**

- Have children identify the number sentence shown by the unfolded paper. Write $6+6=12$ on the board.

- Repeat the activity with the doubles for 5, 7, 4, 9 and 8.

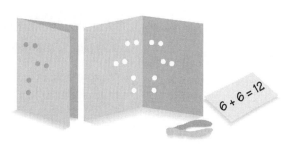

Tips

It may take several rounds of practice before some children understand that the number of holes doubles when the paper is opened.

Develop It!

20 minutes

Doubles and One More

Management whole class
Materials construction paper with holes from Part 1, hole puncher

- Hold up the paper from the first activity that shows double sevens. Ask the class to name the doubles fact shown, then write $7+7=14$ on the board.

- Punch another hole in one side of the paper. Ask children what fact is shown now. Write $7+8=15$.

- Ask children how knowing the double can help you find the double plus-1 fact. **7 + 7 = 14, so 7 + 8 is one more, or 15.**

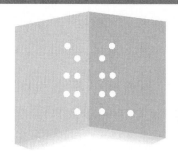

- Write $7+6$ on the chalkboard. Ask children what double can help to find this fact. **6 + 6 and one more; 7 + 7 and one less is also acceptable**

- Write the following facts on the board: $4+5$, $5+6$, $8+7$, $6+7$, $9+8$

- Ask children to identify doubles that can help them give the answers to the number expressions. Then ask, Can you think of a double that will help you find the answer to two of these number expressions at once?

Make It!

Make Doubles Flash Cards

30 minutes

Management individuals

Materials for each child: 16 blue index cards, practice minutes record and certificate (Just the Facts Support Masters 9 and 13)

- Distribute index cards and have children make a flash card for each of the facts shown here.

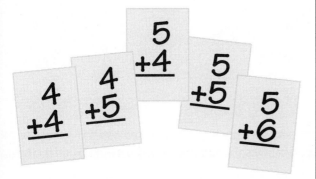

$$
\begin{array}{cccccc}
6 & 6 & 6 & 7 & 7 & 7 \\
+5 & +6 & +7 & +6 & +7 & +8 \\
\end{array}
$$

$$
\begin{array}{ccccc}
8 & 8 & 8 & 9 & 9 \\
+7 & +8 & +9 & +8 & +9 \\
\end{array}
$$

- Working with a partner, children should use their flash cards to practice adding with doubles.

- Children may continue at home, recording practice minutes and returning the completed record to school to be exchanged for a certificate.

Tips

Create a special time for review. Take 10 minutes and have children review facts using different sets of flash cards.

Basic Facts Workshop 12

Strategy: Using Doubles to Subtract

Introduce It!

15 minutes

Doubles Are No Trouble

Management whole class

Materials overhead projector, several teacher-made part-part-whole transparencies (Just the Facts Support Master 2), 20 counters

- Show eight counters on the whole section of a part-part-whole transparency. Ask children how many they see.

- Ask children how many of the eight counters should go on each part if we want to have equal parts. **4** Slide the counters down.

- Cover one part with paper. Then ask children, If the whole is 8 and we know one part is 4, what is the other part? **4** Write 8−4=4.

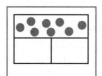 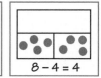

- Repeat, using 10, 12, 6, 14, 18, and 16 counters to identify wholes and parts, and write subtraction sentences.

Tips

Help children to first notice and then describe any patterns they see when doubling numbers.

Develop It!

15 minutes

Near Doubles and the Missing Part

Management whole class

Materials overhead projector, several teacher-made part-part-whole transparencies (Just the Facts Support Master 2), 20 counters

- Show nine counters on the whole section of a part-part-whole transparency. Ask children how many they see.

- Cover the transparency with paper and slide the counters down, putting four on one part and five on the other part. Uncover the transparency to show four counters on one part.

- Write 9 − 4 = . Remind children you started with 9 and they know one part is 4.

- Ask children to determine the other part. Emphasize they should think about doubles to find the missing part. Then ask, Could it be 4? **No** Why? **4 and 4 is only 8. We need one more, or 5, to make 9.**

- Complete the number sentence 9−4=5.

- Then, write 9 − 5 = ____. Ask, How could you find the missing part using doubles? **5 and 5 is 10 and 1 less is 4.**

- Repeat using other examples.

30 minutes

Make Doubles Subtraction Flash Cards

Management individuals or pairs

Materials Each child needs: 16 blue index cards, previously made set of flash cards, practice minutes record and certificate (Just the Facts Support Masters 10 and 14)

- Distribute index cards and have children make flash cards for the doubles and near-doubles facts shown.

$$
\begin{array}{ccccc}
8 & 9 & 9 & 10 & 11 \\
-4 & -4 & -5 & -5 & -6 \\
\end{array}
$$

$$
\begin{array}{ccccc}
11 & 12 & 13 & 13 & 14 \\
-5 & -6 & -6 & -7 & -7 \\
\end{array}
$$

$$
\begin{array}{cccccc}
15 & 15 & 16 & 17 & 17 & 18 \\
-7 & -8 & -8 & -9 & -8 & -9 \\
\end{array}
$$

- When finished, children should find a partner and use their flash cards to practice using doubles to subtract.

- After practicing the doubles subtraction facts at school, children may continue practice at home, recording practice minutes and returning the completed record to school to be exchanged for a certificate.

Tips

If children initially have difficulty with a mixed set of flash cards, separate them into doubles and near doubles for several practice sessions.

Name_____ Date _____

1A BASIC FACTS

Counting

Count. Circle the number that tells how many.

1. ● ●

    1 (2) 3

2. ● ● ● ●

    2 3 4

3. ● ● ● ●
    ● ● ● ●

    6 7 8

4. ● ● ● ● ●
    ● ● ● ● ●

    10 11 12

5. ● ● ●
    ● ● ●

    4 5 6

6. ● ● ●
    ● ● ● ●

    5 6 7

7. ● ● ●

    3 4 5

8. ● ● ● ● ●

    4 5 6

Name_____ Date _____

1B BASIC FACTS

···

Counting

Draw dots. Show how many.

1. 8 • • • • • • • •	**2.** 6
3. 7	**4.** 9
5. 4	**6.** 5
7. 2	**8.** 3

Name_____ Date _____

2A ▶ BASIC FACTS

The Ten-Frame Model

Ring the number.

1.

   (8)   9   10

2.
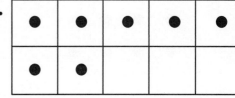

   7   8   9

3.
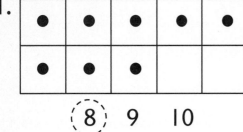

   8   9   10

4.

   4   5   6

5.

   8   9   10

6.
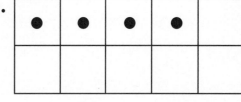

   3   4   5

7.
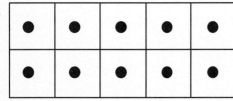

   5   6   7

8.
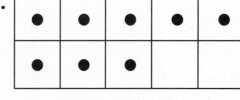

   7   8   9

Name_____ Date _____

2B BASIC FACTS

The Ten-Frame Model

Write the number.

1.

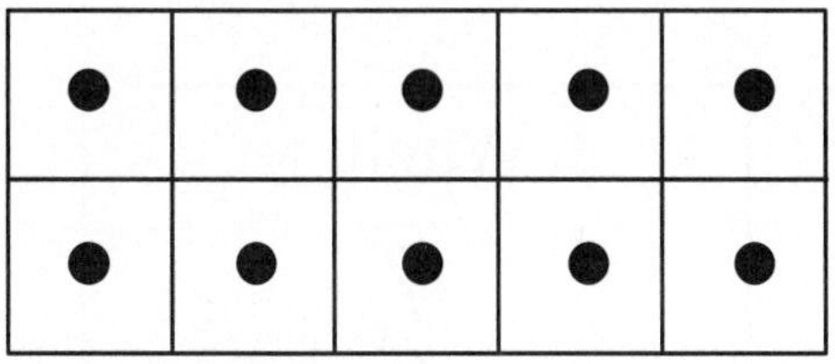

$$--10--$$

2.

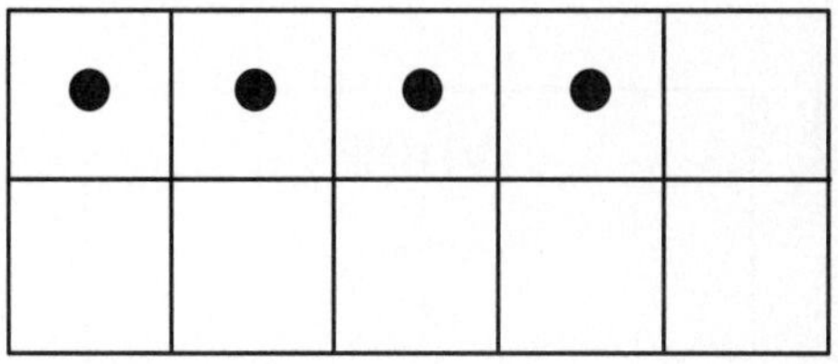

_ _ _ _ _ _ _

3.

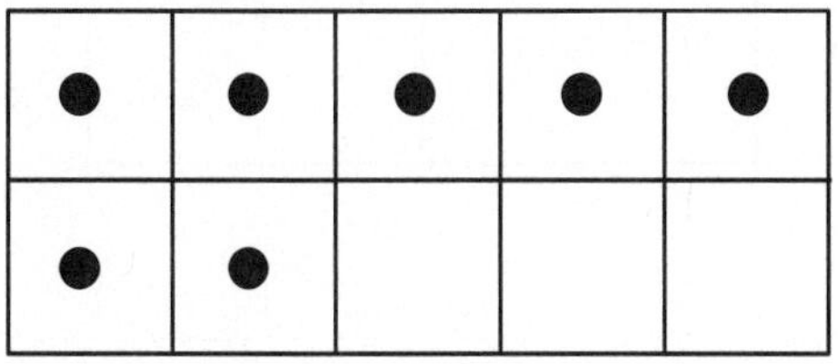

_ _ _ _ _ _ _

4.

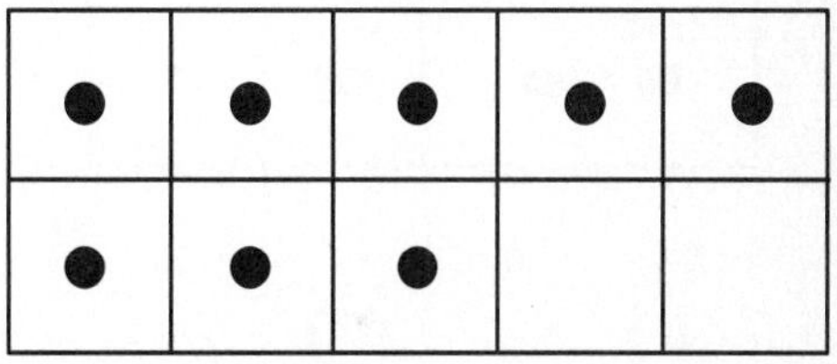

_ _ _ _ _ _ _

5.

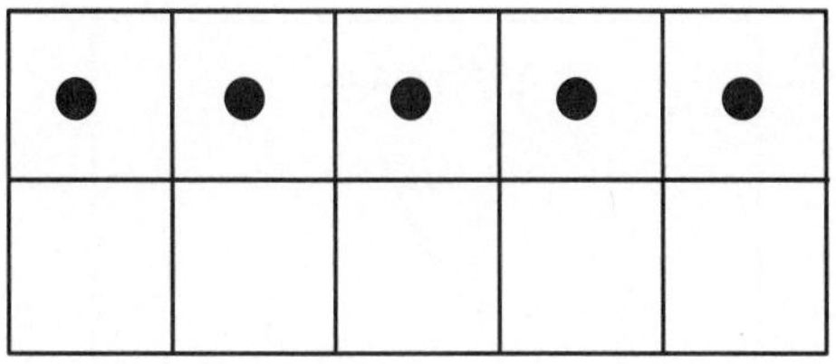

_ _ _ _ _ _ _

6.

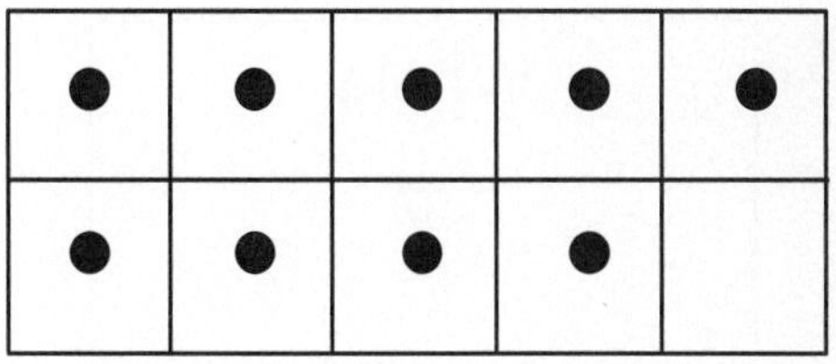

_ _ _ _ _ _ _

7.

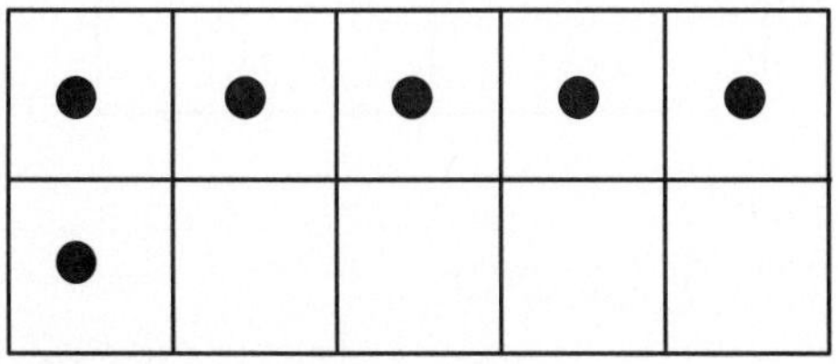

_ _ _ _ _ _ _

8.

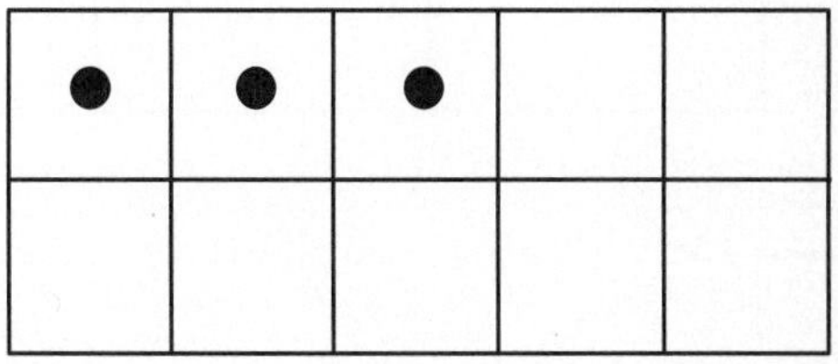

_ _ _ _ _ _ _

Name_____ Date _____

3A ◥ BASIC FACTS

···

Part-Part-Whole Model

Draw dots to show 7. Complete the number sentence.

1.

Whole
7

Part	Part
● ● ● ●	● ● ●

__4__ + __3__ = 7

2.

Whole
7

Part	Part

____ + ____ = 7

3.

Whole
7

Part	Part

____ + ____ = 7

4.

Whole
7

Part	Part

____ + ____ = 7

Name_____ Date _____

3B BASIC FACTS

Part-Part-Whole Model

Write the number sentence.

1.
Whole
6

Part	Part
● ● ● ●	● ●

$$\underline{4} + \underline{2} = \underline{6}$$

2.
Whole
4

Part	Part
● ●	● ●

$$\underline{} + \underline{} = \underline{}$$

3.
Whole
5

Part	Part
● ● ●	● ●

$$\underline{} + \underline{} = \underline{}$$

4.
Whole
3

Part	Part
● ●	●

$$\underline{} + \underline{} = \underline{}$$

Name_____ Date _____

4A BASIC FACTS
··
Part-Part-Whole Model

Use a workmat and counters. Find the whole.
Write the number sentence.

1.

Whole	
9	
Part	Part
8	1

2.

Whole	
Part	Part
5	4

8 + 1 = 9

___ + ___ = ___

3.

Whole	
Part	Part
7	2

4.

Whole	
Part	Part
6	3

___ + ___ = ___   ___ + ___ = ___

Name_____ Date _____

◤4B◢ BASIC FACTS

···

Part-Part-Whole Model

Use a workmat and counters. Find the sum.
Write the numbers.

1.

Whole
10

Part	Part
5	5

5 + 5 = ___10___

2.

Whole

Part	Part

6 + 4 = _____

3.

Whole

Part	Part

10 + 0 = _____

4.

Whole

Part	Part

7 + 3 = _____

Name_____ Date _____

5A BASIC FACTS

....

Exploring Zero

Draw dots. Write the sum.

1.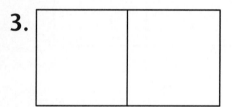

5 + 0 = __5__

2.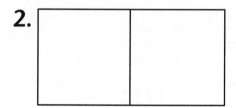

7 + 0 = ____

3.

9 + 0 = ____

4.

6 + 0 = ____

5.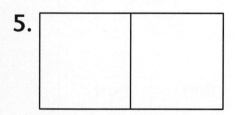

4 + 0 = ____

6.

8 + 0 = ____

Name_____ Date _____

BASIC FACTS
5B

Exploring Zero

Subtract.

1. $6 - 0 = \underline{6}$ 2. $5 - 0 = \underline{}$ 3. $8 - 8 = \underline{}$

4. $1 - 0 = \underline{}$ 5. $2 - 2 = \underline{}$ 6. $9 - 0 = \underline{}$

7. $3 - 3 = \underline{}$ 8. $7 - 0 = \underline{}$ 9. $4 - 0 = \underline{}$

10. $\begin{array}{r} 7 \\ -\ 0 \\ \hline \end{array}$ 11. $\begin{array}{r} 1 \\ -\ 1 \\ \hline \end{array}$ 12. $\begin{array}{r} 7 \\ -\ 7 \\ \hline \end{array}$ 13. $\begin{array}{r} 3 \\ -\ 0 \\ \hline \end{array}$

14. $\begin{array}{r} 9 \\ -\ 9 \\ \hline \end{array}$ 15. $\begin{array}{r} 8 \\ -\ 0 \\ \hline \end{array}$ 16. $\begin{array}{r} 5 \\ -\ 5 \\ \hline \end{array}$ 17. $\begin{array}{r} 6 \\ -\ 6 \\ \hline \end{array}$

18. $\begin{array}{r} 2 \\ -\ 2 \\ \hline \end{array}$ 19. $\begin{array}{r} 9 \\ -\ 0 \\ \hline \end{array}$ 20. $\begin{array}{r} 1 \\ -\ 0 \\ \hline \end{array}$ 21. $\begin{array}{r} 2 \\ -\ 0 \\ \hline \end{array}$

Level 1

Name______________________ Date ______________

6A

BASIC FACTS

Double Ten-Frames

Write the number.

1.

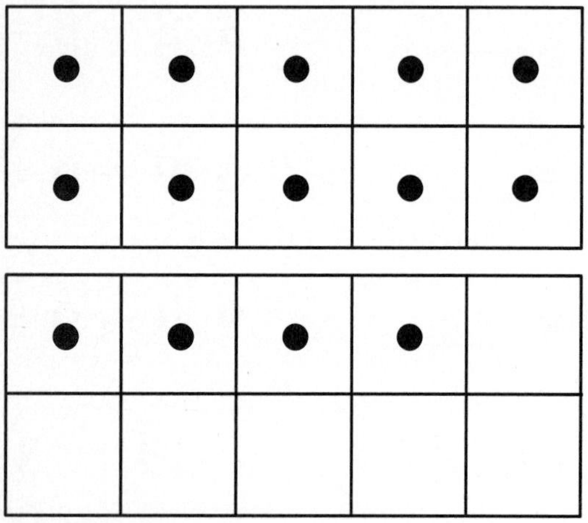

14

2.

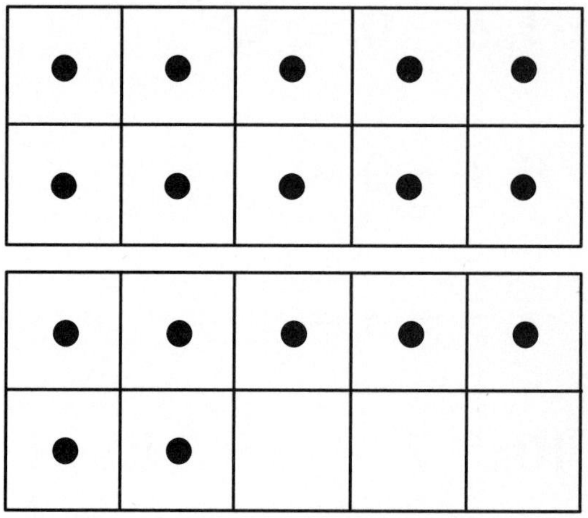

____

3.

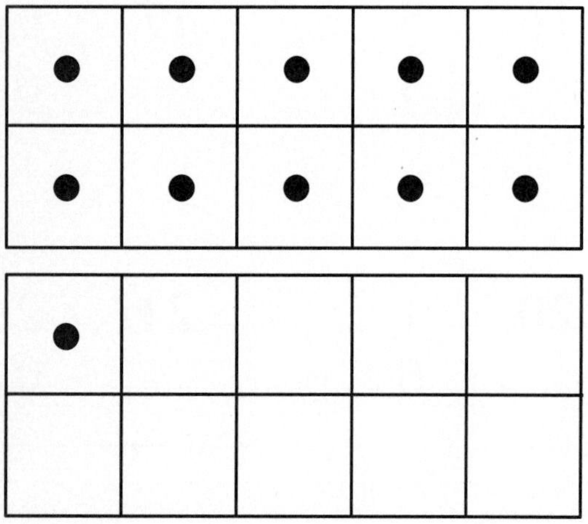

____

4.

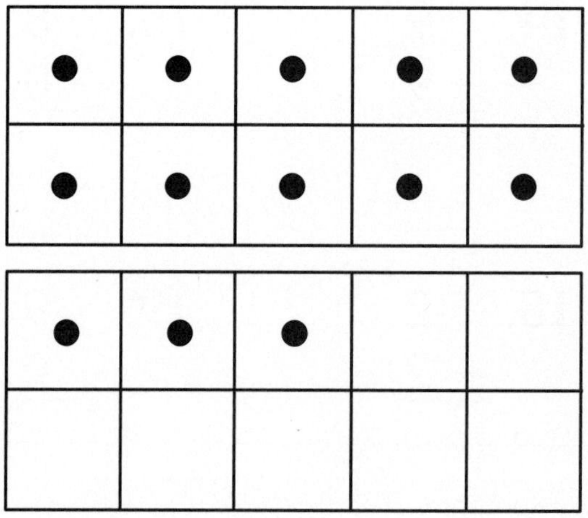

____

Name_____ Date _____

6B BASIC FACTS

....

Double Ten-Frames

Write a matching number sentence.

1.

$$10 + 5 = 15$$

2.

_____

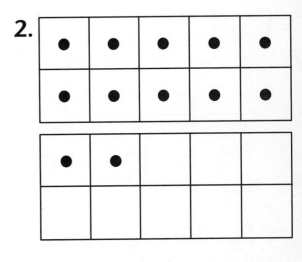

3.

_____

4.

_____

Name_____ Date _____

7A BASIC FACTS

Order Property

Write a number sentence to match.

1.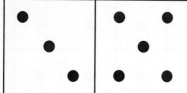

$$\underline{} + \underline{} = \underline{}$$

2.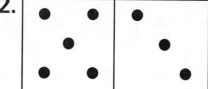

$$\underline{} + \underline{} = \underline{}$$

3.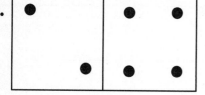

$$\underline{} + \underline{} = \underline{}$$

4.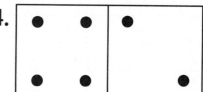

$$\underline{} + \underline{} = \underline{}$$

5.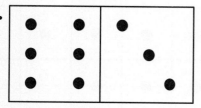

$$\underline{} + \underline{} = \underline{}$$

6.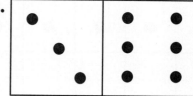

$$\underline{} + \underline{} = \underline{}$$

Name_____ Date _____

7B BASIC FACTS

···

Order Property

Think of order. Add.

1. 1   3
      + 3   + 1
       4   4

2. 1   4
      + 4   + 1

3. 5   1
      + 1   + 5

4. 2   3
      + 3   + 2

5. 6   3
      + 3   + 6

6. 2   4
      + 4   + 2

7. 3   4
      + 4   + 3

8. 3   7
      + 7   + 3

9. 5   3
      + 3   + 5

10. 6   2
       + 2   + 6

11. 2   5
       + 5   + 2

12. 2   7
       + 7   + 2

Name_____ Date _____

8A ▸ BASIC FACTS

Counting On to Add

Count on. Write the sum. Use the dots to help.

1. 3
   + 3 •••
   6

2. 7
   + 1 •

3. 5
   + 2 ••

4. 1
   + 1 •

5. 6
   + 2 ••

6. 8
   + 1 •

7. 9
   + 2 ••

8. 5
   + 1 •

9. 3
   + 2 ••

10. 3
   + 1 •

11. 7
   + 2 ••

12. 9
   + 1 •

13. 2
   + 2 ••

14. 6
   + 1 •

15. 4
   + 2 ••

16. 8
   + 2 ••

17. 4
   + 3 •••

18. 5
   + 3 •••

19. 1
   + 2 ••

20. 6
   + 3 •••

Name_____ Date _____

8B BASIC FACTS

Counting On to Add

Circle the greater number. Count on. Write the sum.

1. (4) + 1 = __5__   2. 3 + 5 = ____   3. 2 + 9 = ____

4. 6 + 3 = ____   5. 3 + 4 = ____   6. 7 + 3 = ____

7. 5 + 3 = ____   8. 3 + 6 = ____   9. 8 + 3 = ____

10.   3
   + 1

11.   1
   + 9

12.   7
   + 2

13.   9
   + 3

14.   1
   + 8

15.   6
   + 1

16.   1
   + 5

17.   1
   + 7

18.   6
   + 2

19.   2
   + 8

20.   2
   + 3

21.   5
   + 1

Name_____ Date _____

9A BASIC FACTS

Counting Back to Subtract

Count back. Write the difference.

1. 4 − 1 **3**	**2.** 6 − 3	**3.** 8 − 1	**4.** 5 − 1
5. 9 − 2	**6.** 3 − 1	**7.** 12 − 3	**8.** 7 − 3
9. 4 − 2	**10.** 6 − 1	**11.** 8 − 2	**12.** 5 − 2
13. 2 − 1	**14.** 11 − 2	**15.** 3 − 2	**16.** 7 − 2
17. 5 − 3	**18.** 7 − 1	**19.** 10 − 3	**20.** 4 − 3

Name_____ Date _____

9B ▶ BASIC FACTS
....
Counting Back to Subtract

Count back to subtract. Write the difference.

1. $5 - 3 =$ _2__

2. $9 - 3 =$ ____

3. $7 - 3 =$ ____

4. $5 - 2 =$ ____

5. $6 - 2 =$ ____

6. $8 - 1 =$ ____

7. $9 - 1 =$ ____

8. $7 - 2 =$ ____

9. $8 - 3 =$ ____

10. $6 - 3 =$ ____

11. $9 - 2 =$ ____

12. $5 - 1 =$ ____

13. $8 - 2 =$ ____

14. $4 - 2 =$ ____

15. $3 - 1 =$ ____

16. $\begin{array}{r} 2 \\ -1 \\ \hline \end{array}$

17. $\begin{array}{r} 8 \\ -3 \\ \hline \end{array}$

18. $\begin{array}{r} 7 \\ -1 \\ \hline \end{array}$

19. $\begin{array}{r} 6 \\ -2 \\ \hline \end{array}$

20. $\begin{array}{r} 4 \\ -1 \\ \hline \end{array}$

21. $\begin{array}{r} 6 \\ -1 \\ \hline \end{array}$

22. $\begin{array}{r} 4 \\ -2 \\ \hline \end{array}$

23. $\begin{array}{r} 5 \\ -3 \\ \hline \end{array}$

Name_____ Date _____

10A BASIC FACTS
···
Counting Up to Subtract

Count up to subtract. Write the difference.

1. 6
  − 5
	2. 8
	  − 7
		3. 10
		  − 9
			4. 5
			  − 4

5. 8
  − 5
	6. 11
	  − 9
		7. 9
		  − 8
			8. 7
			  − 5

9. 10
  − 8
	10. 6
	  − 4
		11. 7
		  − 4
			12. 3
			  − 2

13. 7
  − 6
	14. 11
	  − 8
		15. 8
		  − 6
			16. 9
			  − 7

17. 4
  − 3
	18. 5
	  − 3
		19. 3
		  − 2
			20. 12
			  − 9

Name_____   Date _____

10B BASIC FACTS

Counting Up to Subtract

Subtract. Write the difference. Circle the facts you count up.

1. $8 - 7 =$ __

2. $7 - 2 =$ __

3. $5 - 4 =$ __

4. $7 - 4 =$ __

5. $6 - 2 =$ __

6. $3 - 2 =$ __

7. $8 - 3 =$ __

8. $6 - 3 =$ __

9. $8 - 1 =$ __

Subtract.

10. $\begin{array}{r} 10 \\ -\ 7 \\ \hline \end{array}$

11. $\begin{array}{r} 8 \\ -\ 6 \\ \hline \end{array}$

12. $\begin{array}{r} 9 \\ -\ 8 \\ \hline \end{array}$

13. $\begin{array}{r} 6 \\ -\ 4 \\ \hline \end{array}$

14. $\begin{array}{r} 10 \\ -\ 9 \\ \hline \end{array}$

15. $\begin{array}{r} 7 \\ -\ 5 \\ \hline \end{array}$

16. $\begin{array}{r} 5 \\ -\ 2 \\ \hline \end{array}$

17. $\begin{array}{r} 8 \\ -\ 7 \\ \hline \end{array}$

18. $\begin{array}{r} 9 \\ -\ 7 \\ \hline \end{array}$

19. $\begin{array}{r} 10 \\ -\ 8 \\ \hline \end{array}$

20. $\begin{array}{r} 12 \\ -\ 9 \\ \hline \end{array}$

21. $\begin{array}{r} 7 \\ -\ 3 \\ \hline \end{array}$

Name_____ Date _____

◣ 11A BASIC FACTS

···

Using Doubles to Add

Draw dots to show a double. Complete the number sentence.

1.

4 + _4_ = _8_

2.

6 + ____ = ____

3.

5 + ____ = ____

4.

8 + ____ = ____

5. 7
   + 7

6. 9
   + 9

7. 8
   + 8

8. 6
   + 6

Name_____ Date _____

BASIC FACTS

Using Doubles to Add

Find the sum of the double. Use the double to find the next sums.

1. $\begin{array}{r} 4 \\ + 4 \\ \hline 8 \end{array}$ → → $\begin{array}{r} 4 \\ + 5 \\ \hline 9 \end{array}$ $\begin{array}{r} 5 \\ + 4 \\ \hline 9 \end{array}$

2. $\begin{array}{r} 5 \\ + 5 \\ \hline \end{array}$ → → $\begin{array}{r} 5 \\ + 6 \\ \hline \end{array}$ $\begin{array}{r} 6 \\ + 5 \\ \hline \end{array}$

3. $\begin{array}{r} 6 \\ + 6 \\ \hline \end{array}$ → → $\begin{array}{r} 6 \\ + 7 \\ \hline \end{array}$ $\begin{array}{r} 7 \\ + 6 \\ \hline \end{array}$

4. $\begin{array}{r} 7 \\ + 7 \\ \hline \end{array}$ → → $\begin{array}{r} 7 \\ + 8 \\ \hline \end{array}$ $\begin{array}{r} 8 \\ + 7 \\ \hline \end{array}$

5. $\begin{array}{r} 8 \\ + 8 \\ \hline \end{array}$ → → $\begin{array}{r} 8 \\ + 9 \\ \hline \end{array}$ $\begin{array}{r} 9 \\ + 8 \\ \hline \end{array}$

Name_____ Date _____

12A ◣ BASIC FACTS

Using Doubles to Subtract

Use doubles and near doubles. Subtract.

1. $8 - 4 = \underline{4}$ **2.** $10 - 5 = \underline{}$ **3.** $9 - 5 = \underline{}$

4. $12 - 6 = \underline{}$ **5.** $13 - 7 = \underline{}$ **6.** $11 - 6 = \underline{}$

7. $\begin{array}{r} 13 \\ -\ 7 \\ \hline \end{array}$ **8.** $\begin{array}{r} 14 \\ -\ 7 \\ \hline \end{array}$ **9.** $\begin{array}{r} 16 \\ -\ 8 \\ \hline \end{array}$ **10.** $\begin{array}{r} 13 \\ -\ 6 \\ \hline \end{array}$

11. $\begin{array}{r} 16 \\ -\ 7 \\ \hline \end{array}$ **12.** $\begin{array}{r} 18 \\ -\ 9 \\ \hline \end{array}$ **13.** $\begin{array}{r} 14 \\ -\ 8 \\ \hline \end{array}$ **14.** $\begin{array}{r} 17 \\ -\ 8 \\ \hline \end{array}$

15. $\begin{array}{r} 15 \\ -\ 7 \\ \hline \end{array}$ **16.** $\begin{array}{r} 9 \\ -\ 4 \\ \hline \end{array}$ **17.** $\begin{array}{r} 15 \\ -\ 7 \\ \hline \end{array}$ **18.** $\begin{array}{r} 12 \\ -\ 6 \\ \hline \end{array}$

19. $\begin{array}{r} 17 \\ -\ 9 \\ \hline \end{array}$ **20.** $\begin{array}{r} 14 \\ -\ 7 \\ \hline \end{array}$ **21.** $\begin{array}{r} 15 \\ -\ 8 \\ \hline \end{array}$ **22.** $\begin{array}{r} 8 \\ -\ 4 \\ \hline \end{array}$

Name_____ Date _____

12B ◣ BASIC FACTS
··

Using Doubles to Subtract

Use doubles and near doubles. Subtract.

1. $14 - 7 = \underline{7}$ 2. $11 - 6 = \underline{}$ 3. $12 - 6 = \underline{}$

4. $11 - 5 = \underline{}$ 5. $15 - 8 = \underline{}$ 6. $17 - 9 = \underline{}$

7. $15 - 7 = \underline{}$ 8. $14 - 8 = \underline{}$ 9. $17 - 8 = \underline{}$

10. $\begin{array}{r} 9 \\ -\,4 \\ \hline \end{array}$	11. $\begin{array}{r} 9 \\ -\,5 \\ \hline \end{array}$	12. $\begin{array}{r} 13 \\ -\,6 \\ \hline \end{array}$	13. $\begin{array}{r} 13 \\ -\,7 \\ \hline \end{array}$
14. $\begin{array}{r} 12 \\ -\,6 \\ \hline \end{array}$	15. $\begin{array}{r} 7 \\ -\,4 \\ \hline \end{array}$	16. $\begin{array}{r} 15 \\ -\,8 \\ \hline \end{array}$	17. $\begin{array}{r} 16 \\ -\,7 \\ \hline \end{array}$
18. $\begin{array}{r} 10 \\ -\,5 \\ \hline \end{array}$	19. $\begin{array}{r} 16 \\ -\,8 \\ \hline \end{array}$	20. $\begin{array}{r} 8 \\ -\,4 \\ \hline \end{array}$	21. $\begin{array}{r} 18 \\ -\,9 \\ \hline \end{array}$

Basic Facts Workshop 1

Strategy: Adding and Subtracting Zero

Introduce It!

15 minutes

Adding Zero

Management whole class
Materials two envelopes, 9 counters

- Ask two children to come to the front of the room. Give each child an envelope, one with nine counters and the other one with none.

- Ask the class to find the total number of counters in both envelopes.

- Open the envelope with counters, and have children count them. Write 9 on the board.

- Open the other envelope and ask, How many counters are in this envelope? **none** How many counters are there in all? **9**

- Write the addition sentence $9 + 0 = 9$ on the board.

- Have the children change places. Ask the class to identify the number of counters in the envelopes (0 and 9). How would you write an addition sentence for this? **0 + 9 = 9** Repeat with other examples, adding zero.

- Change the number of counters in one envelope and always leave the other envelope empty.

- Ask three volunteers to repeat the activity. Two children report what's in the envelopes, and the third child writes the addition sentences on the board.

- Repeat with other children.

Develop It!

15 minutes

Subtracting All or None

Management whole class
Materials overhead projector, blank transparency, 9 counters

- Show 7 counters on the overhead projector. Ask children how many they see.

- Ask children to close their eyes. Remove all 7 counters.

- Have children open their eyes and describe what happened.

- Ask the class how to write a number sentence that shows what you just did. Guide them to write $7 - 7 = 0$.

- Repeat with eight counters. Ask children how many they see.

- Have children close their eyes. Do not remove any counters.

- Ask children to open their eyes and describe what happened.

- Ask the class how to write a number sentence that shows what you just did. Guide them to write $8 - 8 = 0$.

- Repeat activity asking one child to put counters on the projector and the other child to record the number sentence.

- Repeat with other children.

Make Zero Flash Cards

20 minutes

Management individuals

Materials 10 triangle-shaped cards (Just the Facts Support Master 4), 2 different-colored markers, large envelope to store triangle flash cards, practice minutes record and certificate (Just the Facts Support Masters 9 and 13)

- Have each child cut ten triangle-shaped flash cards from Support Master 4 and make flash cards as shown.

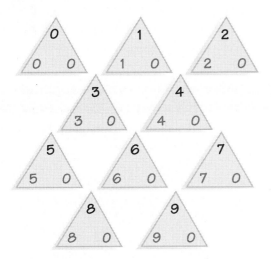

- To use triangle-shaped flash cards, one child holds a card and covers a corner. If the two numbers are the same color, then two addition facts can be stated. If the two numbers are different colors, the subtraction fact is stated.

- Have children work with a partner and practice adding and subtracting with zero. Encourage children to continue at home and record practice using the practice minutes record. The completed record may be returned to school and exchanged for a certificate.

Tips

Remind children that these flash cards will be used all year, so they should put their initials on the back of each card.

Basic Facts Workshop 2

Strategy: Counting On 1, 2, 3 to Add

Introduce It!

15 minutes

Counting On 1, 2, 3

Management whole class
Materials overhead projector, 12 counters

- Show 7 counters on the projector. Ask children how many they see. **7** Cover the counters with a piece of paper. Place two counters beside the paper. Ask, How many more counters do you see? **2** How many counters are there in all? **9** How do you know? Write $7 + 2 = 9$.

- Repeat with other sets of counters, 5, 6, and 8. Always add 1, 2, or 3 more counters. Write number sentences for each example.

- Reverse the order of addends. Show 6 counters on the right side of the projector, cover them, and place 3 counters to the left of the paper. Ask, How many are there in all? **9**

- Write $3 + 6 = 9$. Ask, How is the number sentence different? **Addends have changed position.** Did you count on to find the sum? How? **Remembered 6, then counted on, 7, 8, 9.**

  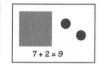

Develop It!

20 minutes

Start with the Greater Number

Management whole class
Materials overhead projector, blank transparency

- Write $3 + 7 =$ on a transparency. Ask the class, How can you use counting on to find the sum? **Possible answer: Think 7, then count 8, 9, 10.** Could you also start at 3 and count on 7 more? Which way is easier? Why?

- Lead children to see that it is easier to start with the greater addend.

$$3 + 7 =$$

Tips

Have children use their fingers to help them count on.

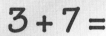

Make It!

Make Counting On Flash Cards

20 minutes

Management individuals
Materials 45 white index cards, storage container for cards, practice minutes record and certificate (Just the Facts Support Masters 9 and 13)

- Distribute 45 white index cards to each child. Remind children to write addends only on the front of the card, and addends and sum on the back of each card. They may want to write their initials or names on the back of each card also.

- Have children make a separate flash card for each of the facts shown.

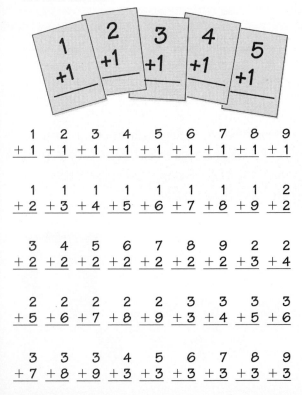

$$
\begin{array}{ccccccccc}
1 & 2 & 3 & 4 & 5 & 6 & 7 & 8 & 9 \\
+1 & +1 & +1 & +1 & +1 & +1 & +1 & +1 & +1 \\
\hline
\end{array}
$$

$$
\begin{array}{ccccccccc}
1 & 1 & 1 & 1 & 1 & 1 & 1 & 1 & 2 \\
+2 & +3 & +4 & +5 & +6 & +7 & +8 & +9 & +2 \\
\hline
\end{array}
$$

$$
\begin{array}{ccccccccc}
3 & 4 & 5 & 6 & 7 & 8 & 9 & 2 & 2 \\
+2 & +2 & +2 & +2 & +2 & +2 & +2 & +3 & +4 \\
\hline
\end{array}
$$

$$
\begin{array}{ccccccccc}
2 & 2 & 2 & 2 & 2 & 3 & 3 & 3 & 3 \\
+5 & +6 & +7 & +8 & +9 & +3 & +4 & +5 & +6 \\
\hline
\end{array}
$$

$$
\begin{array}{ccccccccc}
3 & 3 & 3 & 4 & 5 & 6 & 7 & 8 & 9 \\
+7 & +8 & +9 & +3 & +3 & +3 & +3 & +3 & +3 \\
\hline
\end{array}
$$

- When finished, children should find a partner and use their flash cards to practice adding by counting on.

- After practicing at school, children may continue their practice at home, recording practice minutes and returning the completed record to school to exchange for a certificate.

Basic Facts Workshop 3

Strategy: Counting Back

Introduce It!

15 minutes

Counting Back

Management whole class
Materials none

- First invite ten children to come to the front of the room and stand in a line. Ask, How many children do you see? **10** Then ask two children to kneel down and talk about how to write what happened. Then write 10 − 2 on the board.

- Ask the class how many are left standing. To find out, start at 10 and count back 2. Encourage them to think 10, and then count 9, 8. Ask, How would you

finish the number sentence? Guide children to suggest writing 8 after the equal sign.

- Repeat the activity with 9 children. Have 3 sit down. Record the number sentence, thinking aloud to demonstrate counting back 3. Then repeat with 7 − 2, 5 − 2, and 8 − 3.

Tips

Use a number line to demonstrate, so that children can see the numbers while they count back.

Develop It!

20 minutes

Count Back and Keep Track

Management whole class
Materials 10 connecting cubes, container

- Place 7 cubes in your hand. Show them to the children and ask how many they see.

- Take out 3, and one at a time, drop them into a container.

- Ask children to think 7 and then count back 6, 5, 4 as they hear each cube clink.

- Ask, How many cubes are left? **4** Ask, What number sentence could I write to show what happened? Guide children to suggest writing 7 − 3 = 4 on the board.

- Repeat the activity beginning with other amounts, 10 or less, and have the children count back by 1, 2, or 3 from the starting number. Record the number sentences on the board.

Make It!

20 minutes

Counting Back Flash Cards

Management individuals or pairs

Materials 22 index cards, practice minutes record and certificate (Just the Facts Support Masters 10 and 14)

- Distribute index cards to each child. Remind children to write their initials or names on the back of each.

- Then ask children to make flash cards as shown.

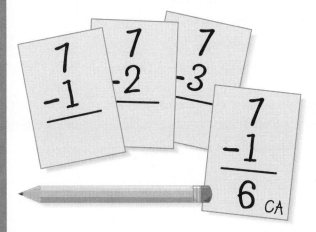

$$
\begin{array}{r} 2 \\ -1 \\ \hline \end{array}
\begin{array}{r} 3 \\ -1 \\ \hline \end{array}
\begin{array}{r} 4 \\ -1 \\ \hline \end{array}
\begin{array}{r} 5 \\ -1 \\ \hline \end{array}
\begin{array}{r} 6 \\ -1 \\ \hline \end{array}
\begin{array}{r} 8 \\ -1 \\ \hline \end{array}
\begin{array}{r} 9 \\ -1 \\ \hline \end{array}
\begin{array}{r} 3 \\ -2 \\ \hline \end{array}
\begin{array}{r} 8 \\ -3 \\ \hline \end{array}
$$

$$
\begin{array}{r} 4 \\ -2 \\ \hline \end{array}
\begin{array}{r} 5 \\ -2 \\ \hline \end{array}
\begin{array}{r} 6 \\ -2 \\ \hline \end{array}
\begin{array}{r} 8 \\ -2 \\ \hline \end{array}
\begin{array}{r} 9 \\ -2 \\ \hline \end{array}
\begin{array}{r} 4 \\ -3 \\ \hline \end{array}
\begin{array}{r} 5 \\ -3 \\ \hline \end{array}
\begin{array}{r} 6 \\ -3 \\ \hline \end{array}
\begin{array}{r} 9 \\ -3 \\ \hline \end{array}
$$

- Invite children to use their flash cards with a partner to practice subtracting by counting back.

- Encourage children to combine these flash cards with their counting on flash cards, and continue to practice at home. Have them record their practice minutes and return the completed record to school to be exchanged for a certificate.

Tips

Remind children to write the expression only on the front of each card and the complete number sentence on the back.

Basic Facts Workshop 4

Strategy: Counting Up

Introduce It!

15 minutes

Counting Up

Management whole class

Materials overhead projector, part-part-whole mat transparency (Just the Facts Support Master 2), large index cards, 10 counters

- Place 7 counters on the whole part of the part-part-whole transparency.

- Ask the children how many they see. Remove the counters and write 7. Slide 5 counters to one part of the mat, slide 2 to the other part, keeping those two covered with a card.

- Ask children how many counters they started with, **7** how many counters are in the part they know, **5** and how many counters they think are in the other part. One way to find out is to count up. Say, Start with 5, count up to 7. Think 6, 7. How many do you count up? **2** Write $7 - 5 = 2$.

- Repeat the activity for other subtraction situations such as $9 - 6$, $8 - 6$, $6 - 5$, and $7 - 4$.

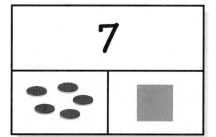

Develop It!

15 minutes

Count Up Flash

Management pairs

Materials 3 index cards labeled numbers 1, 2, and 3

- Write $8 - 5$ on the board.

- Remind children that counting up is a good subtraction strategy to use when numbers are close together.

- Pairs share their answers and hold up the 1, 2, or 3 card. Discuss the correct answer.

- Repeat with the following, $9 - 7$, $10 - 7$, $11 - 8$, $7 - 6$, $7 - 5$, $9 - 6$, $7 - 4$, $9 - 8$, $8 - 6$, and $7 - 6$. Pairs take turns holding up the appropriate card.

Make Counting Up Flash Cards

20 minutes

Management individuals

Materials 18 orange-colored index cards, storage container for flash cards, practice minutes record and certificate (Just the Facts Support Masters 9 and 13)

- Distribute 18 orange-colored index cards to each child.

- Remind children to write the expression only on the front of the card, and the complete number sentence on the back. Also ask children to write their names or initials on the back of each card.

- Have children make a separate flash card for each fact as shown below.

$$
\begin{array}{cccccc}
\dfrac{12}{-9} & \dfrac{11}{-8} & \dfrac{10}{-7} & \dfrac{7}{-5} & \dfrac{5}{-4}
\end{array}
$$

$$
\begin{array}{cccccc}
\dfrac{11}{-9} & \dfrac{10}{-9} & \dfrac{10}{-8} & \dfrac{9}{-8} & \dfrac{9}{-7} & \dfrac{9}{-6} \\
\end{array}
$$

$$
\begin{array}{ccccccc}
\dfrac{8}{-7} & \dfrac{8}{-6} & \dfrac{8}{-5} & \dfrac{7}{-6} & \dfrac{7}{-4} & \dfrac{6}{-5} & \dfrac{6}{-4}
\end{array}
$$

- When finished, children should find a partner and use their flash cards to practice. After practicing at school, children may continue practice at home, recording practice minutes, and returning the completed record to school to be exchanged for a certificate.

Tips

You many want to laminate flash cards so they will last throughout the year.

Basic Facts Workshop 5

Strategy Review

Introduce It!

15 minutes

Choose a Strategy

Management whole class
Materials none

- Write 9 + 2 on the board. Ask, If you can't remember the answer for 9 + 2, how could you figure it out? **Count on from 9.** Would that work for 3 + 7? **Yes, start with 7, count on 3.**

- Then, write 12 − 3 on the board. Ask, How could you figure out the answer if you can't remember it? **Start with 12, count back 3.**

- Next, write the following on the board: 7 + 2, 9 + 3, 8 − 3, 11 + 3, 10 − 2, 15 − 3, and 12 + 1. Ask children to describe how to solve each example by counting on or counting back.

- Finally, write 12 − 9. Ask, Should I count back to find the answer? **No, it would be hard to keep track.** How should I solve the problem? **Start at 9 and count up.**

- Have children count up to find 10 − 8, 13 − 10, 9 − 7, 12 − 10, and 8 − 5.

Tips

Remind children that it is easier to count on when you add 1, 2, or 3; and count back with greater numbers.

Develop It!

15 minutes

Show a Strategy

Management pairs
Materials two different colors of chalk

- Divide children into pairs and have them talk about how they know when to count on, count back, and count up. Ask them to share their ideas with examples. Record their examples on the board.

- Next, draw a triangle on the board, with the number 9 at the top in one color of chalk, and the numbers 2 and 7 at the bottom in another color. Cover the 9, reminding children that since they know the two parts, they can add them. Ask children how they can

figure out 2 + 7 and 7 + 2 if they can't remember them. Write 2 + 7 = 9 and 7 + 2 = 9 underneath the triangle.

- Next, cover the 2, reminding children that since they know the whole and one part, they subtract. Ask how to figure out 9 − 7. Write 9 − 7 = 2. Cover the 7. Ask them how to figure out 9 − 2. Write 9 − 2 = 7.

- Repeat the activity with other numbers.

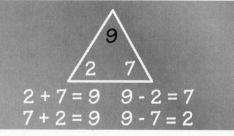

Make It!

Make Triangle Cards

20 minutes

Management individuals or pairs

Materials 24 triangle flash cards (Just the Facts Support Master 4), previously made triangle flash cards, practice minutes record and certificate (Just the Facts Support Masters 11 and 15), two different colored markers

- Have each child cut 24 triangle flash cards from copies of Just the Facts Support Master 4. Remind them to write their initials or first names on the back.

- Children can label flash cards as shown. Tell them to write the top number in one color and the bottom two in the second color.

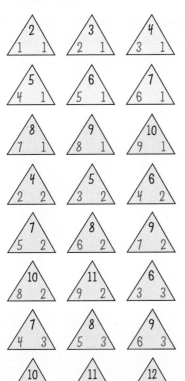

- When finished, divide children into pairs to practice the counting on, counting back, and counting up facts.

- After reviewing these facts at school, children may add in the zero triangle flash cards and practice with them at home. Children should record the time spent working at home on Support Master 11. When they come back to school, the record can be exchanged for a certificate.

Basic Facts Workshop 6

Strategy: Using Doubles to Add

Introduce It!

20 minutes

Where is the Double?

Management whole class

Materials overhead projector, teacher-made transparency of part-part-whole mat (Just the Facts Support Master 2), counters

• Place five counters on one part of the part-part-whole mat. Ask, How many counters should go on the other part to show a double? **5** How many counters are there now? **5 + 5 = 10**

• Place one more counter on one side of the workmat. Ask, How does knowing 5 + 5 help you figure out 5 + 6? **one more than 10; 5 + 6 = 11**

• Then, write 8 + 7. Ask, What double helps with this fact? **7 + 7 and one more, or one less than 8 + 8** Ask a child to model with counters.

• Have children take turns modeling with counters and identifying a helping double for each of the following expressions: 4 + 5, 5 + 7, 7 + 9, 9 + 8, and 6 + 8.

Develop It!

20 minutes

Spin and Double

Management pairs

Materials 2 spinners (Just the Facts Support Masters 5 and 6)

• Distribute to each pair a 6-section spinner labeled, 4, 5, 6, 7, 8, and 9; and a 3-section spinner labeled, double, double + 1, and double + 2.

• First, one partner spins the 6-section spinner to determine a number, and then the 3-section spinner to determine what to do with that number.

• The other partner records the addition fact. For example, if the number spun is 6 and the direction is double + 2, the fact to record is 6 + 8 = 14.

• Players switch roles and continue to play until each partner has written at least 10 facts.

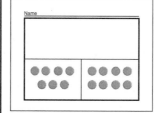

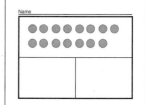

Tips

Write out the possible facts so that children can refer to them when they play.

Make It!

Make Doubles, Near Doubles Flash Cards

25 minutes

Management individuals
Materials 24 blue index cards, practice minutes record and certificate (Just the Facts Support Masters 9 and 13)

- Write a double or near double addition problem on each of sixteen flash cards as shown and display them on the ledge of the board. Distribute sixteen blue index cards to each child.

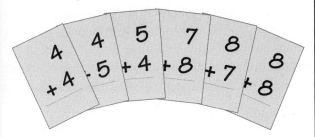

$$\begin{array}{cccccccccc} 4 & 5 & 5 & 5 & 6 & 6 & 6 & 6 & 6 \\ +6 & +5 & +6 & +7 & +4 & +5 & +6 & +7 & +8 \end{array}$$

$$\begin{array}{cccccccccc} 7 & 7 & 7 & 7 & 8 & 8 & 9 & 9 & 9 \\ +5 & +6 & +7 & +9 & +6 & +9 & +7 & +8 & +9 \end{array}$$

- Ask children to copy one addition problem on the front of each card and write the sum on the back of the card. Have children also write their names on the back of each card.

- Then, ask children to use their flash cards to quiz a partner on adding doubles and near doubles.

- After practicing at school, children may bring their flash cards home to practice. Tell children to record the minutes practiced and return the completed record to school to be exchanged for a certificate.

Basic Facts Workshop 7

Strategy: Using Doubles to Subtract

Introduce It!

15 minutes

The Missing Part

Management whole class
Materials 17 counters

- Show 9 counters to children. Ask, How many counters do you see?

- Put all 9 counters in your pocket. Take out 4 counters and show them. Write $9 - 4 = \_\_$ on the board.

- Ask, How many do you think are still in my pocket? Could it be 4? **no** Why? **4 and 4 are only 8, you need one more, or 5, to make 9** Write $9 - 4 = 5$.

- Draw and label a part-part-whole diagram below the

number sentence. Ask children how using doubles can help them find the missing part ($4 + 4 = 8$, so $4 + 5 = 9$, so $9 - 4 = 5$).

- Repeat with 15 counters in your pocket and remove 7; 17 in the pocket and remove 9; and 13 in the pocket and remove 6. Emphasize thinking about doubles to find the missing part.

Tips

Emphasize that with doubles, the two parts on the part-part-whole diagram will be the same.

Develop It!

15 minutes

Name the Doubles

Management whole class
Materials none

- Write $15 - 8 = \_\_$ on the board. Ask, How can you use doubles to help solve this problem? ($8 + 8$

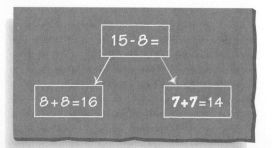

$15 - 8 =$

$8 + 8 = 16$ $7 + 7 = 14$

$= 16$, so $8 + 7 = 15$, so $15 - 8$ must be 7; or $7 + 7 = 14$, so $7 + 8 = 15$, so $15 - 8$ must be 7.)

- Repeat with the following examples: $13 - 7$; $17 - 9$; $15 - 7$; $17 - 8$; and $13 - 6$.

- Ask, Can you use doubles to solve each problem? Some children may solve $13 - 7$ by thinking $7 + 7 = 14$, so $7 + 6 = 13$, so $13 - 7 = 6$, or others may think $6 + 6 = 12$, so $6 + 7 = 13$, so $13 - 7 = 6$.

Tips

Remind children that they should use the doubles that are easiest for them. Not everyone looks at a problem the same way.

Make Doubles, Near Doubles Flash Cards

30 minutes

Management individuals

Materials 21 blue index cards, previously made set of index card flash cards, practice minutes record and certificate (Just the Facts Support Masters 10 and 14)

- Distribute 21 blue index cards to each child.

- Have children make flash cards for the following doubles and near doubles facts:

$$\begin{array}{cccccc} 8 & 9 & 9 & 10 & 11 & 11 \\ -4 & -4 & -5 & -5 & -5 & -6 \\ \hline \end{array}$$

$$\begin{array}{cccccccc} 10 & 10 & 12 & 12 & 13 & 13 & 14 & 14 \\ -4 & -6 & -5 & -6 & -7 & -6 & -6 & -7 \\ \hline \end{array}$$

$$\begin{array}{ccccccc} 15 & 15 & 16 & 16 & 17 & 17 & 18 \\ -7 & -8 & -7 & -8 & -9 & -8 & -9 \\ \hline \end{array}$$

- When finished, children should find a partner and use their flash cards to practice using doubles to subtract.

- After practicing the doubles subtraction facts at school, children may combine these flash cards with previously made flash cards, and continue practicing at home, recording practice minutes and returning the completed record to school to be exchanged for a certificate.

Basic Facts Workshop 8
Strategy Review

Introduce It!

15 minutes

What Strategy Will Help?

Management whole class
Materials chalkboard, large self-adhesive notes

- List the following addition and subtraction strategies on the board as shown: count on, count back, count up, doubles/near doubles.

- Remind children that they have learned each of these strategies as a way to help figure out facts they don't remember. Review strategies if necessary.

- Write $7 + 2 =$ on a self-adhesive note. Show it to the class and ask which strategy could help them figure out this fact if they couldn't remember it. **counting on** Place the self-adhesive note under count on on the board.

count on	count back	count up	doubles/ near doubles
7+2		10-7	8+8

- Repeat, showing the following facts to the class and having them identify the strategy that would be helpful, to find the answer: $10 - 7 =$ **count up**; $8 + 8 =$ **doubles**; $9 + 3 =$ **count on**; $7 + 8 =$ **near doubles**; $8 - 3 =$ **count back**; $6 - 3 =$ **doubles OR count up**; and $11 - 3 =$ **count back**.

Develop It!

15 minutes

Name the Strategy

Management individuals
Materials none

- Have each child fold a paper into four parts and label each part as shown.

- Write $8 + 2 =$ on the board. Ask children which strategy they would use if they couldn't remember the answer. **counting on** Why? **You can keep the greater number in your head and count on**

- Have children write the complete number sentence $8 + 2 = 10$ in the count on section of their paper.

- Repeat with $6 + 6$, having children decide which strategy would be helpful. **doubles** Have them write the complete number sentence in that section, and discuss their decision.

- Repeat, using the following number sentences: $7 + 7$ **doubles**, $13 - 2$ **count back**, $12 - 9$ **count up**, $4 + 3$ **near doubles or counting on**, $8 + 9$ **near doubles**, $9 - 7$ **count up**, $11 - 3$ **count back**, and $9 + 3$ **count on**.

Make It!

15 minutes

Make Doubles Triangle Flash Cards

Management individuals, then pairs

Materials 15 triangle-shaped flash cards (Just the Facts Support Master 4), 2 different-colored markers, practice minutes record and certificate (Just the Facts Support Masters 10 and 14)

- Distribute triangle-shaped flash cards (Support Master 4). Have children make flash cards like the ones shown below. Remind children to write the top number in one color, and the two bottom numbers in a second color.

- When finished, children may find a partner and use the doubles/near doubles flash cards to review addition and subtraction facts.

- After practicing the doubles/near doubles facts, children may add these flash cards to their previously made set of triangle cards and take them home to continue review. Practice minutes may be recorded and forms may be returned to school to exchange for a certificate.

Tips

Remind children that the sum of two odd numbers or two even numbers will always be even, while the sum of an even and odd number will always be odd.

Basic Facts Workshop 9

Strategy: Using Ten to Add

Introduce It!

15 minutes

Make a Ten

Management whole class

Materials overhead projector, double ten-frame workmat (Just the Facts Support Master 3) and teacher-made double ten-frame transparency, 19 counters

- Review adding any number to ten. Have children state answers to 10 + 3, 10 + 8, 10 + 5, 10 + 6, 10 + 9, 10 + 4, 10 + 7, and 10 + 1.

- Show 8 counters on a double ten-frame transparency. Ask children how many they see? **8** Show 6 more counters in the bottom ten frame. Ask children how many more they see? **6** Write 8 + 6 = __.

- Slide 2 counters up to make a ten. Ask children to use the ten fact to find how many counters in all. **14** Write 8 + 6 = 14.

- Distribute a workmat and 20 counters to each child.

- Write the following examples on the chalkboard, having children model each with counters, move counters to make a ten, then find the answer: 9 + 7, 8 + 5, 9 + 8, 7 + 8, 9 + 6, and 8 + 7.

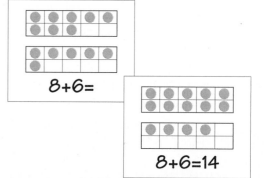

- Repeat the activity with 9 + 4, 8 + 9, 6 + 9, 8 + 7, and 6 + 8.

- Ask children to close their eyes and imagine a double ten frame. Say, Imagine 8 counters on the top ten frame and 5 below. Slide counters up to fill the ten frame and tell how many in all. **10 + 3 = 13**

- Repeat, imagining 9 + 6, 8 + 7, 8 + 6, and 9 + 5.

Develop It!

20 minutes

Imagine a Ten

Management whole class

Materials chalkboard, ten-frame workmat (Just the Facts Support Master 1)

- Have children clear their counters from their ten frames. Write 9 + 4 on the board. Tell the class to look at their workmats and imagine 9 counters on the top ten frame and 4 counters below without really placing any counters on the mat.

- Ask children to imagine sliding a counter up to fill the top frame. Ask, How many counters are there in all? **13** How did you know? **10 + 3 = 13** Write 9 + 4 = 13 on the board.

Make It!

20 minutes

Make a Ten Flash Cards

Management individuals

Materials 20 green index cards, previously made flash cards, practice minutes record and certificate (Just the Facts Support Masters 10 and 14)

- Distribute 20 green index cards to each child. Have children make flash cards for the following make a ten facts:

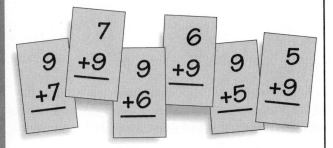

$$
\begin{array}{cccccccc}
9 & 4 & 8 & 7 & 8 & 6 & 8 \\
+4 & +9 & +7 & +8 & +6 & +8 & +5 \\
\end{array}
$$

$$
\begin{array}{ccccccc}
5 & 8 & 4 & 7 & 5 & 7 & 4 \\
+8 & +4 & +8 & +5 & +7 & +4 & +7 \\
\end{array}
$$

- When finished all children may use their flash cards to practice the facts with a partner.

- After practicing at school, children may continue practicing at home, recording the practice minutes and returning the completed record to school to exchange for a certificate.

Tips

Encourage children to create the flash cards in the order of the pattern so that no facts are forgotten. Remind children to write their initials on the back of each card.

Basic Facts Workshop 10

Strategy: Using Ten to Subtract

Introduce It!

15 minutes

Make a Ten

Management whole class

Materials overhead projector, ten-frame and teacher-made ten-frame transparency (Just the Facts Support Master 1), 20 two-sided counters

- Show nine counters of one color on the top ten frame of a transparency. Write 16 − 9 at the top.

- Ask, If you know the whole is 16 and one part is 9, how might you find the other part?

- Use a second color to finish filling the top ten frame and put six counters on the second ten frame. Remind the class that to get from 9 to 16, you need one counter to make ten and another six counters to make 16.

- How many counters did you use for the second part? **7** Write = 7 after 16 − 9 at the top.

- Repeat the activity, having children use ten-frame mats to model 15 − 8, 18 − 9, 13 − 8, 14 − 9, 13 − 7, and 17 − 9. Remind children to show counters for the part they know, then use more counters to make a ten, then add more to get to the whole.

Develop It!

15 minutes

Imagine a Ten

Management whole class

Materials double ten-frame workmat (Just the Facts Support Master 3)

- Write 14 − 8 on the board. Ask children what they know about the whole or parts in the problem. **The whole is 14 and one part is 8.** Ask, How might you find the other part? **Use counters to get from 8 to 14.**

- Tell the class to look at their ten-frame mats and think about the part they know, or eight counters, on the top frame, without really placing any counters on the mat. Ask children to think about putting more counters on the mat to make a ten, then add more to get to 14. Ask, How many counters did you use for the second part? **6**

- Write 14 − 8 = 6 on the board. Repeat the activity with examples such as 13 − 8, 15 − 8, and 14 − 9.

- Next, ask children to turn the ten-frame mats over, and think about double ten frames in their heads. Say, If you want to find the answer to 16 − 9, imagine the 9 counters for the part you know. Now, imagine putting more counters on to get to 16. How many did you use for the other part? **7** Repeat, using 15 − 9, and 17 − 8.

Make It!

Make Ten to Subtract
Flash Cards

Management individuals

Materials 20 green index cards, previously made flash cards, practice minutes record and certificate (Just the Facts Support Masters 10 and 14)

- Distribute 20 green index cards to each child.

- Have children make flash cards for these facts:

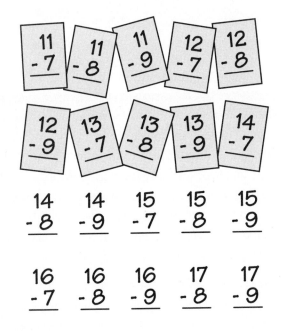

$$\begin{array}{ccccc} 14 & 14 & 15 & 15 & 15 \\ -8 & -9 & -7 & -8 & -9 \end{array}$$

$$\begin{array}{ccccc} 16 & 16 & 16 & 17 & 17 \\ -7 & -8 & -9 & -8 & -9 \end{array}$$

- When finished, children may use the flash cards to practice making a ten to subtract with a partner.

- After practicing at school, children may continue practice at home, recording practice minutes and returning the completed record to school to exchange for a certificate.

Tips

Remind children to write their numbers large enough so the numbers can be read easily.

Basic Facts Workshop 11

Strategy: Using Ten to Subtract

Introduce It!

15 minutes

Tens Again

Management whole class

Materials overhead projector, teacher-made double ten-frame transparency, 20 overhead counters; 20 counters, double ten-frame workmat (Just the Facts Support Master 3) per child

- Show 15 counters 10 on the top frame, and 5 counters on the bottom frame. Ask children how many they see.

- Write 15 − 6 on the top of the transparency. Ask the class what they know about parts and whole in this problem. The whole is 15, and one part is 6. Ask, When you subtract, what do you need to find?

- Remind children that using 10 can help them to subtract 6 from 15 to find the other part. Say, First, you can take 5 away to get to ten, remove counters from the bottom frame. Then you take one more away to get to 9. Ask, What is the other part? Write 15 − 6 = 9.

- Repeat the activity, having children use double ten-frame mats to model 13 − 4, 11 − 4, 14 − 6, 13 − 5, and 12 − 5. Remind children to show counters for the whole, subtract some to go back to ten, then go back further to find the other part.

Develop It!

15 minutes

Imagine a Ten Again

Management whole class

Materials double ten-frame workmat (Just the Facts Support Master 3) per child

- Write 13 − 5 on the board. Have children look at their workmats and *imagine* 13 counters. Ask the class how using a ten could help subtract 5. **Imagine taking off 3 counters to get to ten, then two more to get 8.**

- Repeat the activity with examples such as 11 − 4, 14 − 6, 12 − 5, and 13 − 4. Remind children to imagine the whole, then use the part they know to

count back to ten and further to find the other part. Write 12 − 9 and 12 − 4 on the board. Remind the class that there are two ways to use a ten to subtract. They can start with the whole and use ten to help them subtract one part, or they could start with one part and count up to the whole to find the other part.

- Ask children how they would decide to use a ten to count up or count back. **If the part you know is small, counting back works best; if the part is large, counting up works best.**

- Use the following facts 15 − 9, 14 − 9, 12 − 4, 13 − 5, 12 − 8, 13 − 4, and 13 − 8 to practice the using ten to subtract strategy.

20 minutes

Make Use-a-Ten Flash Cards

Management individuals

Materials 10 triangle flash cards (Just the Facts Support Master 4), 2 different-colored markers, previously made flash cards, practice record form and certificate (Just the Facts Support Masters 11 and 15)

- Distribute triangle-shaped flash cards. Remind children to cut them out and put names or initials on the back. Have children make the flash cards shown below.

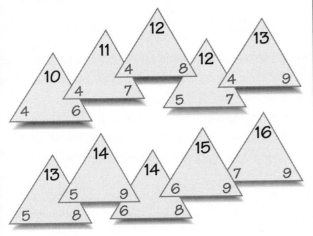

- When finished, children may find a partner and practice addition and subtraction facts with the use-a-ten flash cards.

- After practicing the use-a-ten facts only, children may add these cards to their previously made set of triangle cards and take them home for further practice. Practice minutes may be recorded and records returned to school to be exchanged for a certificate.

Basic Facts Workshop 12
Strategy Review

Introduce It!

15 minutes

Tens Again

Management whole class
Materials overhead projector, teacher-made transparencies of number wheel (Just the Facts Support Master 8)

- Show a number wheel on the overhead projector. Write + 5 in the center. Write the numbers 2-9 in any order in the inner circle.

- Tell children the number wheel will help them practice adding. Ask children to identify each sum, then write it in the outer circle.

- Use a second transparency to make a subtraction wheel. Write − 6 in the center. Write the numbers

7-15 in any order in the inner circle.

- Ask children to identify each difference, then write it in the outer circle.

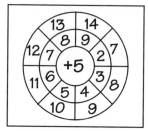 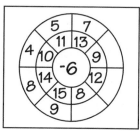

Tips

Remind children to use the count up, count back, doubles and near doubles strategies.

Develop It!

20 minutes

Make a Number Wheel

Management individuals or pairs
Materials number wheel (Just the Facts Support Master 8)

- Distribute 2 number wheels to each child.

- To create an addition wheel, have children write + 6, + 7, + 8, or + 9 in the center. Then, ask them to fill in the inner circle with the numbers 9-17 in any order.

- Children should exchange both number wheels with a partner. Partners write appropriate answers in the outer circles of the wheels, then return the wheels to their partner who will check the answers for accuracy.

 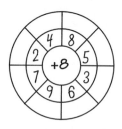 

Tips

Have children write the subtraction sentences if they become confused by the presentation of the numbers in the wheel.

Make It!

15 minutes

Use Flash Cards to Practice

Management pairs
Materials previously made sets of triangle flash cards

- Remind children that they have already practiced all of the addition and subtraction facts. Now they will review to see which ones are now easy for them, and which ones they will want to practice more.

- Have children take out all previously made triangle flash cards.

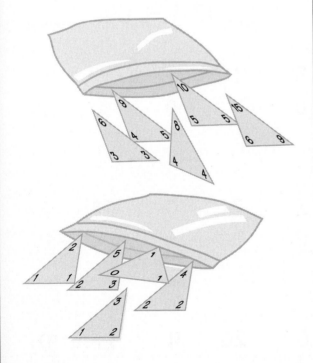

- Working with a partner, each child should go through all cards. If they know all facts for a card, they put it in one pile. If they have difficulty with any facts for a card, they put it in a second pile.

- Each partner should work on facts they have difficulty with for 5-10 minutes. Then have them go through just those cards again.

- Children may want to take their cards home for more practice.

Name_____ Date _____

◤ 1A ◢ BASIC FACTS

Adding and Subtracting Zero

Add.

1. $0 + 7 =$ __7__   2. $0 + 2 =$ _____   3. $3 + 0 =$ _____

4. $2 + 0 =$ _____   5. $1 + 0 =$ _____   6. $0 + 9 =$ _____

7. $4 + 0 =$ _____   8. $0 + 6 =$ _____   9. $0 + 8 =$ _____

10. $8 + 0 =$ _____   11. $5 + 0 =$ _____   12. $0 + 1 =$ _____

13. $\begin{array}{r} 0 \\ +\,1 \\ \hline \end{array}$ 14. $\begin{array}{r} 5 \\ +\,0 \\ \hline \end{array}$ 15. $\begin{array}{r} 8 \\ +\,0 \\ \hline \end{array}$ 16. $\begin{array}{r} 1 \\ +\,0 \\ \hline \end{array}$ 17. $\begin{array}{r} 0 \\ +\,2 \\ \hline \end{array}$

18. $\begin{array}{r} 6 \\ +\,0 \\ \hline \end{array}$ 19. $\begin{array}{r} 5 \\ +\,0 \\ \hline \end{array}$ 20. $\begin{array}{r} 2 \\ +\,0 \\ \hline \end{array}$ 21. $\begin{array}{r} 0 \\ +\,6 \\ \hline \end{array}$ 22. $\begin{array}{r} 7 \\ +\,0 \\ \hline \end{array}$

23. $\begin{array}{r} 0 \\ +\,9 \\ \hline \end{array}$ 24. $\begin{array}{r} 3 \\ +\,0 \\ \hline \end{array}$ 25. $\begin{array}{r} 0 \\ +\,7 \\ \hline \end{array}$ 26. $\begin{array}{r} 4 \\ +\,0 \\ \hline \end{array}$ 27. $\begin{array}{r} 0 \\ +\,4 \\ \hline \end{array}$

Name_____ Date _____

◣1B BASIC FACTS

Adding and Subtracting Zero

Subtract.

1. 2
  − 0
  2

2. 5
  − 5

3. 8
  − 0

4. 3
  − 0

5. 4
  − 0

6. 1
  − 0

7. 3
  − 3

8. 6
  − 0

9. 1
  − 1

10. 4
  − 0

11. 8
  − 8

12. 5
  − 5

13. 9
  − 9

14. 7
  − 0

15. 4
  − 4

16. 6
  − 6

17. 7
  − 7

18. 5
  − 0

19. 6
  − 6

20. 0
  − 0

21. 4
  − 0

22. 8
  − 0

23. 2
  − 2

24. 9
  − 0

25. 5
  − 5

Name_____ Date _____

2A BASIC FACTS

Counting On 1, 2, 3 to Add

Circle the greater addend. Count on to add.

1. $(5) + 3 =$ __8__   2. $2 + 7 =$ _____   3. $1 + 8 =$ _____

4. $9 + 1 =$ _____   5. $3 + 4 =$ _____   6. $5 + 2 =$ _____

7. $1 + 6 =$ _____   8. $8 + 1 =$ _____   9. $7 + 3 =$ _____

Add.

10. $\begin{array}{r} 1 \\ + 9 \\ \hline \end{array}$ 11. $\begin{array}{r} 1 \\ + 2 \\ \hline \end{array}$ 12. $\begin{array}{r} 3 \\ + 8 \\ \hline \end{array}$ 13. $\begin{array}{r} 9 \\ + 2 \\ \hline \end{array}$ 14. $\begin{array}{r} 1 \\ + 3 \\ \hline \end{array}$

15. $\begin{array}{r} 4 \\ + 2 \\ \hline \end{array}$ 16. $\begin{array}{r} 9 \\ + 3 \\ \hline \end{array}$ 17. $\begin{array}{r} 2 \\ + 3 \\ \hline \end{array}$ 18. $\begin{array}{r} 8 \\ + 2 \\ \hline \end{array}$ 19. $\begin{array}{r} 7 \\ + 1 \\ \hline \end{array}$

20. $\begin{array}{r} 3 \\ + 7 \\ \hline \end{array}$ 21. $\begin{array}{r} 6 \\ + 3 \\ \hline \end{array}$ 22. $\begin{array}{r} 2 \\ + 6 \\ \hline \end{array}$ 23. $\begin{array}{r} 4 \\ + 1 \\ \hline \end{array}$ 24. $\begin{array}{r} 1 \\ + 3 \\ \hline \end{array}$

Name_____   Date _____

2B BASIC FACTS

Counting On 1, 2, 3 to Add

Count on to add.

1.   4
   + 2
    6

2.   2
   + 9

3.   1
   + 3

4.   5
   + 3

5.   8
   + 1

6.   2
   + 2

7.   1
   + 9

8.   6
   + 3

9.   9
   + 3

10.   4
   + 3

11.   7
   + 2

12.   8
   + 2

13.   1
   + 4

14.   1
   + 8

15.   5
   + 5

16.   1
   + 5

17.   2
   + 3

18.   3
   + 4

19.   2
   + 6

20.   7
   + 3

21.   3
   + 9

22.   9
   + 2

23.   2
   + 5

24.   8
   + 3

25.   2
   + 4

Name_____   Date _____

3A BASIC FACTS

··

Counting Back

Count back to subtract.

1. 8 − 1 = __*7*__   **2.** 7 − 2 = _____   **3.** 6 − 1 = _____

4. 8 − 3 = _____   **5.** 5 − 1 = _____   **6.** 7 − 3 = _____

7. 9 − 2 = _____   **8.** 6 − 3 = _____   **9.** 4 − 1 = _____

10. 8 − 2 = _____   **11.** 3 − 1 = _____   **12.** 5 − 2 = _____

13. 9
      − 3
      ____

14. 3
      − 2
      ____

15. 2
      − 1
      ____

16. 9
      − 2
      ____

17. 4
      − 1
      ____

18. 4
      − 3
      ____

19. 5
      − 2
      ____

20. 7
      − 1
      ____

21. 4
      − 2
      ____

22. 3
      − 3
      ____

23. 9
      − 1
      ____

24. 8
      − 2
      ____

25. 6
      − 3
      ____

26. 5
      − 3
      ____

27. 6
      − 2
      ____

Name_____ Date _____

3B ▸ BASIC FACTS
....

Counting Back

Count back to subtract.

1. $9 - 3 =$ __6__   2. $9 - 2 =$ _____   3. $7 - 1 =$ _____

4. $8 - 2 =$ _____   5. $7 - 3 =$ _____   6. $6 - 3 =$ _____

7. $4 - 2 =$ _____   8. $4 - 1 =$ _____   9. $5 - 1 =$ _____

10. $9 - 1 =$ _____   11. $5 - 3 =$ _____   12. $3 - 2 =$ _____

13. $\begin{array}{r} 8 \\ -3 \\ \hline \end{array}$ 14. $\begin{array}{r} 6 \\ -1 \\ \hline \end{array}$ 15. $\begin{array}{r} 5 \\ -2 \\ \hline \end{array}$ 16. $\begin{array}{r} 7 \\ -2 \\ \hline \end{array}$ 17. $\begin{array}{r} 4 \\ -3 \\ \hline \end{array}$

18. $\begin{array}{r} 6 \\ -3 \\ \hline \end{array}$ 19. $\begin{array}{r} 7 \\ -3 \\ \hline \end{array}$ 20. $\begin{array}{r} 9 \\ -3 \\ \hline \end{array}$ 21. $\begin{array}{r} 5 \\ -3 \\ \hline \end{array}$ 22. $\begin{array}{r} 6 \\ -2 \\ \hline \end{array}$

23. $\begin{array}{r} 3 \\ -1 \\ \hline \end{array}$ 24. $\begin{array}{r} 9 \\ -2 \\ \hline \end{array}$ 25. $\begin{array}{r} 4 \\ -2 \\ \hline \end{array}$ 26. $\begin{array}{r} 8 \\ -1 \\ \hline \end{array}$ 27. $\begin{array}{r} 3 \\ -2 \\ \hline \end{array}$

Name_____   Date _____

4A BASIC FACTS

Counting Up

Count up to find the missing part.
Write the number sentence.

1.
| Whole |
| 9 |

| Part | Part |
| 6 | *3* |

$$\underline{6} + \underline{3} = \underline{9}$$

2.
| Whole |
| 8 |

| Part | Part |
| 5 | |

$$\underline{} + \underline{} = \underline{}$$

3.
| Whole |
| 7 |

| Part | Part |
| 4 | |

$$\underline{} + \underline{} = \underline{}$$

4.
| Whole |
| 12 |

| Part | Part |
| 9 | |

$$\underline{} + \underline{} = \underline{}$$

◢ BASIC FACTS
4B

Counting Up

Count up to subtract.

1.   12
   − 9
   3
	2. 7
	   − 6
		3. 11
		   − 9
			4. 8
			   − 5
				5. 4
				   − 2

6.   9
   − 6
	7. 3
	   − 2
		8. 10
		   − 9
			9. 7
			   − 4
				10. 5
				   − 2

11.   10
   − 7
	12. 6
	   − 3
		13. 5
		   − 4
			14. 8
			   − 6
				15. 6
				   − 4

16.   9
   − 8
	17. 9
	   − 7
		18. 7
		   − 5
			19. 9
			   − 6
				20. 10
				   − 8

21.   6
   − 5
	22. 11
	   − 8
		23. 5
		   − 3
			24. 12
			   − 9
				25. 6
				   − 4

Name_____ Date _____

5A ▸ BASIC FACTS

Strategy Review

Add or subtract.

1. $\begin{array}{r} 9 \\ + 3 \\ \hline 12 \end{array}$ $\begin{array}{r} 12 \\ - 9 \\ \hline 3 \end{array}$ 2. $\begin{array}{r} 0 \\ + 9 \\ \hline \end{array}$ $\begin{array}{r} 9 \\ - 0 \\ \hline \end{array}$ 3. $\begin{array}{r} 9 \\ + 2 \\ \hline \end{array}$ $\begin{array}{r} 11 \\ - 9 \\ \hline \end{array}$

4. $\begin{array}{r} 1 \\ + 8 \\ \hline \end{array}$ $\begin{array}{r} 9 \\ - 8 \\ \hline \end{array}$ 5. $\begin{array}{r} 4 \\ + 1 \\ \hline \end{array}$ $\begin{array}{r} 5 \\ - 4 \\ \hline \end{array}$ 6. $\begin{array}{r} 4 \\ + 2 \\ \hline \end{array}$ $\begin{array}{r} 6 \\ - 4 \\ \hline \end{array}$

7. $\begin{array}{r} 8 \\ + 3 \\ \hline \end{array}$ $\begin{array}{r} 11 \\ - 8 \\ \hline \end{array}$ 8. $\begin{array}{r} 6 \\ + 2 \\ \hline \end{array}$ $\begin{array}{r} 8 \\ - 7 \\ \hline \end{array}$ 9. $\begin{array}{r} 2 \\ + 8 \\ \hline \end{array}$ $\begin{array}{r} 10 \\ - 8 \\ \hline \end{array}$

10. $\begin{array}{r} 8 \\ + 2 \\ \hline \end{array}$ $\begin{array}{r} 10 \\ - 8 \\ \hline \end{array}$ 11. $\begin{array}{r} 7 \\ + 1 \\ \hline \end{array}$ $\begin{array}{r} 8 \\ - 7 \\ \hline \end{array}$ 12. $\begin{array}{r} 7 \\ + 2 \\ \hline \end{array}$ $\begin{array}{r} 9 \\ - 8 \\ \hline \end{array}$

13. $\begin{array}{r} 1 \\ + 9 \\ \hline \end{array}$ $\begin{array}{r} 10 \\ - 1 \\ \hline \end{array}$ 14. $\begin{array}{r} 0 \\ + 4 \\ \hline \end{array}$ $\begin{array}{r} 4 \\ - 0 \\ \hline \end{array}$ 15. $\begin{array}{r} 7 \\ + 3 \\ \hline \end{array}$ $\begin{array}{r} 10 \\ - 7 \\ \hline \end{array}$

Name_____   Date _____

5B BASIC FACTS

Strategy Review

Count on, back, or up.

1.   2
  − 1
	2. 7
	  + 3
		3. 12
		  − 9
			4. 8
			  − 3
				5. 8
				  + 2

6.   2
  + 6
	7. 8
	  + 3
		8. 11
		  − 9
			9. 7
			  − 3
				10. 2
				  + 7

11.   9
  − 7
	12. 9
	  − 3
		13. 9
		  − 2
			14. 6
			  + 3
				15. 10
				  − 2

16.   7
  − 5
	17. 11
	  − 3
		18. 2
		  + 5
			19. 2
			  + 9
				20. 10
				  − 3

21.   4
  + 3
	22. 8
	  − 5
		23. 2
		  + 4
			24. 6
			  − 4
				25. 9
				  − 6

Name_____ Date _____

6A BASIC FACTS

Using Doubles to Add

Write the sum of the double.
Use the double to write the next sum.

1. $7 + 7 = \underline{14}$ so $8 + 7 = \underline{15}$ so $9 + 7 = \underline{16}$

2. $4 + 4 = \underline{\hphantom{00}}$ so $5 + 4 = \underline{\hphantom{00}}$ so $6 + 4 = \underline{\hphantom{00}}$

3. $5 + 5 = \underline{\hphantom{00}}$ so $6 + 5 = \underline{\hphantom{00}}$ so $7 + 5 = \underline{\hphantom{00}}$

4. $6 + 6 = \underline{\hphantom{00}}$ so $7 + 6 = \underline{\hphantom{00}}$ so $8 + 6 = \underline{\hphantom{00}}$

Write the sum. Use a double when it helps.

5. $\begin{array}{r} 5 \\ + 5 \\ \hline \end{array}$ 6. $\begin{array}{r} 6 \\ + 5 \\ \hline \end{array}$ 7. $\begin{array}{r} 7 \\ + 5 \\ \hline \end{array}$ 8. $\begin{array}{r} 8 \\ + 8 \\ \hline \end{array}$ 9. $\begin{array}{r} 8 \\ + 9 \\ \hline \end{array}$

10. $\begin{array}{r} 7 \\ + 7 \\ \hline \end{array}$ 11. $\begin{array}{r} 7 \\ + 8 \\ \hline \end{array}$ 12. $\begin{array}{r} 8 \\ + 7 \\ \hline \end{array}$ 13. $\begin{array}{r} 4 \\ + 4 \\ \hline \end{array}$ 14. $\begin{array}{r} 5 \\ + 4 \\ \hline \end{array}$

Name_____ Date _____

6B ◣ BASIC FACTS

Using Doubles to Add

Use a double. Add.

1. $4 + 4 = \underline{8}$ so $4 + 5 = \underline{9}$ so $4 + 6 = \underline{10}$

2. $6 + 6 = \underline{\quad}$ so $6 + 7 = \underline{\quad}$ so $6 + 8 = \underline{\quad}$

3. $\begin{array}{r} 4 \\ +4 \\ \hline \end{array}$ 4. $\begin{array}{r} 4 \\ +5 \\ \hline \end{array}$ 5. $\begin{array}{r} 6 \\ +4 \\ \hline \end{array}$ 6. $\begin{array}{r} 7 \\ +8 \\ \hline \end{array}$ 7. $\begin{array}{r} 8 \\ +7 \\ \hline \end{array}$

8. $\begin{array}{r} 8 \\ +8 \\ \hline \end{array}$ 9. $\begin{array}{r} 4 \\ +6 \\ \hline \end{array}$ 10. $\begin{array}{r} 5 \\ +5 \\ \hline \end{array}$ 11. $\begin{array}{r} 5 \\ +6 \\ \hline \end{array}$ 12. $\begin{array}{r} 5 \\ +7 \\ \hline \end{array}$

13. $\begin{array}{r} 6 \\ +4 \\ \hline \end{array}$ 14. $\begin{array}{r} 6 \\ +5 \\ \hline \end{array}$ 15. $\begin{array}{r} 6 \\ +6 \\ \hline \end{array}$ 16. $\begin{array}{r} 6 \\ +7 \\ \hline \end{array}$ 17. $\begin{array}{r} 6 \\ +8 \\ \hline \end{array}$

18. $\begin{array}{r} 7 \\ +5 \\ \hline \end{array}$ 19. $\begin{array}{r} 7 \\ +6 \\ \hline \end{array}$ 20. $\begin{array}{r} 7 \\ +7 \\ \hline \end{array}$ 21. $\begin{array}{r} 7 \\ +9 \\ \hline \end{array}$ 22. $\begin{array}{r} 8 \\ +9 \\ \hline \end{array}$

Name_____ Date _____

7A ◢ BASIC FACTS

··

Using Doubles to Subtract

Think of a double. Write the other part.
Write the number sentence.

1.
Whole
10

Part	Part
5	5

2.
Whole
12

Part	Part
5	

$$10 - 5 = 5$$ ___ − ___ = ___

3.
Whole
11

Part	Part
5	

4.
Whole
14

Part	Part
7	

___ − ___ = ___   ___ − ___ = ___

Name_____   Date _____

7B BASIC FACTS

....

Using Doubles to Subtract

Subtract.

1. $8 - 4 =$ __4__   so $9 - 4 =$ __5__   so $10 - 4 =$ __6__

2. $10 - 5 =$ _____   so $11 - 5 =$ _____   so $12 - 5 =$ _____

3. $12 - 6 =$ _____   so $13 - 6 =$ _____   so $14 - 6 =$ _____

4.	5.	6.	7.	8.
8 -4	10 -5	9 -5	9 -4	11 -5

9.	10.	11.	12.	13.
14 -7	11 -6	13 -7	12 -6	15 -7

14.	15.	16.	17.	18.
14 -6	15 -8	10 -4	18 -9	17 -8

Name_____ Date _____

8A ▸ BASIC FACTS
···
Strategy Review

Count up, on, or back.

1. 10 $-\ 7$ *3*	**2.** 8 $+\ 2$	**3.** 6 $-\ 3$	**4.** 11 $-\ 4$	**5.** 4 $+\ 3$
6. 9 $+\ 1$	**7.** 2 $+\ 9$	**8.** 8 $+\ 3$	**9.** 7 $+\ 3$	**10.** 9 $+\ 2$
11. 10 $-\ 2$	**12.** 10 $-\ 3$	**13.** 10 $-\ 9$	**14.** 9 $-\ 6$	**15.** 9 $+\ 3$
16. 4 $+\ 2$	**17.** 11 $-\ 2$	**18.** 10 $-\ 1$	**19.** 8 $-\ 7$	**20.** 9 $-\ 7$
21. 12 $-\ 9$	**22.** 6 $+\ 2$	**23.** 12 $-\ 3$	**24.** 6 $+\ 1$	**25.** 5 $+\ 3$

Name_____   Date _____

8B ▸ BASIC FACTS

Strategy Review

Think about doubles and near doubles.

1.	8 − 4 **4**	2.	10 − 5	3.	8 + 9	4.	12 − 7	5.	7 + 5

6.	16 − 8	7.	14 − 6	8.	9 − 5	9.	13 − 7	10.	16 − 9

11.	15 − 8	12.	7 + 8	13.	15 − 7	14.	11 − 6	15.	17 − 9

16.	8 + 6	17.	7 + 9	18.	4 + 5	19.	13 − 6	20.	10 − 4

21.	9 + 7	22.	5 + 6	23.	7 + 7	24.	18 − 9	25.	8 + 7

Name_____ Date _____

9A ▷ BASIC FACTS
....

Using Ten to Add

Make a 10. Complete the number sentence.

1. 8 + 4

   10 + _2_ = _12_

2. 9 + 5

   10 + ____ = ____

3. 9 + 7

   10 + ____ = ____

4. 8 + 5

   10 + ____ = ____

5. 9 + 6

   10 + ____ = ____

6. 6 + 8

   10 + ____ = ____

7. 9 + 4

   10 + ____ = ____

8. 8 + 7

   10 + ____ = ____

9. 7 + 4

   10 + ____ = ____

10. 7 + 5

    10 + ____ = ____

Name_____ Date _____

9B BASIC FACTS

···

Using Ten to Add

Make a 10. Complete the number sentence.

1. $8 + 7$

$10 + \underline{}5 = \underline{15}$

2. $9 + 4$

$10 + \underline{} = \underline{}$

3. $8 + 8$

$10 + \underline{} = \underline{}$

4. $9 + 7$

$10 + \underline{} = \underline{}$

5. $9 + 5$

$10 + \underline{} = \underline{}$

6. $8 + 5$

$10 + \underline{} = \underline{}$

7. $9 + 6$

$10 + \underline{} = \underline{}$

8. $8 + 4$

$10 + \underline{} = \underline{}$

9. $5 + 7$

$10 + \underline{} = \underline{}$

10. $4 + 9$

$10 + \underline{} = \underline{}$

Name_____   Date _____

10A BASIC FACTS

Using Ten to Subtract

Make a 10. Subtract.

1. 13
   $-\ 9$
   4

2. 12
   $-\ 9$

3. 16
   $-\ 9$

4. 15
   $-\ 7$

5. 17
   $-\ 9$

6. 11
   $-\ 7$

7. 16
   $-\ 7$

8. 17
   $-\ 9$

9. 14
   $-\ 9$

10. 11
    $-\ 9$

11. 13
    $-\ 8$

12. 11
    $-\ 7$

13. 16
    $-\ 9$

14. 15
    $-\ 8$

15. 18
    $-\ 9$

16. 14
    $-\ 8$

17. 17
    $-\ 9$

18. 14
    $-\ 9$

19. 13
    $-\ 9$

20. 13
    $-\ 8$

21. 15
    $-\ 9$

22. 16
    $-\ 9$

23. 15
    $-\ 9$

24. 17
    $-\ 8$

25. 11
    $-\ 9$

Name_____ Date _____

10B BASIC FACTS

Using Ten to Subtract

Make a 10. Subtract.

1.   12
  − 7
   5
	2. 17
	  − 9
		3. 15
		  − 7
			4. 14
			  − 7
				5. 16
				  − 8

6.   18
  − 9
	7. 12
	  − 9
		8. 15
		  − 8
			9. 17
			  − 8
				10. 13
				  − 9

11.   16
  − 7
	12. 14
	  − 8
		13. 11
		  − 7
			14. 13
			  − 8
				15. 16
				  − 9

16.   15
  − 7
	17. 12
	  − 8
		18. 18
		  − 9
			19. 13
			  − 7
				20. 11
				  − 8

21.   17
  − 9
	22. 16
	  − 7
		23. 14
		  − 8
			24. 11
			  − 9
				25. 13
				  − 9

Name_____ Date _____

11A ◣ BASIC FACTS
··
Using Ten to Subtract

Make a 10. Subtract.

1. 11
   − 4
   ‾‾‾‾
    7

2. 14
   − 6
   ‾‾‾‾

3. 12
   − 5
   ‾‾‾‾

4. 13
   − 4
   ‾‾‾‾

5. 12
   − 7
   ‾‾‾‾

6. 12
   − 4
   ‾‾‾‾

7. 15
   − 9
   ‾‾‾‾

8. 14
   − 9
   ‾‾‾‾

9. 12
   − 4
   ‾‾‾‾

10. 13
    − 5
    ‾‾‾‾

11. 12
    − 8
    ‾‾‾‾

12. 13
    − 8
    ‾‾‾‾

13. 15
    − 6
    ‾‾‾‾

14. 13
    − 5
    ‾‾‾‾

15. 11
    − 4
    ‾‾‾‾

16. 14
    − 6
    ‾‾‾‾

17. 13
    − 4
    ‾‾‾‾

18. 12
    − 5
    ‾‾‾‾

19. 11
    − 7
    ‾‾‾‾

20. 16
    − 9
    ‾‾‾‾

21. 14
    − 5
    ‾‾‾‾

22. 12
    − 7
    ‾‾‾‾

23. 13
    − 9
    ‾‾‾‾

24. 16
    − 7
    ‾‾‾‾

25. 15
    − 9
    ‾‾‾‾

Name_____ Date _____

11B BASIC FACTS

Using Ten to Subtract

Write the answer.

1. $\begin{array}{r} 4 \\ + 4 \\ \hline 8 \end{array}$

2. $\begin{array}{r} 11 \\ - 7 \\ \hline \end{array}$

3. $\begin{array}{r} 13 \\ - 9 \\ \hline \end{array}$

4. $\begin{array}{r} 5 \\ + 8 \\ \hline \end{array}$

5. $\begin{array}{r} 14 \\ - 5 \\ \hline \end{array}$

6. $\begin{array}{r} 12 \\ - 7 \\ \hline \end{array}$

7. $\begin{array}{r} 14 \\ - 6 \\ \hline \end{array}$

8. $\begin{array}{r} 12 \\ - 8 \\ \hline \end{array}$

9. $\begin{array}{r} 6 \\ + 8 \\ \hline \end{array}$

10. $\begin{array}{r} 16 \\ - 9 \\ \hline \end{array}$

11. $\begin{array}{r} 5 \\ + 7 \\ \hline \end{array}$

12. $\begin{array}{r} 9 \\ + 6 \\ \hline \end{array}$

13. $\begin{array}{r} 16 \\ - 7 \\ \hline \end{array}$

14. $\begin{array}{r} 8 \\ + 4 \\ \hline \end{array}$

15. $\begin{array}{r} 10 \\ - 4 \\ \hline \end{array}$

16. $\begin{array}{r} 15 \\ - 9 \\ \hline \end{array}$

17. $\begin{array}{r} 16 \\ - 7 \\ \hline \end{array}$

18. $\begin{array}{r} 9 \\ + 7 \\ \hline \end{array}$

19. $\begin{array}{r} 6 \\ + 9 \\ \hline \end{array}$

20. $\begin{array}{r} 14 \\ - 8 \\ \hline \end{array}$

21. $\begin{array}{r} 13 \\ - 4 \\ \hline \end{array}$

22. $\begin{array}{r} 7 \\ + 9 \\ \hline \end{array}$

23. $\begin{array}{r} 9 \\ + 7 \\ \hline \end{array}$

24. $\begin{array}{r} 5 \\ + 9 \\ \hline \end{array}$

25. $\begin{array}{r} 12 \\ - 5 \\ \hline \end{array}$

Name_____ Date _____

BASIC FACTS

Strategy Review

Add.

1. 1
    + 7

    8

2. 0
    + 9

3. 5
    + 5

4. 8
    + 8

5. 6
    + 5

6. 9
    + 4

7. 9
    + 8

8. 6
    + 5

9. 9
    + 9

10. 7
    + 6

11. 3
    + 4

12. 8
    + 2

13. 6
    + 9

14. 2
    + 7

15. 8
    + 5

16. 4
    + 6

17. 7
    + 7

18. 2
    + 0

19. 7
    + 0

20. 9
    + 7

21. 6
    + 6

22. 4
    + 8

23. 7
    + 9

24. 4
    + 5

25. 8
    + 9

Name_____ Date _____

12B ◣ BASIC FACTS
Strategy Review

Subtract.

1. 8
 − 7
 ⋮

2. 12
 − 5

3. 13
 − 6

4. 11
 − 7

5. 15
 − 9

6. 10
 − 8

7. 11
 − 6

8. 14
 − 8

9. 17
 − 9

10. 16
 − 8

11. 9
 − 3

12. 13
 − 7

13. 17
 − 8

14. 15
 − 9

15. 18
 − 9

16. 12
 − 7

17. 8
 − 4

18. 11
 − 5

19. 13
 − 8

20. 10
 − 7

21. 8
 − 5

22. 13
 − 4

23. 15
 − 6

24. 10
 − 4

25. 10
 − 8

Basic Facts Workshop 1
Addition and Subtraction Facts

Review

🕐 **10 minutes**

Counting On and Back to Add and Subtract

Management whole class

- Write 9 + 3 on the board.

- Ask students how the counting on strategy could help them find the answer. **When adding 1, 2, or 3 to a number, start at the larger number and count on from there.** Repeat with 2 + 9 and 8 + 3.

- Write 11 − 3 on the board.

- Ask students how they could figure out the answer to this basic subtraction fact. **Use the strategy of counting back. Start with the larger number and count back.** Repeat with 10 − 3 and 13 − 4.

- Write 8 − 9 on the board. Ask students if counting back would be a good way to figure out this fact. **No, because it's too hard to keep track of counting back 9 places.**

- Remind students that when subtracting, counting back works well if the number being subtracted is small, and counting on works well if the numbers being subtracted are close together.

- Students can practice these strategies by finding several similar basic facts for which counting on or back will help. For example, 9 − 2, 9 − 6, and 11 − 9.

Practice

🕐 **30 minutes**

Count On and Back with Flash Cards

Management individuals, then pairs
Materials for each student: 2 different-colored markers, 24 triangle flash cards (Just the Facts Support Master 4), practice minutes record and certificate (Just the Facts Support Masters 9 and 13)

- Have students make flash cards like the ones shown, with the top number written in one color and the bottom two numbers written in a second color, for the following fact families: 1,1,2; 1,2,3; 1,3,4; 1,4,5; 1,5,6; 1,6,7; 1,7,8; 1,8,9; 1,9,10; 2,2,4; 2,3,5; 2,4,6; 2,5,7; 2,6,8; 2,7,9; 2,8,10; 2,9,11; 3,3,6; 3,4,7; 3,5,8; 3,6,9; 3,7,10; 3,8,11; and 3,9,12.

- Students work with partners to review their addition and subtraction facts.

- One partner covers each corner in turn. If both numbers the partner sees are the same color, he or she states an addition fact. If the numbers are different colors, the partner states the subtraction fact.

- Encourage students to bring their flash cards home to practice, recording practice minutes. They may exchange completed records at school for a certificate.

Basic Facts Workshop 2

Doubles, Near Doubles Addition and Subtraction Facts

 Review

 25 minutes

Doubles and Near Doubles Facts

Management whole class
Materials overhead projector, blank transparencies, 18 counters

- Draw a vertical line down the center of a transparency. Place 7 counters on one side of the line. Have students count them. Ask, How many would there be if the counters were doubled? **14**

- Place 7 counters on the other half of the transparency. Ask students to name the addition fact shown. **7 + 7 = 14**

- Ask, If the whole is 14 and part is 7, which subtraction fact is known? **14 − 7 = 7**

- Repeat with other doubles facts such as 6 + 6, 8 + 8, and 9 + 9.

- Write 7 + 8 on a transparency. Show a row of 7 counters and a row of 8 counters.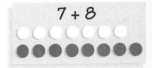

- Ask, How could a double help solve this fact?
  7 − 7 + 1 = 15 or
  8 + 8 − 1 = 15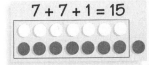

- Write 6 + 8 on a transparency. Place a row of 6 counters and a row of 8 counters on the projector. Ask students to use the double to find the sum.
  6 + 6 + 2 = 14 or 8 + 8 − 2 = 14

 Practice

 30 minutes

Make Doubles, Near Doubles Flash Cards

Management individuals, then pairs
Materials for each student: 2 different-colored markers, 5 triangle flash cards (Just the Facts Support Master 4), 6 index cards, practice minutes record and certificate (Just the Facts Support Masters 10 and 14)

- Remind students that doubles can help when adding two numbers. Tell them that when two numbers being added are close in value, near doubles can be used to find their sum.

- Give students an example of a near doubles fact,

such as 5 + 4. Ask them to identify a double that might be helpful in finding the sum. **4 + 4**

- Ask, How many more need to be added to find the sum? **1** What is the sum? **4 + 4 + 1 = 9**

- Have students make flash cards for the following near doubles facts: 4,5,9; 6,7,13; 8,9,17; 7,8,15; and 5,6,11. Students should also make cards for these doubles facts: 4 + 4; 5 + 5; 6 + 6; 7 + 7; 8 + 8, and 9 + 9. Remind students to write their names or initials on the backs of their cards.

- Students may add these flash cards to their previously made set and take them home to practice. Remind them to record practice minutes. They may exchange completed records for a certificate.

Basic Facts Workshop 3
Using Ten to Add and Subtract

Review

20 minutes

Make a Ten Strategy

Management whole class
Materials overhead projector, 2 double ten-frame transparencies (Just the Facts Support Master 3)

- Write 8 + 5 at the top of a transparency. Show 8 counters on the top ten-frame and 5 below.

8 + 5

- Ask, How could making a ten help you add these numbers?
Move 2 counters up to make
10 + 3 = 13 Write 8 + 5 = 13 at the top.

8 + 5

- Repeat with several examples, such as 9 + 6, 7 + 9, 8 + 6, 7 + 5, and 8 + 5.

- Write 15 − 6 at the top of a transparency. Show 15 counters on the ten-frames, 10 on top and 5 below.

- Ask how the making a ten strategy could help subtract 6 from 15. **Remove 5 counters from the bottom frame and 1 from the top frame.**

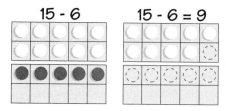

15 - 6   15 - 6 = 9

- Repeat with several examples, such as 13 − 6, 16 − 7, 15 − 8, 14 − 8, and 17 − 9.

Practice

30 minutes

Flash Cards for Make a Ten Facts

Management individuals, then pairs
Materials for each student: 2 different-colored markers, 10 triangle flash cards (Just the Facts Support Master 4), practice minutes record and certificate (Just the Facts Support Masters 10 and 14)

- Have students make flash cards like the ones shown. The top number should be written in one color, the bottom two numbers in another color. Students should make flash cards for the following facts: 4,6,10; 5,7,12; 6,8,14; 7,4,11; 8,4,12; 8,5,13; 9,4,13; 9,5,14; 9,6,15; and 9,7,16.

- When students have completed their make a ten flash cards, have them work with partners to review their addition and subtraction facts. Remind them to write their names or initials on the backs of their cards.

- Encourage students to bring their flash cards home to continue practicing their addition and subtraction facts. Remind them to keep a record of the minutes they practice. They may exchange completed records for a certificate.

Basic Facts Workshop 4

Naming and Using Arrays in Multiplication

Review

15 minutes

Using Arrays to Multiply

Management whole class
Materials overhead projector, hundredths square transparencies (Just the Facts Support Master 7), 35 counters

- Place 3 rows of 4 counters on a grid transparency. Outline the array. Ask students how many counters they see. **12** Then, ask students to name the array and the multiplication sentence it shows. **3 × 4, 3 × 4 = 12**

$3 \times 4 = 12$

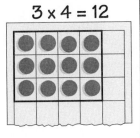

- Remind students that the array shown can be named in two different ways, because when multiplying, the order of the factors does not change the product. Turn the grid transparency 90°. Ask students to name this array. **4 × 3**

$4 \times 3 = 12$

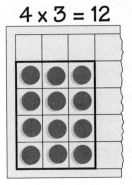

- Repeat the activity, modeling arrays and writing two ways to name them for 2 × 6, 4 × 5, and 5 × 7.

Practice

30 minutes

Naming Arrays

Management pairs
Materials for each pair: a paper clip, a six-section spinner (Just the Facts Support Master 6), 2-3 sheets of hundredths square paper (Just the Facts Support Master 7)

- Distribute a spinner and 2-3 sheets of hundredths square paper to each pair. Have students label the spinner sections 1, 2, 3, 4, 5, and 6.

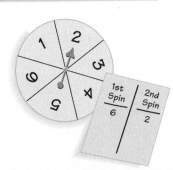

- One partner spins the spinner twice, while the other partner keeps a record of the numbers where the pointer lands.

- Using the two numbers that the pointer landed on, students should draw the array on their paper. Students may either draw circles to represent counters or outline the array. Partners work together to write two multiplication sentences for the array beside it. **Answers will vary. Possible answer:**
  2 × 6 = 12, 6 × 2 = 12

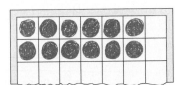

- Partners should switch roles and practice until each partner has had 10 turns.

Basic Facts Workshop 5

Multiplying by 1 and 2

Review

25 minutes

1's and Doubles

Management whole class

Materials overhead projector, hundredths square transparencies (Just the Facts Support Master 7)

- Draw a 1×4 array on a grid transparency. Ask students to name the array and the multiplication sentence it shows. **1×4; $1 \times 4 = 4$**

  1 x 4

- Tell students you are going to double the array. Draw another 1×4 array below the first. Have students name the new array.
  $2 \times 4 = 8$

  2 x 4

- Have students practice naming arrays. Draw a 2×6 array on a grid transparency and ask students to name it. **2×6**

- Repeat with several examples, such as $1 \times 8 = 8$ and $2 \times 8 = 16$; $1 \times 3 = 3$ and $2 \times 3 = 6$; and $1 \times 9 = 9$ and $2 \times 9 = 18$.

- Ask students to picture a 1×3 array and name it. **1×3** Then, ask them to double it and name the doubles multiplication fact. **$2 \times 3 = 6$** Students may have trouble picturing arrays in their minds. If necessary, model arrays with connecting cubes or counters.

- Repeat, using facts such as $1 \times 4 = 4$ and $2 \times 4 = 8$; $1 \times 2 = 2$ and $2 \times 2 = 4$; and $1 \times 7 = 7$ and $2 \times 7 = 14$.

Practice

30 minutes

Make x1 and x2 Flash Cards

Management individuals, then pairs

Materials for each student: 32 index cards, practice minutes record and certificate (Just the Facts Support Masters 9 and 13)

- Distribute index cards to each student and have them make flash cards like the ones below for the following facts: 1×1, 2×1, 3×1, 4×1, 5×1, 6×1, 7×1, 8×1, 9×1, 1×2, 1×3, 1×4, 1×5, 1×6, 1×7, 1×8, 1×9, 2×2, 3×2, 4×2, 5×2, 6×2, 7×2, 8×2, 9×2, 2×3, 2×4, 2×5, 2×6, 2×7, 2×8, and 2×9.

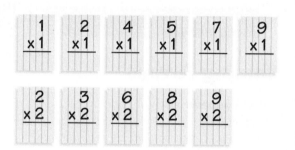

- Remind students to write their names on the backs of each of their flash cards.

- Students should find partners and use their flash cards to practice multiplying by 1 and 2.

- Students should take flash cards home to practice and record practice minutes. Completed records may be exchanged for a certificate.

Basic Facts Workshop 6

Multiplying by 4

Review

15 minutes

4's Are Double Doubles

Management whole class

Materials overhead projector, hundredths square transparencies (Just the Facts Support Master 7)

- Draw a 2 × 4 array on a grid transparency. Have students name the multiplication sentence the array shows. **2 × 4 = 8**

- Ask students to recall how doubles helped them to figure out the 2's multiplication table. **Doubling the 1's multiplication table finds the 2's multiplication table.**

- Tell students that they can double the 2's

multiplication facts to figure out the 4's facts. Draw another 2 × 4 array below the first. Name the new array. **4 × 4** If necessary, point out that 4 × 4 = 16 is the double of 2 × 4 = 8.

- Repeat with several examples, such as 2 × 7 = 14 and 4 × 7 = 28; and 2 × 6 = 12 and 4 × 6 = 24.

- Ask students how to use the 2's multiplication table to figure out 4 × 3 = 12. **2 × 3 = 6, so 4 × 3 is double that, or 12.**

- Repeat with 4 × 5 = 20, 4 × 9 = 36, and 4 × 6 = 24.

- If necessary, model these multiplication sentences by drawing array diagrams.

Practice

30 minutes

Make x4 Flash Cards

Management individuals, then pairs

Materials for each student: 13 index cards, practice minutes record and certificate (Just the Facts Support Masters 10 and 14)

- Distribute index cards to each student and have them make flash cards like those shown below for each of the following facts: 3 × 4, 4 × 3, 4 × 4, 4 × 5, 5 × 4, 4 × 6, 6 × 4, 4 × 7, 7 × 4, 8 × 4, 4 × 8, 4 × 9, and 9 × 4. Remind students to write their names or initials on the backs of their cards.

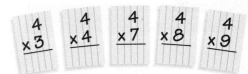

- Have students find partners and use their flash cards to practice multiplying by 4.

- Have students use their previously made flash cards to review the other multiplication facts for 4's that they already know.

- Students may want to take their flash cards home for additional practice. Remind students to keep a record of the minutes that they practice their multiplication facts, and return completed records to school in exchange for a certificate.

Basic Facts Workshop 7
Multiplying by 3

Review
25 minutes

Use 2's to Find 3's

Management whole class

Materials overhead projector, hundredths square transparency (Just the Facts Support Master 7)

- Draw a 2 × 5 array on a grid transparency. Ask students to name the array and the multiplication sentence it shows. **2 × 5, 2 × 5 = 10**

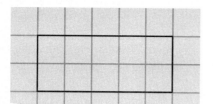

- Draw another row on the array to show 3 × 5. Ask students how knowing 2 × 5 = 10 can help them find 3 × 5. **Another 5 can be added to find the answer to 3 × 5.**

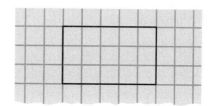

- Repeat the activity, using 2's facts to find 3 × 6, 3 × 4, 3 × 7, 3 × 8, and 3 × 9.

- Remind students that another way to find 3's is to skip-count. Have the class practice skip-counting by 3's to 30. Then ask students how skip-counting could help them figure out 3 × 3, 3 × 6, 3 × 8, and 3 × 9.

Practice
30 minutes

Make x3 Flash Cards

Management individuals, then pairs

Materials for each student: 11 index cards, practice minutes record and certificate (Just the Facts Support Masters 10 and 14)

- Distribute index cards to each student and have them make flash cards like the ones shown below for the following facts: 3 × 3, 3 × 5, 3 × 6, 3 × 7, 3 × 8, 3 × 9, 5 × 3, 6 × 3, 7 × 3, 8 × 3, and 9 × 3.

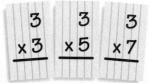

- When students are finished making their cards, they should find partners and use their flash cards to practice multiplying by 3. Remind students to first write their names or initials on the backs of their cards.

- Tell students to add in the flash cards they have already made for 3's facts (3 × 1, 1 × 3, 3 × 2, 2 × 3, 3 × 4, and 4 × 3).

- Encourage students to take all their flash cards home to continue practicing their multiplication facts. Remind students to record the number of minutes they practice at home, and return completed records to school to exchange for a certificate.

Basic Facts Workshop 8

Multiplying by 6

 Review

⏱ **20 minutes**

Use 3's to Find 6's

Management whole class
Materials overhead projector, hundredths square
transparency (Just the Facts Support Master 7)

- Draw a 6 × 4 array on a grid transparency. Then
  draw a line to divide it into two 3 × 4 arrays.

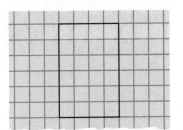

- Cover the bottom array with a piece of paper. Ask
  students how many squares are in the top 3 × 4
  array. **12**

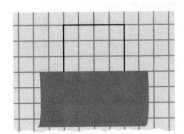

- Uncover the bottom array. Ask students how knowing
  3 × 4 could help them find 6 × 4. **Double the 3 × 4
  array to find 24.**

- Repeat the activity, modeling arrays for 6 × 7,
  6 × 5, 6 × 8, 6 × 6, and 6 × 9, using 3's facts to
  determine 6's.

 Practice

◑ **30 minutes**

Make x6 Flash Cards

Management individuals, then pairs
Materials for each student: 8 index cards, practice
minutes record and certificate (Just the Facts Support Masters
10 and 14)

- Distribute index cards to students and have them
  make flash cards like those shown for the following
  facts: 6 × 5, 5 × 6, 6 × 7, 7 × 6, 6 × 8, 8 × 6,
  6 × 9, and 9 × 6.

- Remind students to add the 6's flash cards they have
  already made (6 × 1, 1 × 6, 6 × 2, 2 × 6, 6 × 3,
  3 × 6, 6 × 4, and 4 × 6) to the new set. Also
  remind them to write their names or initials on the
  backs of their cards. Then have students find partners.
  They can use their flash cards to practice their
  multiplication facts for 6.

- Invite students to take their flash cards home for
  additional practice. Remind them to keep a record of
  the minutes practiced. Students may exchange
  completed records at school for a certificate.

Basic Facts Workshop 9
Multiplying by 5

Review

20 minutes

Skip-Count or Use 10's

Management whole class

- Ask 5 students to stand in a line and hold up their hands as the class skip-counts by 5's to 50.

- Write 3×5 on the board. Ask students how to model this fact with hands or counters. **Holding up three hands or using three rows of five counters shows the fact.**

- Ask, If we know that $3 \times 5 = 15$, what other multiplication fact do we know? $5 \times 3 = 15$

- Repeat the activity, asking volunteers to direct students to show 5×5, 7×5, 4×5, 6×5, 9×5, and 8×5.

- Point out that another way to find 5's is to use 10's. Write $4 \times 10 = 40$ on the board. Ask students how knowing $4 \times 10 = 40$ could help them find 4×5. **4×5 is half of 4×10, or 20.**

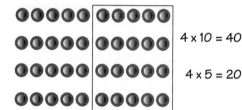

$4 \times 10 = 40$

$4 \times 5 = 20$

- Have students use 10's to find 6×5, 3×5, 2×5, 8×5, 7×5, and 5×5.

- Ask students whether skip-counting or using a 10 is an easier way to find 5's. **Answers will vary.**

Practice

30 minutes

Make x5 Flash Cards

Management individuals, then pairs
Materials for each student: 7 index cards, practice minutes record and certificate (Just the Facts Support Masters 10 and 14)

- Distribute index cards to each student and have them create flash cards like those shown for the following facts: 5×5, 5×7, 7×5, 5×8, 8×5, 5×9, and 9×5.

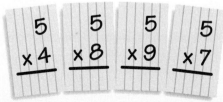

- Remind students to write their names or initials on the backs of their cards. Then, have them find partners and review and practice their multiplication facts for 5.

- Remind students that they already know ten of the facts for 5. Have them add their previously made flash cards (5×1, 1×5, 5×2, 2×5, 5×4, 4×5, 5×3, 3×5, 5×6, and 6×5) to the new ones.

- For additional practice, students may want to take their flash cards home. Remind them to keep a record of the minutes they practice. Students may return completed records to school in exchange for a certificate.

Basic Facts Workshop 10
Multiplying by 9

Review

25 minutes

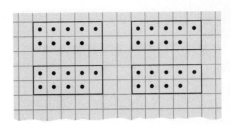

Think Ten to Learn Nines

Management whole class

Materials overhead projector, hundredths square transparencies (Just the Facts Support Master 7)

- Draw four 2 × 5 rectangles on a grid transparency to make ten frames. Ask students how many squares are in 4 tens. **40**

- Draw 9 dots in each ten-frame to model the multiplication fact 4 × 9. Ask the class how much less 4 × 9 is than 40. **It is 4 less** Then, ask students for the answer to 4 × 9. **4 less than 40, or 36**

- Ask students why using the strategy of thinking about tens is a good way to help with 9's facts. **It's easy to multiply by 10 and then subtract.**

- Repeat the activity, modeling 3 × 9, 6 × 9, 5 × 9, and 2 × 9.

- Turn off the projector, and ask students to visualize ten-frames. Have them use tens to find the products for these multiplication facts: 7 × 9, 8 × 9, and 9 × 9.

Practice

30 minutes

Make x9 Flash Cards

Management individuals, then pairs

Materials for each student: 6 index cards, practice minutes record and certificate (Just the Facts Support Masters 10 and 14)

- Distribute index cards and have students make flash cards like the ones shown for the following facts: 7 × 9, 9 × 7, 8 × 9, 9 × 8, 9 × 9, and 9 × 5.

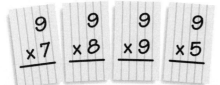

- When students complete their flash cards, have them add in the 9's cards they have already made. Then, have them practice multiplying by 9 with partners.

- Encourage students to take all of their flash cards home for additional practice. Remind them to keep a record of the number of minutes they work at home. Students may return completed records to school in exchange for a certificate.

Basic Facts Workshop 11
Multiplying by 7

Review

25 minutes

Use What You Know for 7's

Management whole class

Materials overhead projector, blank transparency, hundredths square transparencies (Just the Facts Support Master 7)

- Remind the class that they have already practiced multiplying by 1's, 2's, 3's, 4's, 5's, 6's, and 9's. On a transparency write equations as shown. Have students determine the missing numbers. **2, 5, 1, 4, 3**

☐ × 7 = 14
☐ × 7 = 35
☐ × 7 = 7
☐ × 7 = 28
☐ × 7 = 21

- Ask students to identify which facts for 7 are missing from the list. **6 × 7 = 42, 7 × 7 = 49, 8 × 7 = 56, and 9 × 7 = 63**

- Draw a 7 × 7 array on a grid transparency. Tell students that if they cannot remember the product of 7 × 7, they could use the facts they do know to find the answer.

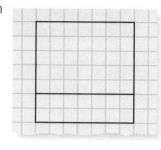

Discuss different ways they might split the array into parts to find the product for 7 × 7.

7 × 5 plus 7 × 2; 7 × 1 plus 7 × 6; 7 × 3 plus 7 × 4

- Draw a 7 × 8 array on a grid transparency. In the event that students cannot remember the product, ask how they might split the array to use facts they do know to find 7 × 8. **7 × 4 plus 7 × 4; 7 × 2 plus 7 × 6; 7 × 3 plus 7 × 5**

Practice

30 minutes

Make x7 Flash Cards

Management individuals, then pairs

Materials for each student: 3 index cards, practice minutes record and certificate (Just the Facts Support Masters 11 and 15)

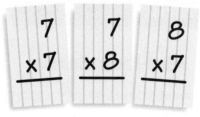

- Distribute index cards to each student.

- Have students make flash cards for the 3 remaining multiplication facts for 7: 7 × 7, 7 × 8, and 8 × 7. Remind them to write their names or initials on the backs of their cards.

- After they complete their flash cards, have students work with partners to practice multiplying by 7.

- For additional practice, students should take their flash cards home. Remind them to keep a record of the minutes that they practice. Students may return completed records to school in exchange for a certificate.

Basic Facts Workshop 12
Multiplying by 8

Review

25 minutes

Only One 8

Management whole class
Materials overhead projector, blank transparency, hundredths square transparency (Just the Facts Support Master 7)

- Remind students that they have already practiced multiplying by 1's, 2's, 3's, 4's, 5's, 6's, 7's, and 9's. On a blank transparency, write equations as shown. Have students name the missing factors. **2, 7, 5, 4, 9, 3, 6**

$$\square \times 8 = 16$$
$$\square \times 8 = 56$$
$$\square \times 8 = 40$$
$$\square \times 8 = 32$$
$$\square \times 8 = 72$$
$$\square \times 8 = 24$$
$$\square \times 8 = 48$$

- Ask students to identify any facts for 8 other than 1 or 0 that are missing from the list. **The only fact left to learn is 8 × 8.**

- Draw an 8×8 array on a grid transparency. Tell students that if they cannot remember the answer to 8×8, they might use facts that they already know to figure out the product.

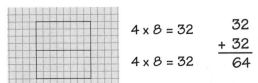

$$4 \times 8 = 32$$
$$4 \times 8 = 32$$

$$\begin{array}{r} 32 \\ + 32 \\ \hline 64 \end{array}$$

- Discuss different ways they might split the array into parts to find the product for 8×8. **Answers will vary. Possible answers: 4 × 8 plus 4 × 8; 1 × 8 plus 7 × 8; 2 × 8 plus 6 × 8; 3 × 8 plus 5 × 8.**

Practice

30 minutes

Make x8 Flash Cards

Management individuals, then pairs
Materials for each student: 1 index card, practice minutes record and certificate (Just the Facts Support Masters 11 and 15)

- Distribute index cards to students. Have them make flash cards as shown for the following fact: 8×8.

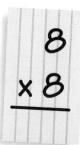

$$\begin{array}{r} 8 \\ \times 8 \\ \hline \end{array}$$

- Have students add this card to their previously made sets of 8's facts (8×1, 1×8, 8×2, 2×8, 8×3, 3×8, 8×4, 4×8, 8×5, 5×8, 8×6, 6×8, 8×7, 7×8, 8×9, and 9×8).

- Have students use their flash cards to practice 8's multiplication facts with a partner.

- For additional practice, students may want to take their flash cards home. Remind them to keep track of the number of minutes they practice. Students may return completed records to school in exchange for a certificate.

Name_____ Date _____

1A BASIC FACTS
....
Addition and Subtraction Facts

Add.

1. 2 + 4	**2.** 3 + 5	**3.** 8 + 1	**4.** 3 + 4	**5.** 7 + 2
6. 1 + 0	**7.** 2 + 6	**8.** 2 + 8	**9.** 7 + 1	**10.** 0 + 6

Add or subtract. Find a pattern. Write the next number sentence.

11. 1 + 6 = _____

2 + 6 = _____

3 + 6 = _____

_____ + _____ = _____

12. 3 + 3 = _____

4 + 3 = _____

5 + 3 = _____

_____ + _____ = _____

13. 7 − 2 = _____

8 − 2 = _____

9 − 2 = _____

_____ − _____ = _____

14. 9 − 5 = _____

9 − 6 = _____

9 − 7 = _____

_____ − _____ = _____

Name_____   Date _____

1B BASIC FACTS

....

Addition and Subtraction Facts

Find the greater number. Count on to add.

1. $6 + 1 =$ _____   **2.** $3 + 4 =$ _____   **3.** $5 + 2 =$ _____

4. $3 + 7 =$ _____   **5.** $6 + 2 =$ _____   **6.** $1 + 8 =$ _____

7. $2 + 9 =$ _____   **8.** $3 + 5 =$ _____   **9.** $4 + 2 =$ _____

Find the difference.

10. $\begin{array}{r} 5 \\ -3 \\ \hline \end{array}$	**11.** $\begin{array}{r} 7 \\ -4 \\ \hline \end{array}$	**12.** $\begin{array}{r} 8 \\ -6 \\ \hline \end{array}$	**13.** $\begin{array}{r} 10 \\ -7 \\ \hline \end{array}$	**14.** $\begin{array}{r} 4 \\ -0 \\ \hline \end{array}$
15. $\begin{array}{r} 6 \\ -5 \\ \hline \end{array}$	**16.** $\begin{array}{r} 4 \\ -2 \\ \hline \end{array}$	**17.** $\begin{array}{r} 9 \\ -6 \\ \hline \end{array}$	**18.** $\begin{array}{r} 6 \\ -4 \\ \hline \end{array}$	**19.** $\begin{array}{r} 7 \\ -6 \\ \hline \end{array}$
20. $\begin{array}{r} 5 \\ -2 \\ \hline \end{array}$	**21.** $\begin{array}{r} 6 \\ -3 \\ \hline \end{array}$	**22.** $\begin{array}{r} 8 \\ -5 \\ \hline \end{array}$	**23.** $\begin{array}{r} 7 \\ -3 \\ \hline \end{array}$	**24.** $\begin{array}{r} 6 \\ -0 \\ \hline \end{array}$
25. $\begin{array}{r} 9 \\ -3 \\ \hline \end{array}$	**26.** $\begin{array}{r} 8 \\ -2 \\ \hline \end{array}$	**27.** $\begin{array}{r} 9 \\ -5 \\ \hline \end{array}$	**28.** $\begin{array}{r} 4 \\ -3 \\ \hline \end{array}$	**29.** $\begin{array}{r} 7 \\ -5 \\ \hline \end{array}$

Name_____ Date _____

◤ 2A ◢ BASIC FACTS

···

Doubles, Near Doubles Addition and Subtraction Facts

Write a double that helps. Add.

1.   6
    + 5   + _____

2.   8
    + 9   + _____

3.   7
    + 6   + _____

4.   6
    + 5   + _____

5.   8
    + 9   + _____

6.   7
    + 6   + _____

Find the difference.

7.   5
    − 3

8.   7
    − 4

9.   8
    − 6

10. 10
    − 5

11. 4
    − 0

12. 16
    − 8

13. 4
    − 2

14. 12
    − 6

15. 8
    − 4

16. 7
    − 6

Look for doubles first. Then add.

17. $2 + 3 + 4 =$ _____

18. $3 + 3 + 5 =$ _____

19. $4 + 5 + 5 =$ _____

20. $2 + 7 + 3 =$ _____

Name_____   Date _____

◣2B BASIC FACTS

Doubles, Near Doubles Addition and Subtraction Facts

Add.

1. $\begin{array}{r} 4 \\ +\ 4 \\ \hline \end{array}$

2. $\begin{array}{r} 7 \\ +\ 6 \\ \hline \end{array}$

3. $\begin{array}{r} 2 \\ +\ 8 \\ \hline \end{array}$

4. $\begin{array}{r} 6 \\ +\ 3 \\ \hline \end{array}$

5. $\begin{array}{r} 4 \\ +\ 5 \\ \hline \end{array}$

6. $\begin{array}{r} 9 \\ +\ 9 \\ \hline \end{array}$

7. $\begin{array}{r} 5 \\ +\ 5 \\ \hline \end{array}$

8. $\begin{array}{r} 3 \\ +\ 3 \\ \hline \end{array}$

9. $\begin{array}{r} 5 \\ +\ 6 \\ \hline \end{array}$

10. $\begin{array}{r} 8 \\ +\ 7 \\ \hline \end{array}$

11. $\begin{array}{r} 8 \\ +\ 8 \\ \hline \end{array}$

12. $\begin{array}{r} 1 \\ +\ 2 \\ \hline \end{array}$

13. $\begin{array}{r} 6 \\ +\ 6 \\ \hline \end{array}$

14. $\begin{array}{r} 7 \\ +\ 7 \\ \hline \end{array}$

15. $\begin{array}{r} 3 \\ +\ 7 \\ \hline \end{array}$

Draw a line to match. Subtract.

16. $16 - 8 =$ _____

A. $\begin{array}{r} 18 \\ -\ 9 \\ \hline \end{array}$

17. $9 - 5 =$ _____

B. $\begin{array}{r} 16 \\ -\ 8 \\ \hline \end{array}$

18. $18 - 9 =$ _____

C. $\begin{array}{r} 9 \\ -\ 5 \\ \hline \end{array}$

Name_____   Date _____

3A BASIC FACTS

··

Using Ten to Add and Subtract

Add. Make a ten to help.

1. 9 + 5 = _____   **2.** 4 + 7 = _____   **3.** 5 + 8 = _____

4. 6 + 8 = _____   **5.** 4 + 9 = _____   **6.** 7 + 9 = _____

7. 8 + 9 = _____   **8.** 4 + 8 = _____   **9.** 9 + 6 = _____

Subtract.

10. $\begin{array}{r} 10 \\ -3 \\ \hline \end{array}$	**11.** $\begin{array}{r} 6 \\ -4 \\ \hline \end{array}$	**12.** $\begin{array}{r} 7 \\ -5 \\ \hline \end{array}$	**13.** $\begin{array}{r} 9 \\ -6 \\ \hline \end{array}$	**14.** $\begin{array}{r} 8 \\ -3 \\ \hline \end{array}$
15. $\begin{array}{r} 6 \\ -2 \\ \hline \end{array}$	**16.** $\begin{array}{r} 10 \\ -2 \\ \hline \end{array}$	**17.** $\begin{array}{r} 11 \\ -1 \\ \hline \end{array}$	**18.** $\begin{array}{r} 10 \\ -8 \\ \hline \end{array}$	**19.** $\begin{array}{r} 11 \\ -9 \\ \hline \end{array}$
20. $\begin{array}{r} 8 \\ -5 \\ \hline \end{array}$	**21.** $\begin{array}{r} 7 \\ -4 \\ \hline \end{array}$	**22.** $\begin{array}{r} 7 \\ -6 \\ \hline \end{array}$	**23.** $\begin{array}{r} 8 \\ -2 \\ \hline \end{array}$	**24.** $\begin{array}{r} 9 \\ -7 \\ \hline \end{array}$
25. $\begin{array}{r} 11 \\ -3 \\ \hline \end{array}$	**26.** $\begin{array}{r} 10 \\ -7 \\ \hline \end{array}$	**27.** $\begin{array}{r} 8 \\ -6 \\ \hline \end{array}$	**28.** $\begin{array}{r} 10 \\ -4 \\ \hline \end{array}$	**29.** $\begin{array}{r} 8 \\ -4 \\ \hline \end{array}$

Name_____ Date _____

3B BASIC FACTS

Using Ten to Add and Subtract

Subtract. Make a ten to help.

1. $13 - 8 =$ _____

2. $15 - 9 =$ _____

3. $16 - 8 =$ _____

4. $12 - 9 =$ _____

5. $14 - 8 =$ _____

6. $17 - 8 =$ _____

Add or subtract.

7. $9 + 6 =$ _____

8. $16 - 8 =$ _____

9. $4 + 9 =$ _____

10. $18 - 9 =$ _____

11. $13 - 5 =$ _____

12. $7 + 7 =$ _____

13. $11 - 6 =$ _____

14. $14 - 8 =$ _____

15. $7 + 8 =$ _____

16. $12 - 7 =$ _____

17. $6 + 6 =$ _____

18. $10 - 6 =$ _____

19. $17 - 9 =$ _____

20. $9 + 7 =$ _____

21. $13 - 8 =$ _____

22. $15 - 8 =$ _____

23. $5 + 6 =$ _____

24. $7 + 9 =$ _____

Find the missing number.

25. $12 -$ _____ $= 3$

26. $14 -$ _____ $= 7$

27. $11 -$ _____ $= 9$

28. $16 -$ _____ $= 7$

29. $13 -$ _____ $= 5$

30. $12 -$ _____ $= 7$

Name_____   Date _____

4A ▶ BASIC FACTS

Naming and Using Arrays in Multiplication

Write one addition sentence and one multiplication sentence to describe each array.

1. • • • • •
   • • • • •
   • • • • •

_____ = _____

_____ = _____

2. • • • • • • •
   • • • • • • •

_____ = _____

_____ = _____

Solve.

3. $2 + 2 =$ _____

$2 \times 2 =$ _____

4. $2 + 2 + 2 =$ _____

$3 \times 2 =$ _____

5. $2 + 2 + 2 + 2 =$ _____

$4 \times 2 =$ _____

6. $2 + 2 + 2 + 2 + 2 =$ _____

$5 \times 2 =$ _____

7. $9 \times 2 =$ _____

8. $8 \times 2 =$ _____

Draw counters to show the array. Then write the product.

9.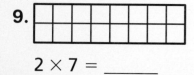

$2 \times 7 =$ _____

10.

$6 \times 2 =$ _____

11.

$4 \times 2 =$ _____

Name_____   Date _____

4B ▶ BASIC FACTS

Naming and Using Arrays in Multiplication

Draw counters to show the array. Then find the product.

1.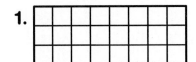

$3 \times 6 =$ _____

2.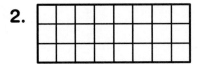

$3 \times 8 =$ _____

3.

$3 \times 5 =$ _____

Multiply. Think of doubles or the order property.

4. $2 \times 7 =$ _____   **5.** $6 \times 2 =$ _____   **6.** $2 \times 9 =$ _____

7. $4 \times 2 =$ _____   **8.** $2 \times 8 =$ _____   **9.** $2 \times 5 =$ _____

10. $2 \times 3 =$ _____   **11.** $9 \times 2 =$ _____   **12.** $2 \times 2 =$ _____

13. $5 \times 3 =$ _____   **14.** $4 \times 3 =$ _____   **15.** $3 \times 7 =$ _____

Use estimation. Write < or >.

16. $4 \times 3 = 12$, so 3×3 _____ 12   **17.** $7 \times 2 = 14$, so 7×3 _____ 14

18. $3 \times 2 = 6$, so 4×2 _____ 6   **19.** $8 \times 3 = 24$, so 9×3 _____ 24

20. $3 \times 3 = 9$, so 4×3 _____ 9   **21.** $6 \times 3 = 18$, so 7×3 _____ 18

Name_____ Date _____

5A BASIC FACTS

Multiplying by 1 and 2

Multiply.

1. $\begin{array}{r} 1 \\ \times 2 \\ \hline \end{array}$	**2.** $\begin{array}{r} 2 \\ \times 3 \\ \hline \end{array}$	**3.** $\begin{array}{r} 4 \\ \times 1 \\ \hline \end{array}$	**4.** $\begin{array}{r} 1 \\ \times 7 \\ \hline \end{array}$	**5.** $\begin{array}{r} 6 \\ \times 2 \\ \hline \end{array}$
6. $\begin{array}{r} 1 \\ \times 1 \\ \hline \end{array}$	**7.** $\begin{array}{r} 7 \\ \times 1 \\ \hline \end{array}$	**8.** $\begin{array}{r} 9 \\ \times 2 \\ \hline \end{array}$	**9.** $\begin{array}{r} 1 \\ \times 8 \\ \hline \end{array}$	**10.** $\begin{array}{r} 1 \\ \times 5 \\ \hline \end{array}$
11. $\begin{array}{r} 4 \\ \times 2 \\ \hline \end{array}$	**12.** $\begin{array}{r} 1 \\ \times 6 \\ \hline \end{array}$	**13.** $\begin{array}{r} 2 \\ \times 2 \\ \hline \end{array}$	**14.** $\begin{array}{r} 1 \\ \times 4 \\ \hline \end{array}$	**15.** $\begin{array}{r} 1 \\ \times 3 \\ \hline \end{array}$
16. $\begin{array}{r} 2 \\ \times 5 \\ \hline \end{array}$	**17.** $\begin{array}{r} 2 \\ \times 7 \\ \hline \end{array}$	**18.** $\begin{array}{r} 6 \\ \times 1 \\ \hline \end{array}$	**19.** $\begin{array}{r} 2 \\ \times 4 \\ \hline \end{array}$	**20.** $\begin{array}{r} 1 \\ \times 9 \\ \hline \end{array}$

Use mental math. Write just the answer.

21. $5 \times 1 \times 2 =$ _____

22. $7 \times 0 \times 2 =$ _____

23. $1 \times 2 \times 8 =$ _____

24. $3 \times 2 \times 1 =$ _____

25. $4 \times 2 \times 1 =$ _____

26. $2 \times 2 \times 1 =$ _____

Name_____   Date _____

5B ◢ BASIC FACTS

Multiplying by 1 and 2

Multiply. Think of doubles.

1. $2 \times 3 =$ _____   **2.** $2 \times 5 =$ _____   **3.** $2 \times 4 =$ _____

4. $2 \times 9 =$ _____   **5.** $2 \times 2 =$ _____   **6.** $2 \times 8 =$ _____

Multiply.

7. $1 \times 4 =$ _____   **8.** $1 \times 8 =$ _____   **9.** $6 \times 2 =$ _____

10. $9 \times 1 =$ _____   **11.** $1 \times 3 =$ _____   **12.** $2 \times 2 =$ _____

13. $1 \times 5 =$ _____   **14.** $7 \times 2 =$ _____   **15.** $2 \times 9 =$ _____

16. $\begin{array}{r} 1 \\ \times\, 2 \\ \hline \end{array}$	**17.** $\begin{array}{r} 7 \\ \times\, 1 \\ \hline \end{array}$	**18.** $\begin{array}{r} 5 \\ \times\, 2 \\ \hline \end{array}$	**19.** $\begin{array}{r} 1 \\ \times\, 9 \\ \hline \end{array}$	**20.** $\begin{array}{r} 2 \\ \times\, 1 \\ \hline \end{array}$
21. $\begin{array}{r} 1 \\ \times\, 1 \\ \hline \end{array}$	**22.** $\begin{array}{r} 1 \\ \times\, 6 \\ \hline \end{array}$	**23.** $\begin{array}{r} 8 \\ \times\, 2 \\ \hline \end{array}$	**24.** $\begin{array}{r} 1 \\ \times\, 4 \\ \hline \end{array}$	**25.** $\begin{array}{r} 2 \\ \times\, 6 \\ \hline \end{array}$
26. $\begin{array}{r} 8 \\ \times\, 1 \\ \hline \end{array}$	**27.** $\begin{array}{r} 1 \\ \times\, 3 \\ \hline \end{array}$	**28.** $\begin{array}{r} 3 \\ \times\, 2 \\ \hline \end{array}$	**29.** $\begin{array}{r} 2 \\ \times\, 7 \\ \hline \end{array}$	**30.** $\begin{array}{r} 4 \\ \times\, 2 \\ \hline \end{array}$

Name_____ Date _____

6A ◢ BASIC FACTS

Multiplying by 4

Write one addition sentence and one multiplication sentence to describe each array.

1. • • • •
• • • •

2. • • •
• • •
• • •
• • •

_____ = _____

_____ = _____

_____ = _____

_____ = _____

Multiply.

3. $4 \times 3 =$ _____

4. $4 \times 8 =$ _____

5. $7 \times 4 =$ _____

6. $5 \times 4 =$ _____

7. $4 \times 2 =$ _____

8. $4 \times 4 =$ _____

9. $\begin{array}{r} 4 \\ \times\ 7 \\ \hline \end{array}$

10. $\begin{array}{r} 4 \\ \times\ 4 \\ \hline \end{array}$

11. $\begin{array}{r} 4 \\ \times\ 3 \\ \hline \end{array}$

12. $\begin{array}{r} 9 \\ \times\ 4 \\ \hline \end{array}$

13. $\begin{array}{r} 5 \\ \times\ 4 \\ \hline \end{array}$

14. $\begin{array}{r} 4 \\ \times\ 6 \\ \hline \end{array}$

15. $\begin{array}{r} 3 \\ \times\ 4 \\ \hline \end{array}$

16. $\begin{array}{r} 7 \\ \times\ 4 \\ \hline \end{array}$

17. $\begin{array}{r} 4 \\ \times\ 8 \\ \hline \end{array}$

18. $\begin{array}{r} 2 \\ \times\ 4 \\ \hline \end{array}$

Name_____ Date _____

6B BASIC FACTS

....

Multiplying by 4

Multiply. Think of doubles or the order property.

1. $2 \times 7 =$ _____   **2.** $6 \times 2 =$ _____   **3.** $2 \times 9 =$ _____

4. $4 \times 2 =$ _____   **5.** $2 \times 8 =$ _____   **6.** $2 \times 5 =$ _____

7. $2 \times 3 =$ _____   **8.** $9 \times 2 =$ _____   **9.** $2 \times 2 =$ _____

Multiply.

10. $4 \times 3 =$ _____   **11.** $4 \times 8 =$ _____   **12.** $7 \times 4 =$ _____

13. $5 \times 4 =$ _____   **14.** $4 \times 2 =$ _____   **15.** $4 \times 4 =$ _____

16. $9 \times 4 =$ _____   **17.** $4 \times 6 =$ _____   **18.** $8 \times 4 =$ _____

19. $1 \times 4 =$ _____   **20.** $2 \times 4 =$ _____   **21.** $6 \times 4 =$ _____

22. $4 \times 7 =$ _____   **23.** $4 \times 1 =$ _____   **24.** $4 \times 9 =$ _____

25. $3 \times 4 =$ _____   **26.** $4 \times 5 =$ _____   **27.** $4 \times 6 =$ _____

28. $4 \times 8 =$ _____   **29.** $4 \times 2 =$ _____   **30.** $7 \times 4 =$ _____

Name_____   Date _____

7A ▸ BASIC FACTS

Multiplying by 3

Multiply.

1.	2 × 3	2.	5 × 3	3.	6 × 3	4.	4 × 3
5.	9 × 3	6.	8 × 3	7.	7 × 3	8.	3 × 3
9.	3 × 9	10.	3 × 5	11.	3 × 6	12.	3 × 2

Think of multiplication facts. Complete the tables.

	x	2
13.	6	12
14.	7	
15.	3	
16.	4	
17.	5	

	x	3
18.		27
19.	6	
20.		12
21.		24
22.		15

Name_____   Date _____

7B BASIC FACTS

....

Multiplying by 3

Match.

1. $3 \times 4 =$ _____   **a.** 9×1

2. $3 \times 5 =$ _____   **b.** 9×2

3. $3 \times 6 =$ _____   **c.** 6×2

4. $7 \times 3 =$ _____   **d.** 5×3

5. $3 \times 2 =$ _____   **e.** 1×3

6. $3 \times 3 =$ _____   **f.** 3×7

7. $3 \times 1 =$ _____   **g.** 6×1

Write pairs of factors for each product.

8. _____ $\times$ _____ $= 4$ **9.** _____ $\times$ _____ $= 8$

10. _____ $\times$ _____ $= 3$ **11.** _____ $\times$ _____ $= 5$

12. _____ $\times$ _____ $= 6$ **13.** _____ $\times$ _____ $= 10$

14. _____ $\times$ _____ $= 7$ **15.** _____ $\times$ _____ $= 9$

16. _____ $\times$ _____ $= 12$ **17.** _____ $\times$ _____ $= 15$

Name_____ Date _____

8A ◣ BASIC FACTS

Multiplying by 6

Multiply.

1. $\begin{array}{r} 3 \\ \times 6 \\ \hline \end{array}$	**2.** $\begin{array}{r} 5 \\ \times 6 \\ \hline \end{array}$	**3.** $\begin{array}{r} 6 \\ \times 2 \\ \hline \end{array}$	**4.** $\begin{array}{r} 4 \\ \times 6 \\ \hline \end{array}$	**5.** $\begin{array}{r} 0 \\ \times 6 \\ \hline \end{array}$
6. $\begin{array}{r} 1 \\ \times 6 \\ \hline \end{array}$	**7.** $\begin{array}{r} 6 \\ \times 4 \\ \hline \end{array}$	**8.** $\begin{array}{r} 9 \\ \times 6 \\ \hline \end{array}$	**9.** $\begin{array}{r} 8 \\ \times 6 \\ \hline \end{array}$	**10.** $\begin{array}{r} 6 \\ \times 2 \\ \hline \end{array}$

Compare. Write <, >, or =.

11. 5×6 _____ 3×6　　　　**12.** 4×3 _____ 2×6

13. 3×3 _____ 6×2　　　　**14.** 3×2 _____ 6×1

Multiply.

15. $6 \times 3 =$ _____　　**16.** $6 \times 0 =$ _____　　**17.** $9 \times 6 =$ _____

18. $5 \times 6 =$ _____　　**19.** $6 \times 1 =$ _____　　**20.** $7 \times 6 =$ _____

21. $2 \times 6 =$ _____　　**22.** $6 \times 4 =$ _____　　**23.** $6 \times 6 =$ _____

24. $6 \times 8 =$ _____　　**25.** $3 \times 6 =$ _____　　**26.** $6 \times 5 =$ _____

Name_____ Date _____

◤8B◢ BASIC FACTS

Multiplying by 6

Draw an array for each multiplication sentence. Find the product.

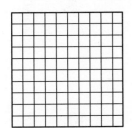 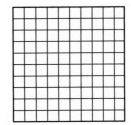

1. $6 \times 3 =$ _____   **2.** $2 \times 6 =$ _____

Multiply.

3.   6
     $\times\,6$

4.   6
     $\times\,4$

5.   9
     $\times\,6$

6.   3
     $\times\,6$

7.   6
     $\times\,2$

8.   7
     $\times\,6$

9.   8
     $\times\,6$

10.   4
      $\times\,6$

11.   0
      $\times\,6$

12.   6
      $\times\,8$

13.   2
      $\times\,9$

14.   5
      $\times\,6$

15.   8
      $\times\,3$

16.   6
      $\times\,1$

17.   3
      $\times\,2$

Name_____   Date _____

9A ▸ BASIC FACTS

Multiplying by 5

Multiply.

1. $\begin{array}{r} 3 \\ \times\,5 \\ \hline \end{array}$	**2.** $\begin{array}{r} 5 \\ \times\,6 \\ \hline \end{array}$	**3.** $\begin{array}{r} 7 \\ \times\,5 \\ \hline \end{array}$	**4.** $\begin{array}{r} 2 \\ \times\,5 \\ \hline \end{array}$	**5.** $\begin{array}{r} 5 \\ \times\,8 \\ \hline \end{array}$
6. $\begin{array}{r} 5 \\ \times\,4 \\ \hline \end{array}$	**7.** $\begin{array}{r} 9 \\ \times\,5 \\ \hline \end{array}$	**8.** $\begin{array}{r} 6 \\ \times\,5 \\ \hline \end{array}$	**9.** $\begin{array}{r} 8 \\ \times\,5 \\ \hline \end{array}$	**10.** $\begin{array}{r} 5 \\ \times\,9 \\ \hline \end{array}$

Compare. Write < or >.

11. 5×6 _____ 3×6

12. 5×7 _____ 9×5

13. 5×8 _____ $5 + 8$

14. 5×9 _____ 4×8

Complete the multiplication table.

	x	6
15.	6	
16.	2	
17.	8	
18.	7	
19.	9	

Name_____ Date _____

9B ◢ BASIC FACTS
....
Multiplying by 5

Multiply.

1. $5 \times 2 =$ _____

2. $3 \times 5 =$ _____

3. $4 \times 5 =$ _____

$2 \times 5 =$ _____

$5 \times 3 =$ _____

$5 \times 4 =$ _____

Find the products. Write whether each product is *greater than*, *less than*, or *equal to* 40.

4. $8 \times 5 =$ _____   _____

5. $5 \times 6 =$ _____   _____

6. $2 \times 5 =$ _____   _____

7. $9 \times 5 =$ _____   _____

8. $5 \times 10 =$ _____   _____

Multiply.

9. $8 \times 5 =$ _____

10. $5 \times 3 =$ _____

11. $8 \times 2 =$ _____

12. $9 \times 5 =$ _____

13. $4 \times 5 =$ _____

14. $6 \times 5 =$ _____

15. $0 \times 5 =$ _____

16. $7 \times 5 =$ _____

17. $5 \times 2 =$ _____

Name_____ Date _____

BASIC FACTS

Multiplying by 9

Complete the multiplication table. Use the table to complete the number sentences.

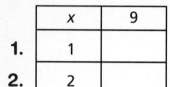

	x	9
1.	1	
2.	2	
3.	3	
4.	4	
5.	5	

6. 9
  × 2
  ☐

7. 4
  × 9
  ☐

8. 1
  × ☐
  9

9. ☐
  × 9
  36

Multiply.

10. 9
  × 7

11. 9
  × 4

12. 9
  × 3

13. 9
  × 2

14. 4
  × 9

15. 8
  × 9

16. 5
  × 9

17. 9
  × 9

18. 3
  × 9

19. 2
  × 9

Name_____ Date _____

10B BASIC FACTS

Multiplying by 9

Complete the chart below, using what you know about nines facts.

1.	1×9	=	
2.	2×9	=	
3.	3×9	=	
4.	4×9	=	
5.	5×9	=	
6.	6×9	=	
7.	7×9	=	
8.	8×9	=	
9.	9×9	=	

Multiply.

10. $\begin{array}{r} 9 \\ \times\, 4 \\ \hline \end{array}$

11. $\begin{array}{r} 9 \\ \times\, 6 \\ \hline \end{array}$

12. $\begin{array}{r} 4 \\ \times\, 5 \\ \hline \end{array}$

13. $\begin{array}{r} 7 \\ \times\, 6 \\ \hline \end{array}$

14. $\begin{array}{r} 7 \\ \times\, 9 \\ \hline \end{array}$

15. $9 \times 5 = $ _____

16. $9 \times 1 = $ _____

17. $0 \times 9 = $ _____

Fill in the blanks.

18. $2 \times$ _____ $= 18$

19. $3 \times 9 = $ _____

20. $9 \times$ _____ $= 9$

21. _____ $\times 9 = 36$

22. _____ $\times 9 = 9$

23. $9 \times$ _____ $= 45$

Name_____ Date _____

11A BASIC FACTS

Multiplying by 7

Find the products. Write whether each product is *greater than*, *less than*, or *equal to* 30.

1. $7 \times 3 =$ _____

2. $7 \times 8 =$ _____

3. $6 \times 7 =$ _____

4. $5 \times 7 =$ _____

Multiply.

5. $\begin{array}{r} 3 \\ \times 7 \\ \hline \end{array}$ **6.** $\begin{array}{r} 4 \\ \times 7 \\ \hline \end{array}$ **7.** $\begin{array}{r} 7 \\ \times 6 \\ \hline \end{array}$ **8.** $\begin{array}{r} 5 \\ \times 7 \\ \hline \end{array}$ **9.** $\begin{array}{r} 7 \\ \times 5 \\ \hline \end{array}$

10. $\begin{array}{r} 8 \\ \times 7 \\ \hline \end{array}$ **11.** $\begin{array}{r} 2 \\ \times 7 \\ \hline \end{array}$ **12.** $\begin{array}{r} 1 \\ \times 7 \\ \hline \end{array}$ **13.** $\begin{array}{r} 0 \\ \times 7 \\ \hline \end{array}$ **14.** $\begin{array}{r} 9 \\ \times 7 \\ \hline \end{array}$

Use estimation. Write < or >.

15. $7 \times 3 = 21$, so 7×4 ____ 21   **16.** $7 \times 2 = 14$, so 7×1 ____ 14

17. $7 \times 5 = 35$, so 7×4 ____ 35   **18.** $7 \times 6 = 42$, so 7×7 ____ 42

Name_____ Date _____

11B ◢ BASIC FACTS

Multiplying by 7

Multiply.

x	7
1. 8	
2. 3	
3. 9	
4. 6	
5. 7	

6. $7 \times 7 =$ _____

7. $6 \times 8 =$ _____

8. $1 \times 7 =$ _____

9. $8 \times 7 =$ _____

10. $7 \times 4 =$ _____

11. $7 \times 3 =$ _____

12. $4 \times 7 =$ _____

13. $6 \times 7 =$ _____

14. $7 \times 9 =$ _____

15. $7 \times 8 =$ _____

16. $3 \times 9 =$ _____

17. $2 \times 7 =$ _____

Multiply and add using mental math. Work from left to right. Write just the answer.

18. $7 \times 8 + 3 =$ _____

19. $7 \times 4 + 2 =$ _____

20. $2 \times 7 + 4 =$ _____

21. $3 \times 7 + 3 =$ _____

Name_____ Date _____

12A BASIC FACTS

Multiplying by 8

Multiply.

1. $\begin{array}{r} 8 \\ \times\,6 \\ \hline \end{array}$	2. $\begin{array}{r} 8 \\ \times\,7 \\ \hline \end{array}$	3. $\begin{array}{r} 8 \\ \times\,3 \\ \hline \end{array}$	4. $\begin{array}{r} 6 \\ \times\,8 \\ \hline \end{array}$	5. $\begin{array}{r} 5 \\ \times\,8 \\ \hline \end{array}$
6. $\begin{array}{r} 7 \\ \times\,8 \\ \hline \end{array}$	7. $\begin{array}{r} 8 \\ \times\,4 \\ \hline \end{array}$	8. $\begin{array}{r} 0 \\ \times\,8 \\ \hline \end{array}$	9. $\begin{array}{r} 8 \\ \times\,8 \\ \hline \end{array}$	10. $\begin{array}{r} 1 \\ \times\,8 \\ \hline \end{array}$

Complete the table.

	x	8
11.	2	
12.		64
13.	7	
14.	4	
15.		40

Multiply and add using mental math. Work from left to right. Write just the answer.

16. $5 \times 8 + 2 =$ _____   17. $1 \times 8 + 4 =$ _____

18. $8 \times 2 + 2 =$ _____   19. $3 \times 8 + 1 =$ _____

Name_____   Date _____

12B ▷ BASIC FACTS

Multiplying by 8

Multiply.

1. $8 \times 7 =$ _____

2. $8 \times 5 =$ _____

3. $8 \times 3 =$ _____

4. $1 \times 8 =$ _____

5. $4 \times 8 =$ _____

6. $8 \times 2 =$ _____

7. $8 \times 4 =$ _____

8. $8 \times 1 =$ _____

9. $6 \times 8 =$ _____

Complete the table with the facts you have learned. One column has been completed for you.

	x	2	3	4	5	6	7	8	9
10.	2			8					
11.	3			12					
12.	4			16					
13.	5			20					
14.	6			24					
15.	7			28					
16	8			32					
17.	9			36					

Compare. Write <, >, or =.

18. 2×8 ___ 3×5

19. 3×8 ___ 4×8

20. 8×4 ___ 5×9

21. 4×6 ___ 3×8

22. 2×8 ___ 3×5

23. 1×8 ___ $1 + 8$

Basic Facts Workshop 1
Fact Families

Review

20 minutes

Modeling Fact Families with Arrays

Management whole class

Materials overhead projector, 20 counters, hundredths square transparency (Just the Facts Support Master 7)

- Show 3 rows of 4 counters on the transparency. Ask, What multiplication fact does this array show?

  3 × 4 = 12

- Turn the transparency. Ask, What other multiplication fact does the array show now? **4 × 3 = 12**

- Next, draw the division sign over the 3 × 4 array. Ask what division fact the array shows. **12 ÷ 3 = 4** Turn

the transparency again. Ask students what division fact the array shows now. **12 ÷ 4 = 3**

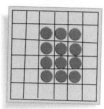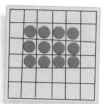

- Tell students that they have found all four facts for a fact family: 3 × 4 = 12, 4 × 3 = 12, 12 ÷ 3 = 4, and 12 ÷ 4 = 3.

- Repeat with the numbers 3, 5, and 15. Use counters to demonstrate; write the fact families.

- Repeat with the numbers 3, 3, and 9. Point out that only 2 facts are in this fact family. Show that both the 3 × 3 = 9 and the 9 ÷ 3 = 3 arrays are recorded the same way, even when turned.

Practice

30 minutes

Drawing Fact Families

Management pairs

Materials hundredths square paper (Just the Facts Support Master 7)

- Distribute several copies of Support Master 7 to each pair of students.

- Ask students to work with their partners to draw on the grid an array showing each of the facts in the fact family for the numbers 2, 5, and 10. They should label each of their four drawings.

- Check with each pair to see that they have accurately drawn arrays for 2 × 5 = 10, 5 × 2 = 10, 10 ÷ 2 = 5, and 10 ÷ 5 = 2.

- Repeat with several fact families. Have partners work together to draw the arrays and record the facts in the fact families for 3, 6, and 18; 3, 4, and 12; and 2, 6, and 12.

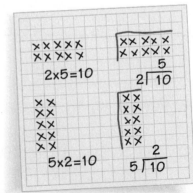

Basic Facts Workshop 2

Multiplying and Dividing by 2

Review

20 minutes

Multiplying and Dividing by 2

Management whole class

Materials overhead projector, 2 different-colored markers, 18 counters, hundredths square transparency (Just the Facts Support Master 7)

- Display 2 rows of 4 counters on a transparency. Ask students how many counters they see. **8** Ask, What multiplication fact names this array? **2 × 4 = 8** Turn the transparency. Ask, what multiplication fact names this array now? **4 × 2 = 8** Point out that multiplying a number by 2 is the same

as doubling that number.

- Remind students to use the multiplication facts they know to find division facts. Draw the division sign over the 2 × 4 array. Ask, What division fact does this show? **8 ÷ 2 = 4** Repeat wth the 4 × 2 array. Ask, What division fact does this show? **8 ÷ 4 = 2**

- Write the numbers 2, 4, 8 on the transparency as shown. Ask students to name the four facts in the fact family for these numbers.
  2 × 4 = 8, 4 × 2 = 8, 8 ÷ 2 = 4, and 8 ÷ 4 = 2

- Repeat, showing arrays and naming four facts for 1, 2, 2; 2, 3, 6; 2, 5, 10; 2, 6, 12; 2, 7, 14; 2, 8, 16; and 2, 9, 18. Then, repeat naming the two facts for 2, 2, 4. As students supply facts, write the numbers in triangle shapes.

Practice

30 minutes

Make 2's Flash Cards

Management individuals, then pairs

Materials for each student: 2 different-colored markers, 9 triangle flash cards (Just the Facts Support Master 4), practice minutes record and certificate (Just the Facts Support Masters 9 and 13)

- Direct each student to make nine flash cards. Students should print the products in one color and the factors in a second color.

- Students should make cards for the following fact families: 1, 2, 2; 2, 2, 4; 2, 3, 6;

2, 4, 8; 2, 5, 10; 2, 6, 12; 2, 7, 14; 2, 8, 16; and 2, 9, 18. Remind them to write their names or initials on the back of each card.

- Have students find partners. One student holds up a card and covers each corner in turn. If the partner sees two numbers in the same color, he or she states the two multiplication facts for the fact family. If the two numbers are different colors, the partner states the division fact.

- Students may take flash cards home to practice, recording practice minutes. Completed records may be returned to school and exchanged for a certificate.

Basic Facts Workshop 3
Multiplying and Dividing by 4

20 minutes

Multiplying and Dividing by 4

Management whole class

Materials overhead projector, 36 counters, blank transparency, hundredths square transparency (Just the Facts Support Master 7)

- Use counters to show 4 rows of 5 on the transparency. Ask, What multiplication fact does this array show? **4 × 5 = 20** Turn the transparency. Ask, what multiplication fact names this array now? **5 × 4 = 20**

- Remind students that they can use multiplication facts they know to find division facts. Draw a division

symbol over the array. Ask, What two division facts does the array show? **20 ÷ 4 = 5, 20 ÷ 5 = 4**

- Write the numbers 4, 5, and 20 in a triangle on the transparency, with 20 at the top. Remind students that they have found all four members of the fact family. Ask them to name the fact family as you write. Repeat with other fact families for 4.

- Tell students there is another way to think about 4's. If you know the facts for 2, you can use them to remember the facts for 4. Replace the grid transparency with a blank transparency. Write 2 × 3 = 6. Then, write 4 × 3 = ? Ask, If you know that 2 × 3 = 6, how could you figure out what 4 × 3 is? **Use the strategy of doubling the product to get 12.** Ask, If you know that 4 × 3 = 12, what is the rest of the fact family? **3 × 4 = 12, 12 ÷ 4 = 3, and 12 ÷ 3 = 4** Repeat with other examples.

30 minutes

Make 4's Flash Cards

Management individuals, then pairs

Materials for each student: 2 different-colored markers, 8 triangle flash cards (Just the Facts Support Master 4), practice minutes record and certificate (Just the Facts Support Masters 10 and 14)

- Direct each student to make eight triangle flash cards like those shown for the following fact families: 1, 4, 4; 3, 4, 12; 4, 4, 16; 4, 5, 20; 4, 6, 24; 4, 7, 28; 4, 8, 32; and 4, 9, 36.

- Students print the product in one color and the two factors in another color. They should also write their names or initials on the back of each card. When finished, students add in the 4-2-8 flash card from their previously made set to complete the 4's.

- Have students find partners. One student holds up a card and covers each corner, one at a time. Seeing two numbers in the same color, the partner states the two multiplication facts for the fact family. Seeing two numbers in different colors, the partner states the division fact. Students should state all four facts for each card except the 4-4-16 card, which has only two facts.

- Students add these flash cards to their complete set and take them home to practice. Remind students to keep track of minutes practiced at home. Completed practice records may be exchanged for a certificate.

Basic Facts Workshop 4
Multiplying and Dividing by 5

Review

20 minutes

Multiplying and Dividing by 5

Management whole class

Materials overhead projector, blank transparencies, 45 counters

- Place 7 rows of 5 counters on the transparency on the overhead projector. Ask, What multiplication facts does this represent? Write $5 \times 7 = 35$ and $7 \times 5 = 35$. Ask, How can skip-counting help you multiply by 5? Repeat, showing 6, 8, 9, and 4 rows of 5 counters. Have students name the two 5's facts represented by each.

- Remind students of another way to figure out 5's. Write 10×4 on a transparency, and ask, What is the product? Write $10 \times 4 = 40$. Write $5 \times 4 = ?$ directly below. Ask, How can knowing 10's help you with 5's facts? **You can figure out a 10 fact and find half of it.** If $10 \times 4 = 40$, then $5 \times 4 = 20$. Repeat with 10×6 and 5×6; 10×8 and 5×8; 10×5 and 5×5; 10×3 and 5×3; and 10×7 and 5×7.

- Write 5×6 on a transparency. Ask, Can you name the four facts in the fact family? Write $5 \times 6 = 30$, $6 \times 5 = 30$, $30 \div 6 = 5$, and $30 \div 5 = 6$. Repeat with fact families for 5×8, 5×4, 5×9, and 5×7.

Practice

30 minutes

Make 5's Flash Cards

Management individuals, then pairs

Materials for each student: 2 different-colored markers, 7 triangle flash cards (Just the Facts Support Master 4), practice minutes record and certificate (Just the Facts Support Masters 10 and 14)

- Remind students that they already know some of the 5's facts. Ask them to pull the 2×5 and 4×5 flash cards from their previously made set.

- Have each student make seven flash cards like those shown for the following facts: 1, 5, 5; 5, 3, 15; 5, 5, 25; 5, 6, 30; 5, 7, 35; 5, 8, 40; and 5, 9, 45. Remind them to print the products in one color and

the factors in another color. Ask students to put their initials or names on the back of each card.

- When finished, students may practice 5's with a partner. Students should add these cards to their complete set and continue practicing at home, recording practice minutes. Completed records may be exchanged for a certificate.

Basic Facts Workshop 5

Multiplying and Dividing by 1

Review

20 minutes

Multiplying and Dividing by 1

Management whole class

Materials overhead projector, 9 counters, hundredths square transparency (Just the Facts Support Master 7)

- Display one row of 6 counters on the transparency. Ask, How many counters do you see? **6 counters** What is the multiplication fact that names this array? **1 × 6 = 6**

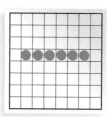

$$1 \times 6 = 6$$

- Turn the transparency 90°. Ask, What multiplication fact names this array? **6 × 1 = 6**

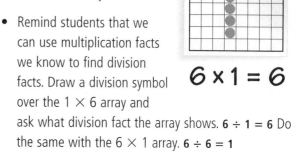

$$6 \times 1 = 6$$

- Remind students that we can use multiplication facts we know to find division facts. Draw a division symbol over the 1 × 6 array and ask what division fact the array shows. **6 ÷ 1 = 6** Do the same with the 6 × 1 array. **6 ÷ 6 = 1**

- Ask, What happens when you multiply any number by 1? **The product is the original number.** If we know 7 × 1 = 7, what are the other facts in the fact family? **1 × 7 = 7, 7 ÷ 1 = 7, 7 ÷ 7 = 1**

- Have students name the fact families for 8 × 1, 1 × 5, 9 × 1, and 1 × 4.

Practice

20 minutes

Make 1's Flash Cards

Management individuals, then pairs

Materials for each student: 2 different-colored markers, 6 triangle flash cards (Just the Facts Support Master 4), practice minutes record and certificate (Just the Facts Support Masters 10 and 14)

- Have students pull the 2 × 1, 4 × 1, and 5 × 1 flash cards from their previously made set.

- Students should make the six flash cards as shown, with the products printed in one color and the two factors in another color. Students should make cards for the following fact families: 1, 1, 1; 1, 3, 3; 1, 6, 6; 1, 7, 7; 1, 8, 8; and 1, 9, 9. Ask students to print their names or initials on the back of each card.

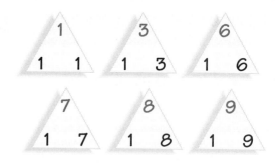

- When finished, students may practice 1's with a partner. After practicing the 1's, students may add those cards to their complete set and continue to practice at home, recording practice minutes. Completed records can be exchanged for a certificate.

Basic Facts Workshop 6
Multiplying and Dividing by 3

Review

15 minutes

Multiplying and Dividing by 3

Management whole class

Materials overhead projector, 27 counters, hundredths square transparencies (Just the Facts Support Master 7)

- Use a projector to display 3 rows of 4 counters on a transparency. Ask students how many counters they see. **12** Ask, What multiplication fact names this array? **3 × 4 = 12**

- Ask, How could skip-counting help you figure out the answer? **Counters in each column are 3, 6, 9, 12.**

- Ask, How could you use the strategy of using 2's to find 3's? **2 × 4 = 8, so I add another 4. 3 fours are 12, so 3 × 4 = 12.**

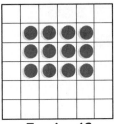

$$3 \times 4 = 12$$

- Ask, If we know $3 \times 4 = 12$, what are the other facts in this fact family? **4 × 3 = 12, 12 ÷ 4 = 3, 12 ÷ 3 = 4**

- Ask a student to show a 3×6 array on the projector, then write the fact family as class members name it.

- Repeat with 3×8, 3×9, 3×5, and 3×7.

Practice

30 minutes

Make 3's Flash Cards

Management individuals, then pairs

Materials for each student: 2 different-colored markers, 5 triangle flash cards (Just the Facts Support Master 4), practice minutes record and certificate (Just the Facts Support Masters 11 and 15)

- Remind students that they already know some 3's. Have them pull the 2×3, 4×3, 5×3, and 1×3 flash cards from their previously made set.

- Then, instruct each student to make 5 triangle flash cards as shown for the following fact families: 3, 3, 9; 3, 6, 18; 3, 7, 21; 3, 8, 24; and 3, 9, 27. Ask students

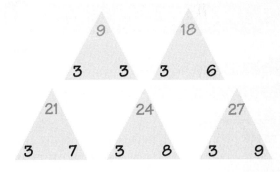

to write their names or initials on the back of each card.

- When finished, students may practice 3's with a partner. Students can add these cards to their complete set and continue practice at home, recording practice minutes. Completed records may be exchanged for a certificate.

Basic Facts Workshop 7

Reviewing 1's-5's and 0's

Review

20 minutes

Multiplying and Dividing by 0

Management whole class
Materials overhead projector, 6 transparent plastic cups, 8 counters

- Show 4 plastic cups in a row. Put 2 counters in each one. Have students name the multiplication fact that describes how many counters there are in all.

4 × 2 = 8

$$4 \times 2 = 8$$

- Show 3 cups with no counters in them. Ask the class to name the multiplication fact that describes how many counters there are in all. **3 × 0 = 0**

- Repeat, showing 5, 2, 6, and 4 empty cups. Have students name the multiplication facts. Discuss what happens when you multiply any number by 0. **The product is 0.**

- Have 6 students stand. Ask the class to divide them into 3 equal groups, then write 6 ÷ 3 = 2 on the board; two equal groups, then write 6 ÷ 2 = 3 on the board; no equal groups, then write not possible.

- Have students sit down. Write 0 ÷ 4 = ? Ask, If we have 0 people to divide into 4 groups, how many people would be in each group? **0 ÷ 4 = 0**

Practice

30 minutes

Showing 0 and Reviewing 1's-5's

Management pairs
Materials large sheet of drawing paper for each pair, practice minutes record and certificate (Just the Facts Support Masters 11 and 15)

- Have students work in pairs. Ask each pair to divide a piece of paper into three parts with the following headings: Multiplying by 0; Dividing 0 by any number; and Dividing by 0.

- Students work with partners to write, illustrate, or show examples for what happens when they multiply

by 0 (the answer is always 0); divide 0 by any number (the answer is always 0); and divide by 0 (it's not possible, so the answer is the dividend). Students can share their work with other pairs or with the class.

- Because dividing by 0 is impossible, students will not make triangle flash cards for 0 facts. They may take home their previously made flash cards to continue practicing 1's through 5's, recording practice minutes. Completed practice records may be returned to school to exchange for a certificate.

Basic Facts Workshop 8

Multiplying and Dividing by 9

Review

20 minutes

Using a Hundredths Square to find 9's

Management whole class

Materials for each student: scissors, hundredths square (Just the Facts Support Master 7)

- Distribute copies of Support Master 7. Have students cut out the hundredths square.

- Ask students to fold back five rows of the square to show 6×10. Have them record $6 \times 10 = 60$.

- Ask students to fold back the last column to show 6×9. Have them record $6 \times 9 = 54$.

- Tell students to record the rest of the fact family for 6×9. **$9 \times 6 = 54$; $54 \div 9 = 6$; $54 \div 6 = 9$**

- Repeat the folding and recording activity for 4×9, 8×9, 3×9, 7×9, 9×9, and 2×9.

Practice

30 minutes

Make 9's Flash Cards

Management individuals, then pairs

Materials for each student: 2 different-colored markers, 4 triangle flash cards (Just the Facts Support Master 4), practice minutes record and certificate (Just the Facts Support Masters 10 and 14)

- Remind students that they already know some 9's. Have them pull the 1×9, 2×9, 3×9, 4×9, and 5×9 flash cards from their previously made sets. Then, have each student cut out 4 triangle flash cards and write his or her name on the backs.

- Instruct students to make 4 cards each, as shown.

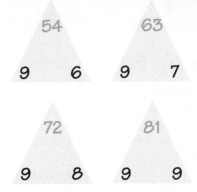

- When finished, students may practice with a partner. Students may add the 9's cards to the set they have made and continue practice at home, recording practice minutes. Completed records may be exchanged for a certificate.

Basic Facts Workshop 9
Multiplying and Dividing by 6

Review

20 minutes

Finding 6's with Arrays

Management whole class, then pairs

Materials overhead projector, hundredths square transparencies (Just the Facts Support Master 7)

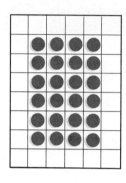
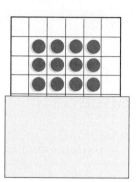

- Draw or use counters to make a 6 × 4 array on a transparency. Cover the bottom three rows with paper to show a 3 × 4 array. Ask students how knowing 3 × 4 = 12 can help them find 6 × 4. **Use the doubles strategy.** Write 6 × 4 = 24.

- Repeat the activity, doubling 3's facts to find 3 × 7 and 6 × 7, 3 × 5 and 6 × 5, 3 × 8 and 6 × 8, 3 × 9 and 6 × 9, and 3 × 6 and 6 × 6.

- Remind students that once you know a multiplication fact, you can write the other facts in the fact family. Have students work with partners to write the fact families for each of the facts above.

Practice

30 minutes

Make 6's Flash Cards

Management individuals, then pairs

Materials for each student: 2 different-colored markers, three triangle flash cards (Just the Facts Support Master 4), practice minutes record and certificate (Just the Facts Support Masters 10 and 14)

- When finished, have students add these cards to the set they have already made, then have them practice with a partner. They should continue to practice at home, recording practice minutes. Completed records may be exchanged for a certificate.

- Remind students that they already know some 6's multiplication facts. Have them pull the 1 × 6, 2 × 6, 3 × 6, 4 × 6, 5 × 6, and 9 × 6 flash cards from their previously made sets.

- Have each student cut out three triangle flash cards and write his or her name on the backs. Instruct students to make the following three flash cards to complete the 6's: 6, 6, 36; 6, 7, 42; 6, 8, 48.

Basic Facts Workshop 10

Multiplying and Dividing by 7

Review

20 minutes

Using Arrays to Find 7's

Management whole class

Materials overhead projector, blank transparency, 2 hundredths square transparencies (Just the Facts Support Master 7)

* Remind students that they have already practiced many of the 7's facts. Ask, What is 2 × 7? **14** What is 4 × 7? **28**

* Draw a 6 × 7 array on a grid transparency. Draw a line across the array to divide it into a 2 × 7 array and a 4 × 7 array. Ask, How could knowing the

products of 2 × 7 and 4 × 7 help you to figure out 6 × 7? **Add the products: 14 + 28 = 42.** Ask, Could you use any other parts of the 6 × 7 array to help you? **Yes, you could use 1 × 7 plus 5 × 7, or 3 × 7 plus 3 × 7.**

* Repeat the activity, drawing arrays for 7 × 7 and 8 × 7. Have students think of possible combinations of facts they know that could help them determine the products.

* Remind the class that once you know a multiplication fact, you can write the fact family. Have students work with partners to write the fact families for 6 × 7, 7 × 7, 8 × 7, and 9 × 7. Ask them to share their results.

Practice

30 minutes

Make 7's Flash Cards

Management individuals, then pairs

Materials for each student: 2 different-colored markers, 2 triangle flash cards (Just the Facts Support Master 4), practice minutes record and certificate (Just the Facts Support Masters 11 and 15)

* Distribute two triangle flash cards to each student. Students should cut out the cards, and write their name or initials on the backs.

* Instruct students to make flash cards as shown for the following fact families: 7, 7, 49 and 7, 8, 56. Remind the class to write the product in one color and the factors in another color.

* When finished, students should add these cards to the set they have already made (1 × 7, 2 × 7, 3 × 7, 4 × 7, 5 × 7, 6 × 7, and 9 × 7). Then they can find partners and practice 7's with them. Students may take their sets home to continue practice, recording practice minutes. They may return completed records to school in exchange for a certificate.

Basic Facts Workshop 11

Multiplying and Dividing by 8

Review

20 minutes

Finding 8's with Arrays

Management whole class

Materials overhead projector, hundredths square transparencies (Just the Facts Support Master 7)

- Draw or use counters to make an 8 × 3 array on a transparency.

- Cover the bottom 4 rows with paper to show a 4 × 3 array. Ask, How can knowing 4 × 3 = 12 help you find 8 × 3? **Use the doubles strategy.** Write 4 × 3 = 12. Under it, write 8 × 3 = 24.

- Repeat the activity, doubling 4's facts to find 8 × 5, 8 × 6, 8 × 8, and 8 × 7.

- Remind the class that once you know a multiplication fact, you can write the whole fact family. Have students work with partners to write the fact families for each of the 8's facts above.

- Have students share and discuss their fact families. Ask, Do all of the fact families have 4 facts? **No, 8 × 8 has only 3 facts.** Ask, Is it easier to use 4's facts and double them than to memorize the 8's facts? **Answers will vary. Possible answer: it depends on the individual. Some people like to use the strategy; some like to memorize.**

Practice

30 minutes

Make 8's Flash Cards

Management individuals, then pairs

Materials for each student: 2 different-colored markers, 1 triangle flash card (Just the Facts Support Master 4), practice minutes record and certificate (Just the Facts Support Masters 11 and 15)

- Distribute 1 triangle flash card to each student. Students should cut out the card, write their name or initials on the back, then make the flash card as shown to complete the 8's. Remind students to write the product in one color and the factors in another color.

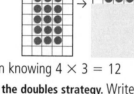

- Remind students that they have already made flash cards and practiced many 8's facts. Have them find the following cards from their previously made sets: 1 × 8, 2 × 8, 3 × 8, 4 × 8, 5 × 8, 6 × 8, 7 × 8, and 9 × 8. Students should add these cards to the card they completed.

- Students should find partners to practice their 8's facts with. Then, they may take their sets home to continue practice, recording practice minutes. They may exchange completed records for a certificate.

Basic Facts Workshop 12

Review 6, 7, 8, and 9

Review

20 minutes

Number Wheel Practice

Management whole class, then pairs
Materials overhead projector, number wheel transparencies (Just the Facts Support Master 8)

- Tell students that they can make a number wheel to practice multiplication. Write × 6 in the center of a number wheel transparency. Write the numbers 2-9 in any order in the inner circle.

- Ask the class to identify each product, then write it in the outer circle.

- Tell students that they can also make a number wheel

to practice division. Write × 7 in the center of a number wheel transparency. Leave the inner circle empty, and fill in the following numbers in the outer circle in any order: 7, 14, 21, 28, 35, 42, 49, 56, and 63.

- Ask the class how making a number wheel like this would help them to divide. **I need to know what number I multiply by 7 to get the answer. Division reverses the multiplication process.** Ask students to help you fill in the inner circle.

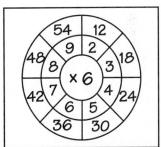

Practice

30 minutes

Make Your Own

Management individuals, then pairs
Materials 2 number wheels for each student (Just the Facts Support Master 8)

- Have students make one multiplication and one division number wheel. They should choose a different number— 6, 7, 8, or 9— to put in the center of each wheel.

- Tell students to fill in the inner circle of the multiplication wheel with the numbers 2-9 in any order, and to leave the outer circle blank.

- Have students fill in the outer circle of the division wheel with products of the center number and the numbers 2-9. Students should leave the inner circle blank.

- Students should exchange both number wheels with a partner. Partners fill in appropriate answers in either inner or outer circles as required, then return wheels to the maker, who will check answers for accuracy.

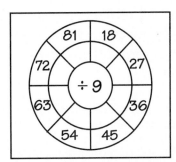

Basic Facts Workshop 13

Review Multiplication and Division Facts

Review

20 minutes

All of the Facts

Management whole class
Materials none

- Draw a 9 × 3 array on the board. Ask, What fact family does this array show? **9 × 3 = 27; 3 × 9 = 27; 27 ÷ 9 = 3; 27 ÷ 3 = 9**

- Ask, If you couldn't remember that 9 × 3 = 27, what strategies could you use to help you? **Answers will vary. Possible answers: 10 × 3 = 30, subtract 3; 9 × 2 = 18, add another 9**

- Ask, If you couldn't remember 27 ÷ 3, how could knowing a multiplication fact help you? **9 × 3 = 27, so 27 ÷ 3 = 9**

- Write the following sentences on the board: 6 × 4, 7 × 3, 5 × 7, and 8 × 6. Have students discuss strategies that might help them figure out these sentences. Suggestions might include doubling, skip-counting, or using facts they know.

- Have students write the fact families for each fact.

Practice

30 minutes

Help Wanted

Management pairs
Materials practice minutes record and certificate (Just the Facts Support Masters 12 and 16)

- Remind students that they have already practiced all of the multiplication and division facts. Now, they will review to determine if any facts still need more practice.

- Have students take out all previously made triangle flash cards.

- Students should go through all of the cards with a partner, naming the entire fact family for each card.

If they can easily state the fact family, they should place the card into a "known facts" pile. If they have difficulty with any facts for a card, they should put them into a second "help wanted" pile.

- The other partner then goes through every card, making a pile of "known facts" and a pile of "help wanted" cards.

- Partners may use their "help wanted" cards to help each other discuss strategies for remembering their most difficult facts. They should continue to practice only these facts.

Name_____ Date _____

◤1A BASIC FACTS

Fact Families

Write two multiplication facts.

1. • • • •
   • • • •
   • • • •

   _____

   _____

2. • • • • • •
   • • • • • •
   • • • • • •

   _____

   _____

3. • • • • • •
   • • • • •
   • • • • •

   _____

   _____

Use the order property. Complete.

4. $4 \times 5 =$ _____ $\times$ _____

5. $2 \times 6 =$ _____ $\times$ _____

6. $7 \times 3 =$ _____ $\times$ _____

7. $8 \times 2 =$ _____ $\times$ _____

Write a multiplication fact.

8. 3 sevens = _____

9. 5 fives = _____

Write a division number sentence.

10. • • • • • •
    • • • • • •

11. • • • • •
    • • • • •
    • • • • •

    _____   _____

Name_____ Date _____

◤1B BASIC FACTS

Fact Families

Draw an array. Then multiply.

1. 2
   $\times\,3$

2. 4
   $\times\,4$

3. 3
   $\times\,6$

4. 2
   $\times\,8$

5. 5
   $\times\,3$

6. 4
   $\times\,2$

7. 2
   $\times\,7$

8. 3
   $\times\,4$

9. 5
   $\times\,2$

10. 2
    $\times\,6$

11. 3
    $\times\,3$

12. 5
    $\times\,4$

Draw an array. Then divide.

13. $8 \div 2 =$ _____

14. $15 \div 3 =$ _____

15. $6 \div 3 =$ _____

16. $18 \div 3 =$ _____

17. $6 \div 2 =$ _____

18. $18 \div 2 =$ _____

19. $10 \div 2 =$ _____

20. $12 \div 3 =$ _____

21. $16 \div 2 =$ _____

Name_____   Date _____

2A BASIC FACTS

Multiplying and Dividing by 2

Look at the multiplication sentences below. Write a related division fact for each.

   1. 2 × 2 = 4 _____

   2. 2 × 5 = 10 _____

   3. 2 × 6 = 12 _____

List the first ten multiples.

   4. of 2 ____ ____ ____ ____ ____ ____ ____ ____ ____ ____

Draw a picture of the groups in the division fact.

   5. 8 ÷ 2   **6.** 14 ÷ 2

Write the correct sign. Choose +, × , or ÷.

   7. 45 ___ 5 = 9   **8.** 4 ___ 3 = 12   **9.** 9 ___ 9 = 18

Write a multiplication sentence. Then solve.

   10. 8 ÷ 4 = ____ _____   **11.** 5 ÷ 5 = ____ _____

   12. 2 ÷ 1 = ____ _____   **13.** 14 ÷ 7 = ____ _____

Name_____ Date _____

2B ◢ BASIC FACTS

Multiplying and Dividing by 2

Multiply. Think of doubles or the order property.

1. $2 \times 7 =$ _____

2. $6 \times 2 =$ _____

3. $2 \times 9 =$ _____

4. $4 \times 2 =$ _____

5. $2 \times 8 =$ _____

6. $2 \times 5 =$ _____

7. $2 \times 3 =$ _____

8. $1 \times 2 =$ _____

9. $2 \times 2 =$ _____

10. $\begin{array}{r} 2 \\ \times\, 5 \\ \hline \end{array}$

11. $\begin{array}{r} 2 \\ \times\, 3 \\ \hline \end{array}$

12. $\begin{array}{r} 8 \\ \times\, 2 \\ \hline \end{array}$

13. $\begin{array}{r} 9 \\ \times\, 2 \\ \hline \end{array}$

14. $\begin{array}{r} 2 \\ \times\, 4 \\ \hline \end{array}$

15. $\begin{array}{r} 2 \\ \times\, 6 \\ \hline \end{array}$

Divide.

16. $8 \div 2 =$ _____

17. $6 \div 2 =$ _____

18. $18 \div 2 =$ _____

19. $10 \div 2 =$ _____

20. $16 \div 2 =$ _____

21. $12 \div 2 =$ _____

22. $14 \div 2 =$ _____

23. $2 \div 1 =$ _____

24. $4 \div 2 =$ _____

Write a division sentence. Then solve.

25. $2 \times 7 =$ ____ _____

26. $2 \times 3 =$ ____ _____

27. $2 \times 4 =$ ____ _____

28. $2 \times 8 =$ ____ _____

Name_____ Date _____

3A ▸ BASIC FACTS

Multiplying and Dividing by 4

Find the missing factor. Complete.

1. $9 \times$ _____ $= 36$ **2.** $4 \times$ _____ $= 32$ **3.** $4 \times$ _____ $= 12$

4. $7 \times 4 = 4 \times$ _____   **5.** $4 \times 5 = 5 \times$ _____   **6.** _____ $\times 7 = 28$

7. $4 \times$ _____ $= 16$ **8.** $2 \times$ _____ $= 4 \times 2$ **9.** $4 \times$ _____ $= 24$

List the first ten multiples.

10. of 4 ____ ____ ____ ____ ____ ____ ____ ____ ____ ____

Write a related multiplication fact. Then divide.

11. $10 \div 2 =$ _____   **12.** $8 \div 4 =$ _____   **13.** $16 \div 4 =$ _____

_____   _____   _____

14. $14 \div 2 =$ _____   **15.** $24 \div 4 =$ _____   **16.** $20 \div 4 =$ _____

_____   _____   _____

17. $32 \div 4 =$ _____   **18.** $18 \div 2 =$ _____   **19.** $28 \div 4 =$ _____

_____   _____   _____

Name_____ Date _____

3B BASIC FACTS

Multiplying and Dividing by 4

Divide. Check by multiplying.

1. $4\overline{)8}$

_____

2. $4\overline{)32}$

_____

3. $4\overline{)24}$

_____

4. $4\overline{)16}$

_____

5. $4\overline{)36}$

_____

6. $4\overline{)12}$

_____

7. $28 \div 4 = $ _____

_____

8. $20 \div 4 = $ _____

_____

9. $12 \div 4 = $ _____

_____

Multiply.

10. $\begin{array}{r} 6 \\ \times\,4 \\ \hline \end{array}$

11. $\begin{array}{r} 5 \\ \times\,4 \\ \hline \end{array}$

12. $\begin{array}{r} 7 \\ \times\,4 \\ \hline \end{array}$

13. $\begin{array}{r} 4 \\ \times\,8 \\ \hline \end{array}$

14. $\begin{array}{r} 4 \\ \times\,9 \\ \hline \end{array}$

15. $\begin{array}{r} 3 \\ \times\,4 \\ \hline \end{array}$

16. $\begin{array}{r} 4 \\ \times\,4 \\ \hline \end{array}$

17. $\begin{array}{r} 9 \\ \times\,4 \\ \hline \end{array}$

18. $\begin{array}{r} 8 \\ \times\,4 \\ \hline \end{array}$

19. $\begin{array}{r} 4 \\ \times\,5 \\ \hline \end{array}$

20. $4 \times 3 = $ _____

21. $2 \times 7 = $ _____

22. $6 \times 4 = $ _____

Name_____ Date _____

4A ▶ BASIC FACTS

···

Multiplying and Dividing by 5

Multiply.

1. $5 \times (1 \times 8) =$ _____

2. $(3 \times 5) \times 1 =$ _____

3. $5 \times 2 =$ _____

4. $5 \times 5 =$ _____

5. $5 \times 8 =$ _____

6. $5 \times 9 =$ _____

Complete.

7. $6 \times (1 \times 5) =$ _____

8. $1 \times 5 \times 6 =$ _____

List the first ten multiples.

9. of 5 ____ ____ ____ ____ ____ ____ ____ ____ ____ ____

Divide. Think of multiplication.

10. $40 \div 5 =$ ____

11. $35 \div 5 =$ ____

12. $25 \div 5 =$ ____

13. $10 \div 5 =$ ____

14. $20 \div 5 =$ ____

15. $30 \div 5 =$ ____

16. $15 \div 5 =$ ____

17. $45 \div 5 =$ ____

18. $5 \div 1 =$ ____

19. $40 \div 8 =$ ____

20. $35 \div 7 =$ ____

21. $45 \div 9 =$ ____

Name_____ Date _____

4B ▶ BASIC FACTS

Multiplying and Dividing by 5

What is the quotient? Think of multiplication.

1. $5\overline{)25}$ **2.** $5\overline{)30}$ **3.** $5\overline{)45}$ **4.** $5\overline{)40}$

5. $5\overline{)35}$ **6.** $5\overline{)50}$ **7.** $5\overline{)15}$ **8.** $5\overline{)20}$

List the multiples

9. of 4 up to 50

_____

Complete the number sentence.

10. $45 = \underline{\quad} \times \underline{\quad}$ **11.** $25 \div 5 = \underline{\quad}$ **12.** $\underline{\quad} = 7 \times 5$

13. $5 \times 8 = \underline{\quad}$ **14.** $3 \times 7 = \underline{\quad}$ **15.** $18 = \underline{\quad} \times 2$

16. $54 = \underline{\quad} \times \underline{\quad}$ **17.** $20 = \underline{\quad} \times \underline{\quad}$ **18.** $50 \div \underline{\quad} = 10$

19. $30 = \underline{\quad} \times \underline{\quad}$ **20.** $10 \div 2 = \underline{\quad}$ **21.** $\underline{\quad} \div 5 = 9$

22. $15 \div 5 = \underline{\quad}$ **23.** $6 \times 4 = \underline{\quad}$ **24.** $9 \div 3 = \underline{\quad}$

Name_____ Date _____

5A ◤ BASIC FACTS
....

Multiplying and Dividing by 1

Use multiplication and division properties to complete.

1. 8 ÷ _____ = 1   2. (6 × 2) × 1 = 1 × _____

3. (3 × _____) × 5 = 1 × (3 × 5)   4. _____ ÷ 1 = 10

Multiply.

5. 1	6. 7	7. 5	8. 1	9. 2	10. 1
× 2	× 1	× 1	× 9	× 1	× 1

11. 1	12. 8	13. 1	14. 6	15. 1	16. 1
× 6	× 1	× 4	× 1	× 7	× 3

Write a multiplication sentence. Then solve.

17. 5 ÷ 5 = ____ _____   18. 3 ÷ 1 = ____ _____

What is the quotient? Think of multiplication.

19. 1)$\overline{5}$ 20. 1)$\overline{1}$ 21. 1)$\overline{8}$ 22. 1)$\overline{3}$

Name_____ Date _____

◢5B BASIC FACTS

Multiplying and Dividing by 1

Multiply.

1. $1 \times 4 =$ _____

2. $1 \times 8 =$ _____

3. $6 \times 2 =$ _____

4. $9 \times 1 =$ _____

5. $1 \times 3 =$ _____

6. $2 \times 4 =$ _____

7. $1 \times 5 =$ _____

8. $7 \times 1 =$ _____

9. $2 \times 9 =$ _____

10. $\begin{array}{r} 2 \\ \times 2 \\ \hline \end{array}$

11. $\begin{array}{r} 1 \\ \times 7 \\ \hline \end{array}$

12. $\begin{array}{r} 5 \\ \times 4 \\ \hline \end{array}$

13. $\begin{array}{r} 1 \\ \times 9 \\ \hline \end{array}$

14. $\begin{array}{r} 2 \\ \times 1 \\ \hline \end{array}$

15. $\begin{array}{r} 1 \\ \times 2 \\ \hline \end{array}$

16. $\begin{array}{r} 1 \\ \times 6 \\ \hline \end{array}$

17. $\begin{array}{r} 8 \\ \times 4 \\ \hline \end{array}$

18. $\begin{array}{r} 4 \\ \times 1 \\ \hline \end{array}$

19. $\begin{array}{r} 2 \\ \times 7 \\ \hline \end{array}$

Divide.

20. $4 \div 1 =$ _____

21. $6 \div 1 =$ _____

22. $2 \div 1 =$ _____

23. $18 \div 2 =$ _____

24. $12 \div 1 =$ _____

25. $24 \div 3 =$ _____

26. $25 \div 5 =$ _____

27. $24 \div 4 =$ _____

28. $8 \div 1 =$ _____

29. $40 \div 5 =$ _____

30. $11 \div 1 =$ _____

31. $16 \div 4 =$ _____

Name_____ Date _____

6A ◢ BASIC FACTS

Multiplying and Dividing by 3

Complete each fact family.

1. $3 \times 2 =$ _____ $6 \div 2 =$ _____

$2 \times 3 =$ _____ $6 \div 3 =$ _____

2. $6 \times 3 =$ _____ $18 \div 6 =$ _____

$3 \times 6 =$ _____ $18 \div 3 =$ _____

3. $8 \times 3 =$ _____ $24 \div 3 =$ _____

$3 \times 8 =$ _____ $24 \div 8 =$ _____

4. $3 \times 9 =$ _____ $27 \div 9 =$ _____

$9 \times 3 =$ _____ $27 \div 3 =$ _____

5. $5 \times 3 =$ _____ $15 \div 3 =$ _____

$3 \times 5 =$ _____ $15 \div 5 =$ _____

Write four number sentences for each fact family.

6. 3, 4, 12 _____ _____ _____ _____

7. 3, 7, 21 _____ _____ _____ _____

6B BASIC FACTS

Multiplying and Dividing by 3

Write a related multiplication fact. Then divide.

1. $6 \div 3 =$ ____

____ $\times$ ____ $=$ ____

2. $21 \div 3 =$ ____

____ $\times$ ____ $=$ ____

3. $12 \div 3 =$ ____

____ $\times$ ____ $=$ ____

4. $3 \div 3 =$ ____

____ $\times$ ____ $=$ ____

5. $9 \div 3 =$ ____

____ $\times$ ____ $=$ ____

6. $24 \div 3 =$ ____

____ $\times$ ____ $=$ ____

7. $15 \div 3 =$ ____

____ $\times$ ____ $=$ ____

8. $0 \div 3 =$ ____

____ $\times$ ____ $=$ ____

9. $18 \div 3 =$ ____

____ $\times$ ____ $=$ ____

10. $27 \div 3 =$ ____

____ $\times$ ____ $=$ ____

Check by multiplying. Correct any mistakes.

11. $12 \div 3 = 6$

_____

12. $9 \div 3 = 3$

_____

13. $15 \div 3 = 4$

_____

Name_____ Date _____

7A ◢ BASIC FACTS

....

Reviewing 1's - 5's and 0's

Multiply.

1. $0 \times 4 =$ _____   **2.** $1 \times 8 =$ _____   **3.** $6 \times 0 =$ _____

4. $9 \times 1 =$ _____   **5.** $0 \times 3 =$ _____   **6.** $2 \times 0 =$ _____

7. $1 \times 5 =$ _____   **8.** $7 \times 0 =$ _____   **9.** $0 \times 9 =$ _____

10. $\begin{array}{r} 7 \\ \times\ 1 \\ \hline \end{array}$ **11.** $\begin{array}{r} 5 \\ \times\ 5 \\ \hline \end{array}$ **12.** $\begin{array}{r} 3 \\ \times\ 0 \\ \hline \end{array}$ **13.** $\begin{array}{r} 2 \\ \times\ 1 \\ \hline \end{array}$ **14.** $\begin{array}{r} 1 \\ \times\ 0 \\ \hline \end{array}$

15. $\begin{array}{r} 8 \\ \times\ 0 \\ \hline \end{array}$ **16.** $\begin{array}{r} 1 \\ \times\ 4 \\ \hline \end{array}$ **17.** $\begin{array}{r} 1 \\ \times\ 3 \\ \hline \end{array}$ **18.** $\begin{array}{r} 6 \\ \times\ 2 \\ \hline \end{array}$ **19.** $\begin{array}{r} 2 \\ \times\ 7 \\ \hline \end{array}$

20. $\begin{array}{r} 3 \\ \times\ 3 \\ \hline \end{array}$ **21.** $\begin{array}{r} 3 \\ \times\ 7 \\ \hline \end{array}$ **22.** $\begin{array}{r} 8 \\ \times\ 3 \\ \hline \end{array}$ **23.** $\begin{array}{r} 3 \\ \times\ 5 \\ \hline \end{array}$ **24.** $\begin{array}{r} 4 \\ \times\ 3 \\ \hline \end{array}$

25. $\begin{array}{r} 2 \\ \times\ 5 \\ \hline \end{array}$ **26.** $\begin{array}{r} 5 \\ \times\ 4 \\ \hline \end{array}$ **27.** $\begin{array}{r} 2 \\ \times\ 4 \\ \hline \end{array}$ **28.** $\begin{array}{r} 4 \\ \times\ 4 \\ \hline \end{array}$ **29.** $\begin{array}{r} 5 \\ \times\ 0 \\ \hline \end{array}$

Name_____ Date _____

7B ◣ BASIC FACTS

Reviewing 1's - 5's and 0's

Find the quotient. Think of multiplication.

1. $1\overline{)5}$ 2. $5\overline{)0}$ 3. $1\overline{)4}$ 4. $8\overline{)0}$

5. $7\overline{)14}$ 6. $9\overline{)0}$ 7. $1\overline{)9}$ 8. $8\overline{)8}$

9. $3\overline{)15}$ 10. $1\overline{)8}$ 11. $1\overline{)3}$ 12. $6\overline{)0}$

13. $6\overline{)6}$ 14. $2\overline{)0}$ 15. $4\overline{)16}$ 16. $1\overline{)7}$

Write a multiplication sentence. Then solve.

17. $0 \div 4 =$ _____ _____   18. $5 \div 5 =$ _____ _____

19. $3 \div 1 =$ _____ _____   20. $10 \div 2 =$ _____ _____

21. $6 \div 3 =$ _____ _____   22. $0 \div 3 =$ _____ _____

23. $8 \div 1 =$ _____ _____   24. $14 \div 2 =$ _____ _____

25. $4 \div 1 =$ _____ _____   26. $9 \div 3 =$ _____ _____

27. $3 \div 3 =$ _____ _____   28. $16 \div 1 =$ _____ _____

Name_____ Date _____

8A ◢ BASIC FACTS

Multiplying and Dividing by 9

Find two multiplication facts.

1. • • • • • • • •
   • • • • • • • •
   • • • • • • • •

   _____

   _____

2. • • • • • • • •
   • • • • • • • •

   _____

   _____

Find the missing factor. Complete.

3. ____ $\times$ 3 = 27

4. 9 $\times$ ____ = 72

5. 6 $\times$ 9 = 9 $\times$ ____

Complete the number sentence.

6. 36 = ____ $\times$ ____

7. 18 = ____ $\times$ ____

8. 45 = ____ $\times$ ____

Multiply.

9. 5
   $\times$ 9

10. 7
    $\times$ 9

11. 3
    $\times$ 9

12. 4
    $\times$ 9

13. 9
    $\times$ 9

14. 6
    $\times$ 9

15. 9
    $\times$ 5

16. 2
    $\times$ 9

17. 1
    $\times$ 9

18. 8
    $\times$ 9

Name_____ Date _____

BASIC FACTS

Multiplying and Dividing by 9

Divide.

1. $0 \div 9 =$ _____

2. $9 \div 1 =$ _____

3. $5 \div 1 =$ _____

4. $9 \div 9 =$ _____

5. $54 \div 6 =$ _____

6. $27 \div 9 =$ _____

7. $9 \div 3 =$ _____

8. $18 \div 9 =$ _____

9. $45 \div 9 =$ _____

10. $63 \div 9 =$ _____

11. $36 \div 9 =$ _____

12. $81 \div 9 =$ _____

13. $72 \div 9 =$ _____

14. $27 \div 9 =$ _____

15. $54 \div 9 =$ _____

Compare. Write >, <, or =.

16. $18 \div 2$ ____ $18 \div 9$

17. $9 \div 9$ ____ $3 \div 3$

18. $27 \div 9$ ____ $25 \div 5$

19. $24 \div 6$ ____ $36 \div 4$

Divide.

20. $2\overline{)18}$

21. $9\overline{)81}$

22. $9\overline{)27}$

23. $9\overline{)9}$

24. $9\overline{)36}$

25. $6\overline{)54}$

26. $5\overline{)45}$

27. $8\overline{)72}$

Name_____ Date _____

◢9A BASIC FACTS

Multiplying and Dividing by 6

Multiply.

1. $3 \times 3 =$ _____ $6 \times 3 =$ _____   **2.** $3 \times 2 =$ _____ $6 \times 2 =$ _____

3. $3 \times 7 =$ _____ $6 \times 7 =$ _____   **4.** $3 \times 4 =$ _____ $6 \times 4 =$ _____

5. $3 \times 9 =$ _____ $6 \times 9 =$ _____   **6.** $3 \times 5 =$ _____ $6 \times 5 =$ _____

7. $3 \times 8 =$ _____ $6 \times 8 =$ _____   **8.** $3 \times 6 =$ _____ $6 \times 6 =$ _____

9. $\begin{array}{r} 4 \\ \times\, 6 \\ \hline \end{array}$
10. $\begin{array}{r} 3 \\ \times\, 6 \\ \hline \end{array}$
11. $\begin{array}{r} 5 \\ \times\, 6 \\ \hline \end{array}$
12. $\begin{array}{r} 7 \\ \times\, 6 \\ \hline \end{array}$
13. $\begin{array}{r} 6 \\ \times\, 6 \\ \hline \end{array}$

14. $\begin{array}{r} 6 \\ \times\, 1 \\ \hline \end{array}$
15. $\begin{array}{r} 2 \\ \times\, 6 \\ \hline \end{array}$
16. $\begin{array}{r} 6 \\ \times\, 0 \\ \hline \end{array}$
17. $\begin{array}{r} 9 \\ \times\, 6 \\ \hline \end{array}$
18. $\begin{array}{r} 8 \\ \times\, 6 \\ \hline \end{array}$

19. $\begin{array}{r} 6 \\ \times\, 5 \\ \hline \end{array}$
20. $\begin{array}{r} 6 \\ \times\, 7 \\ \hline \end{array}$
21. $\begin{array}{r} 6 \\ \times\, 4 \\ \hline \end{array}$
22. $\begin{array}{r} 6 \\ \times\, 3 \\ \hline \end{array}$
23. $\begin{array}{r} 7 \\ \times\, 3 \\ \hline \end{array}$

24. $\begin{array}{r} 6 \\ \times\, 2 \\ \hline \end{array}$
25. $\begin{array}{r} 6 \\ \times\, 8 \\ \hline \end{array}$
26. $\begin{array}{r} 6 \\ \times\, 9 \\ \hline \end{array}$
27. $\begin{array}{r} 5 \\ \times\, 5 \\ \hline \end{array}$
28. $\begin{array}{r} 8 \\ \times\, 2 \\ \hline \end{array}$

Name_____   Date _____

9B BASIC FACTS
....

Multiplying and Dividing by 6

Write four number sentences for each fact family.

1. 6, 7, 42   _____ × _____ = _____

                       _____ × _____ = _____

                       _____ ÷ _____ = _____

                       _____ ÷ _____ = _____

2. 5, 6, 30   _____ × _____ = _____

                       _____ × _____ = _____

                       _____ ÷ _____ = _____

                       _____ ÷ _____ = _____

3. 6, 8, 48   _____ × _____ = _____

                       _____ × _____ = _____

                       _____ ÷ _____ = _____

                       _____ ÷ _____ = _____

4. 6, 9, 54   _____ × _____ = _____

                       _____ × _____ = _____

                       _____ ÷ _____ = _____

                       _____ ÷ _____ = _____

5. 4, 6, 24   _____ × _____ = _____

                       _____ × _____ = _____

                       _____ ÷ _____ = _____

                       _____ ÷ _____ = _____

Name_____   Date _____

10A # BASIC FACTS

Multiplying and Dividing by 7

Write a related multiplication fact. Then divide.

1. $7 \div 7 =$ ___

___ $\times$ ___ $=$ ___

2. $21 \div 7 =$ ___

___ $\times$ ___ $=$ ___

3. $35 \div 7 =$ ___

___ $\times$ ___ $=$ ___

4. $56 \div 7 =$ ___

___ $\times$ ___ $=$ ___

5. $42 \div 7 =$ ___

___ $\times$ ___ $=$ ___

6. $63 \div 7 =$ ___

___ $\times$ ___ $=$ ___

7. $14 \div 7 =$ ___

___ $\times$ ___ $=$ ___

8. $28 \div 7 =$ ___

___ $\times$ ___ $=$ ___

9. $49 \div 7 =$ ___

___ $\times$ ___ $=$ ___

Write four number sentences for each fact family.

10. 7, 9, 63

_____ $\times$ _____ $=$ _____

_____ $\times$ _____ $=$ _____

_____ $\div$ _____ $=$ _____

_____ $\div$ _____ $=$ _____

11. 7, 8, 56

_____ $\times$ _____ $=$ _____

_____ $\times$ _____ $=$ _____

_____ $\div$ _____ $=$ _____

_____ $\div$ _____ $=$ _____

Name_____   Date _____

◢10B◣ BASIC FACTS

Multiplying and Dividing by 7

Multiply.

1. $7 \times 2 =$ _____

2. $7 \times 5 =$ _____

3. $7 \times 7 =$ _____

4. $7 \times 4 =$ _____

5. $7 \times 3 =$ _____

6. $7 \times 8 =$ _____

7. $7 \times 9 =$ _____

8. $7 \times 6 =$ _____

9. $7 \times 1 =$ _____

10. $\begin{array}{r} 7 \\ \times\, 0 \\ \hline \end{array}$

11. $\begin{array}{r} 2 \\ \times\, 7 \\ \hline \end{array}$

12. $\begin{array}{r} 6 \\ \times\, 7 \\ \hline \end{array}$

13. $\begin{array}{r} 8 \\ \times\, 7 \\ \hline \end{array}$

14. $\begin{array}{r} 4 \\ \times\, 7 \\ \hline \end{array}$

15. $\begin{array}{r} 1 \\ \times\, 7 \\ \hline \end{array}$

16. $\begin{array}{r} 9 \\ \times\, 7 \\ \hline \end{array}$

17. $\begin{array}{r} 5 \\ \times\, 7 \\ \hline \end{array}$

18. $\begin{array}{r} 7 \\ \times\, 7 \\ \hline \end{array}$

19. $\begin{array}{r} 3 \\ \times\, 7 \\ \hline \end{array}$

20. $\begin{array}{r} 0 \\ \times\, 7 \\ \hline \end{array}$

21. $\begin{array}{r} 7 \\ \times\, 1 \\ \hline \end{array}$

Divide.

22. $63 \div 7 =$ _____

23. $21 \div 7 =$ _____

24. $7 \div 7 =$ _____

25. $14 \div 7 =$ _____

26. $56 \div 7 =$ _____

27. $42 \div 7 =$ _____

28. $28 \div 7 =$ _____

29. $49 \div 7 =$ _____

30. $35 \div 7 =$ _____

Name_____ Date _____

BASIC FACTS

Multiplying and Dividing by 8

Find two multiplication facts.

1. • • • • • • • •
   • • • • • • • •
   • • • • • • • •

   _____

   _____

2. • • • • • • • •
   • • • • • • • •

   _____

   _____

3. • • • • • • • •
   • • • • • • • •
   • • • • • • • •
   • • • • • • • •

   _____

   _____

Write a multiplication fact.

4. 6 eights = _____

5. 5 eights = _____

6. 7 eights = _____

7. 9 eights = _____

8. 4 eights = _____

9. 8 eights = _____

Draw an array. Find the product.

10. $6 \times 8 =$ _____

11. $3 \times 8 =$ _____

Multiply.

12. $\begin{array}{r} 6 \\ \times\ 8 \\ \hline \end{array}$

13. $\begin{array}{r} 8 \\ \times\ 5 \\ \hline \end{array}$

14. $\begin{array}{r} 7 \\ \times\ 8 \\ \hline \end{array}$

15. $\begin{array}{r} 8 \\ \times\ 4 \\ \hline \end{array}$

Name_____   Date _____

11B BASIC FACTS

Multiplying and Dividing by 8

Write the missing numbers.

1. ___ × 8 = 40

2. ___ × 8 = 56

3. ___ × 8 = 24

4. ___ × 8 = 64

5. ___ × 8 = 48

6. ___ × 8 = 72

7. 72 = ___ × ___

8. 56 = ___ × ___

9. 24 = ___ × ___

Divide.

10. 8)‾32‾

11. 8)‾16‾

12. 8)‾40‾

13. 8)‾24‾

14. 8)‾48‾

15. 8)‾8‾

16. 8)‾56‾

17. 8)‾64‾

Check by multiplying. Correct any quotients that are wrong.

18. 40 ÷ 8 = 6

19. 16 ÷ 8 = 3

20. 64 ÷ 8 = 7

_____

_____

_____

21. 24 ÷ 8 = 4

22. 56 ÷ 8 = 6

23. 32 ÷ 8 = 5

_____

_____

_____

Name_____   Date _____

12A ◢ BASIC FACTS

Review 6, 7, 8, and 9

Multiply.

1. $\begin{array}{r} 4 \\ \times\ 8 \\ \hline \end{array}$	**2.** $\begin{array}{r} 9 \\ \times\ 2 \\ \hline \end{array}$	**3.** $\begin{array}{r} 5 \\ \times\ 8 \\ \hline \end{array}$	**4.** $\begin{array}{r} 9 \\ \times\ 4 \\ \hline \end{array}$	**5.** $\begin{array}{r} 8 \\ \times\ 8 \\ \hline \end{array}$
6. $\begin{array}{r} 9 \\ \times\ 3 \\ \hline \end{array}$	**7.** $\begin{array}{r} 9 \\ \times\ 7 \\ \hline \end{array}$	**8.** $\begin{array}{r} 1 \\ \times\ 8 \\ \hline \end{array}$	**9.** $\begin{array}{r} 5 \\ \times\ 9 \\ \hline \end{array}$	**10.** $\begin{array}{r} 7 \\ \times\ 9 \\ \hline \end{array}$
11. $\begin{array}{r} 9 \\ \times\ 9 \\ \hline \end{array}$	**12.** $\begin{array}{r} 8 \\ \times\ 6 \\ \hline \end{array}$	**13.** $\begin{array}{r} 9 \\ \times\ 8 \\ \hline \end{array}$	**14.** $\begin{array}{r} 3 \\ \times\ 9 \\ \hline \end{array}$	**15.** $\begin{array}{r} 8 \\ \times\ 7 \\ \hline \end{array}$
16. $\begin{array}{r} 6 \\ \times\ 8 \\ \hline \end{array}$	**17.** $\begin{array}{r} 9 \\ \times\ 5 \\ \hline \end{array}$	**18.** $\begin{array}{r} 2 \\ \times\ 8 \\ \hline \end{array}$	**19.** $\begin{array}{r} 7 \\ \times\ 7 \\ \hline \end{array}$	**20.** $\begin{array}{r} 8 \\ \times\ 5 \\ \hline \end{array}$
21. $\begin{array}{r} 7 \\ \times\ 8 \\ \hline \end{array}$	**22.** $\begin{array}{r} 3 \\ \times\ 8 \\ \hline \end{array}$	**23.** $\begin{array}{r} 4 \\ \times\ 9 \\ \hline \end{array}$	**24.** $\begin{array}{r} 7 \\ \times\ 4 \\ \hline \end{array}$	**25.** $\begin{array}{r} 9 \\ \times\ 6 \\ \hline \end{array}$
26. $\begin{array}{r} 6 \\ \times\ 7 \\ \hline \end{array}$	**27.** $\begin{array}{r} 3 \\ \times\ 9 \\ \hline \end{array}$	**28.** $\begin{array}{r} 4 \\ \times\ 6 \\ \hline \end{array}$	**29.** $\begin{array}{r} 6 \\ \times\ 6 \\ \hline \end{array}$	**30.** $\begin{array}{r} 2 \\ \times\ 7 \\ \hline \end{array}$

Name_____ Date _____

12B BASIC FACTS

....

Review 6, 7, 8, and 9

Divide.

1. $9\overline{)36}$ 2. $6\overline{)30}$ 3. $8\overline{)8}$ 4. $8\overline{)64}$ 5. $6\overline{)24}$

6. $6\overline{)54}$ 7. $7\overline{)42}$ 8. $9\overline{)9}$ 9. $8\overline{)56}$ 10. $9\overline{)72}$

11. $7\overline{)21}$ 12. $8\overline{)72}$ 13. $9\overline{)45}$ 14. $8\overline{)0}$ 15. $6\overline{)12}$

16. $9\overline{)0}$ 17. $9\overline{)54}$ 18. $6\overline{)0}$ 19. $7\overline{)49}$ 20. $9\overline{)81}$

21. $6\overline{)36}$ 22. $6\overline{)48}$ 23. $7\overline{)35}$ 24. $7\overline{)7}$ 25. $7\overline{)28}$

26. $8\overline{)16}$ 27. $9\overline{)18}$ 28. $8\overline{)48}$ 29. $8\overline{)32}$ 30. $7\overline{)63}$

31. $6\overline{)18}$ 32. $7\overline{)56}$ 33. $5\overline{)30}$ 34. $3\overline{)21}$ 35. $8\overline{)24}$

Name_____ Date _____

BASIC FACTS

··

Review Multiplication and Division Facts

Write the fact family for each of the arrays.

1. • • • • • • • •
   • • • • • • • •
   • • • • • • • •
   • • • • • • • •

   _____ × _____ = _____

   _____ × _____ = _____

   _____ ÷ _____ = _____

   _____ ÷ _____ = _____

2. • • • • • • • • •
   • • • • • • • • •
   • • • • • • • • •

   _____ × _____ = _____

   _____ × _____ = _____

   _____ ÷ _____ = _____

   _____ ÷ _____ = _____

Multiply.

3.

x	7
8	56
3	
9	
6	
7	

4.

x	9
3	
	63
	54
	45
9	

5. 9
  × 3

6. 4
  × 9

7. 8
  × 9

8. 5
  × 9

9. 9
  × 9

Name_____ Date _____

13B BASIC FACTS

Review Multiplication and Division Facts

Write four number sentences for each fact family.

1. 5, 7, 35 _____ _____ _____ _____

2. 6, 8, 48 _____ _____ _____ _____

Complete.

3. $4 \times 8 =$ _____ $32 \div 8 =$ _____

   $8 \times 4 =$ _____ $32 \div 4 =$ _____

4. $6 \times 7 =$ _____ $42 \div 7 =$ _____

   $7 \times 6 =$ _____ $42 \div 6 =$ _____

5. $8 \times 5 =$ _____ $40 \div 5 =$ _____

   $5 \times 8 =$ _____ $40 \div 8 =$ _____

6. $4 \times 9 =$ _____ $36 \div 9 =$ _____

   $9 \times 4 =$ _____ $36 \div 4 =$ _____

Divide.

7. $9\overline{)45}$ **8.** $5\overline{)40}$ **9.** $6\overline{)54}$ **10.** $7\overline{)28}$

Basic Skills Workshop 1

Addition and Subtraction: Mental Math Strategies

Number Sense

15 minutes

Strategies for Basic Facts

Management whole class or small group
Materials chart paper

- Elicit from students examples of times when they add or subtract using mental math. Students may give real-world examples such as figuring out how many people will be at dinner when two families eat together.

- Have students brainstorm a list of strategies for finding basic addition and subtraction facts without using manipulatives or counting out each amount.

Write all ideas on a group or class chart.

- To spark additional ideas, first write some basic addition facts on the board with the sums left blank. Ask students to tell different ways to find these sums: 8 + 3, 9 + 7, 6 + 5.

- Repeat with subtraction examples such as 15 − 7, 8 − 3, 11 − 9

- Students may name familiar strategies, such as Counting On, Making a Ten, or Doubles, Near Doubles, or they may describe their own methods. Add these to the list of strategies.

- Students should explain how they use their strategies. Example: For 15 − 7, I thought of a double: 7 + 7 = 14. I know 15 is 1 more than 14. So the answer has to be 1 more than 7. The answer is 8.

Skill Application

30 minutes

Totals Greater than 20

Management whole class, then pairs
Materials Just the Facts Support Master 20

- Explain that even with greater addends, such as 28 + 9, a basic fact strategy such as Making a Ten can be used to find the sum. Ask students how this strategy might help. Then model ways to find 28 + 9.

A ten near 28 is 30. Count on 2. $28 + 2 = 30$
That leaves 7 more to add. $30 + 7 = 37$
The answer is 37, because: $28 + 2 + 7 = 37$

or

Nine is one less than ten. Add 10. $28 + 10 = 38$
I added 1 to get 10. $9 + 1 = 10$
Subtract 1. $38 - 1 = 37$
The answer is 37, because: $28 + 10 - 1 = 37$

- Ask how doubles might help in finding 46 + 6, or 98 − 4. **Double 6 is 12. 40 + 12 = 52; Double 4 is 8. 98 − 4 = 94.**

- Ask students to give new examples where another strategy, such as Counting On, might be helpful.

- In pairs, have each partner create 10 exercises like the above examples. Each sum or difference should include a 2-digit number and a 1-digit number. Have partners trade papers. After they write each answer, partners tell each other how they figured it out.

- List some strategies on the board. Have partners create exercises that use these strategies.

Basic Skills Workshop 2

Multiplication and Division: Mental Math Strategies

 Number Sense

 15 minutes

Basic Multiplication Facts

Management whole class or small group

- Ask students to give real-world examples of multiplying with mental math. Model a situation such as figuring out how many slices are in pizzas. Since pizzas usually have 8 slices, ask how many slices are there all together? Have students describe how they might find 6×8 using mental math. If they have the fact "memorized," encourage them to describe how they "remember" it. Model examples, like the following:

Find: 6×8

Strategy: Use a double

| I know $3 \times 8 = 24$ |
| I know 6 is double 3. |

$3 \times 8 = 24$
$24 + 24 = 48$

Strategy: Use patterns

| $8 = 2 \times 2 \times 2$ |
| I can double the 2 three times. |

$6 \times 2 = 12$
$12 \times 2 = 24$
$24 \times 2 = 48$

Strategy: Use a close fact

| I know 8 is |
| close to 10. |

8×10
$10 - 2 = 8$
$(6 \times 10) - (6 \times 2)$
$60 - 12 = 48$

- Students may name familiar strategies, such as those given in the example, or they may name a method of their own. As students tell their strategies, they should describe how to use them. Point out that many different strategies may be used to find basic facts.

 Skill Application

 30 minutes

Basic Division Facts

Management whole class, then pairs
Materials 2 hundredths square (Just the Facts Support Master 7) per student, Just the Facts Support Master 20

- Solving basic division facts often presents more of a challenge than finding basic multiplication facts. Set up the pizza example differently: Suppose you order 6 pizzas. Each has 8 slices. 16 people want pizza. How many slices can each person have?

- Demonstrate two ideas that are helpful in learning basic division facts and solving such problems:

Step 1. Learn to recognize numbers that are products for a basic multiplication fact. Some students can recall a short series of numbers if they have heard them or seen them repeated often. Provide examples: 2, 4, 6, 8. . .; 3, 6, 9, 12. . .

Step 2. Learn to recognize patterns of divisibility. Numbers divisible by 5, for example, have a 0 or 5 in the ones place. Numbers divisible by 9 have digits that total 9, such as 27, 36, and 45.

- Ask students to explain how either of the above strategies can help them solve the pizza problem.

- Have students review division facts with a partner, using a hundredths square. The first partner asks a division question using a product as the dividend and a factor as the divisor. Example: How many 8's are in 24? The other partner uses a blank grid to locate the answer, using mental math strategy. Partners reverse roles.

Basic Skills Workshop 3
Adding 2- and 3-Digit Whole Numbers

 Number Sense

15 minutes

Estimating to Add

Management whole class or small group

- Elicit from students real-world examples of times they would need to estimate the sum of 2- or 3-digit numbers. Encourage them to think of examples that use money, numbers of people, amounts of food, and so on.

- Ask students to think of estimation strategies they could use to add two numbers together. Students' strategies should include front-end estimation and estimation with rounding.

- Write a sample addition problem on the board. Try to connect it to one of the real-world examples students mentioned. If a student gave an example of estimating the numbers of students in two homeroom classrooms, for example, write on the board 34 + 28.

- Ask students to estimate the sum using the estimation strategy that makes sense to them. Discuss with the class which kinds of estimates they feel work best for which kinds of situations. Discuss with students how over- and under-estimating affects estimations, and in which situations one might be preferable to the other.

 Skill Application

30 minutes

Finding Exact Sums

Management whole class, then pairs
Materials Just the Facts Support Master 20

- Give students an example of adding two numbers when an exact answer is needed. For example, they want to count school attendance for the fifth grade for Monday and Tuesday. On Monday, 239 students were present. On Tuesday, 273 students were present. Have students estimate first, and write down their estimates.

Find: 239 + 273

Step 1. Add the ones.
Do you need to regroup?

$$\begin{array}{r} \overset{1}{} \\ 239 \\ + 273 \\ \hline 2 \end{array}$$

Step 2. Add the tens.
Do you need to regroup?

$$\begin{array}{r} \overset{1\;1}{} \\ 239 \\ + 273 \\ \hline 12 \end{array}$$

Step 3. Add the hundreds.

$$\begin{array}{r} \overset{1\;1}{} \\ 239 \\ + 273 \\ \hline 512 \end{array}$$

- Have students compare the answer to their estimates. Then, ask students what strategies might be helpful in checking the addition. For example, rounding to the nearest hundred: 200 + 300 = 500.

- Now, have students write ten similar 2- and 3-digit addition exercises and then trade exercises with a partner. Partners should take turns finding sums and explaining their reasoning.

Basic Skills Workshop 4

Subtracting 2- and 3-Digit Whole Numbers

 Number Sense

15 minutes

2-Digit Subtraction

Management whole class or small group

- Give students a real-world situation for which they need to subtract a 2-digit number from another. For example: The class raises $82 from a talent show. The students spend $46 on books. How much money is left?

- Ask students why it is a good idea to estimate before finding the difference. Elicit from the class methods of estimation. Students will probably suggest front-end estimation or rounding. Write problems on the board for students to solve using front-end estimation or rounding.

- Now model the steps to find an exact answer to the talent show problem. Challenge students to name and explain each step.

Step 1.
Regroup one ten as ten ones, if necessary.

$$\begin{array}{r} {}^{7\,12} \\ 8\,\not{2} \\ -\ 4\,6 \\ \hline \end{array}$$

Step 2.
Subtract the ones.

$$\begin{array}{r} {}^{7\,12} \\ 8\,\not{2} \\ -\ 4\,6 \\ \hline 6 \end{array}$$

Step 3.
Subract the tens.

$$\begin{array}{r} {}^{7\,12} \\ 8\,\not{2} \\ -\ 4\,6 \\ \hline 3\,6 \end{array}$$

 Skill Application

30 minutes

3-Digit Subtraction

Management whole class, then pairs
Materials Just the Facts Support Master 20

- Help students apply what they already know about subtraction to subtract greater numbers. Model the steps to find 342 − 116. Have students estimate first, and then write down their estimates.

Step 1. Subtract the ones.
Regroup a ten if necessary.

$$\begin{array}{r} {}^{3\,12} \\ 3\,4\,\not{2} \\ -\ 1\,1\,6 \\ \hline 6 \end{array}$$

Regroup

Step 2. Subtract the tens.
Regroup a hundred if necessary.

$$\begin{array}{r} {}^{3\,12} \\ 3\,4\,\not{2} \\ -\ 1\,1\,6 \\ \hline 2\,6 \end{array}$$

Not necessary to regroup

Step 3. Subtract the hundreds.

$$\begin{array}{r} {}^{3\,12} \\ 3\,4\,\not{2} \\ -\ 1\,1\,6 \\ \hline 2\,2\,6 \end{array}$$

Don't regroup

- Model checking the answer by addition.
226 + 116 = 342.

- Ask students how they might check an answer for reasonableness. Now, ask student pairs to write and exchange 10 exercises similar to the 3-digit examples shown above. Then have students check each other's work using estimation, as well as pencil and paper addition.

Basic Skills Workshop 5

Multiplying 2-Digit Numbers

Number Sense

15 minutes

Multiplication Strategies

Management whole class or small group

- Ask students to give examples of times they can use estimation strategies to multiply by 2-digit numbers. Elicit real world examples by modeling one, such as determining how many eggs a bakery uses to make 200 cakes a week. Each cake requires 12 eggs. Ask students to describe how they would multiply these numbers together.

- As students describe these strategies and others of their own, write down the steps on the board.

Emphasize any intermediate steps.

Strategy:	12×200
Use factors with zeros	$12 \times 2 = 24$; Ones times hundreds are hundreds. So, 12×200 are 24 hundreds or 2400.

Strategy:	12×200
Use front-end estimation	12×2 is 24. 24 hundred is 2400.

Strategy:	12×200
Use doubling and halving	Double 12 is 24. Half of 200 is 100. $24 \times 100 = 2400$.

Skill Application

30 minutes

Multiplying Exact Products

Management whole class, then pairs
Materials Just the Facts Support Master 20

- Give students a real-world example in which they need to multiply a number by a 2-digit number. For example, camels can walk up to 40 miles a day. How many miles could a camel walk in a year? First, ask students to make an estimate and write that number down. Then, model 365×40.

Step 1.
Multiply by the ones digit.

```
  365
× 40
  000
```

Step 2. Multiply by the tens digit.

```
  365
×  40
  000
 1460
```

Step 3. Add.

```
   365
×   40
   000
+ 1460
 14,600
```

- Ask students which estimation strategies they used to check their answers for reasonableness. Then, have students practice by creating a sheet of 10 exercises with 2- and 3-digit multiplication problems. Have students trade their sheets with a partner. Ask students to make an estimate and write it down before solving each problem.

Basic Skills Workshop 6

Dividing by 1-Digit Divisors

Number Sense

20 minutes

Divisibility

Management whole class or small group
Materials Just the Facts Support Master 7

- Give students a real-world example using division. You buy 36 tickets at a carnival. How many 4-ticket rides can you go on? Will you have any tickets left? Elicit real-world examples from students.

- How can you tell whether a number is divisible by another number? Point out that fact families can be used to help with divisibility. ($4 \times 9 = 36$, $36 \div 9 = 4$) Use this fact family to elicit the quotient from the carnival problem.

- Have students give divisibility rules for 2 (all even numbers) and 10 (numbers with a 0 in the ones place).

- Distribute Just the Facts Support Master 7, and have students use the grid to create their own divisibility charts like the one below. Students should work in small groups to complete charts for the divisors: 2, 3, 4, 5, 6, 7, 8, 9, 10, 11. Have student groups find a rule or pattern for divisibility for 3, 4, 6, and 9.

2	3	4	5	6	7	8	9	10	11
4	6	8	10	12	14	16	18	20	22
6	9	12	15	18	21	28	27	30	33

Skill Application

40 minutes

Division Step-by-Step

Management whole class, then pairs
Materials completed divisibility charts (Just the Facts Support Master 7), Just the Facts Support Master 20

- Give students a division problem with a remainder.

$$9 \overline{)65} \quad 7$$

65 is not evenly divisible by 7. Ask for a number close to 65 that is compatible with 7. **63**

$63 \div 7 = 9$. So the exact quotient will be close to 9 rides. Explain that compatible numbers are used to make an estimate and to find an exact quotient. Use another example to illustrate how steps for dividing repeat. Label the steps as you model them.

Divide the hundreds.
$$\begin{array}{r} 7 \\ 9\overline{)6570} \end{array}$$

Multiply. $\boxed{9 \times 7 = 63}$
$$\begin{array}{r} 7 \\ 9\overline{)6570} \\ -63 \end{array}$$

Subtract. $\boxed{65 - 63 = 2}$
$$\begin{array}{r} 7 \\ 9\overline{)6570} \\ -63 \\ \hline 2 \end{array}$$

Divide the tens.
Then repeat the steps.
$$\begin{array}{r} 730 \\ 9\overline{)6570} \\ -63 \\ \hline 27 \\ -27 \\ \hline 00 \end{array}$$

- Ask students to write 10 division exercises similar to the one above. Partners should trade papers, find the answers, and check each other's work.

Basic Skills Workshop 7

Fractions: Comparing and Ordering

 Number Sense

 15 minutes

Using Benchmarks

Management whole class or small group
Materials overhead projector, number line transparency (Just the Facts Support Master 17)

- Ask for real-world examples using fractions. Elicit examples such as using measuring cups.

- Benchmarks can help you estimate the value of fractions. Label the number line as shown. Model $\frac{3}{8}$.

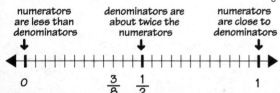

numerators are less than denominators

denominators are about twice the numerators

numerators are close to denominators

$0 \qquad \frac{3}{8} \quad \frac{1}{2} \qquad 1$

- Ask students to name a fraction that is closer to 1 than to $\frac{1}{2}$. Repeat with fractions close to zero and close to $\frac{1}{2}$.

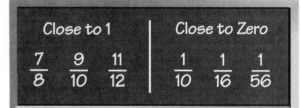

Close to 1			Close to Zero		
$\frac{7}{8}$	$\frac{9}{10}$	$\frac{11}{12}$	$\frac{1}{10}$	$\frac{1}{16}$	$\frac{1}{56}$

- Record each response on the board, and model them on the number line. Ask small groups to name fractions close to and closer to other benchmarks, such as $\frac{1}{4}$, $\frac{1}{3}$, $\frac{2}{3}$, and $\frac{3}{4}$.

 Skill Application

 30 minutes

Using Least Common Denominators

Management whole class, then pairs
Materials scissors and 20 small squares of paper for each pair, Just the Facts Support Master 20

- Model a method for comparing fractions with different denominators. Write the following fractions and steps for comparing their values: $\frac{1}{5}$, $\frac{1}{2}$, $\frac{1}{4}$

Step 1. Find the least common multiple (LCM) of the denominators.

$\frac{1}{5}$ 5:   5, 10, 15, **20**, 25, 30, 35, 40

$\frac{1}{2}$ 2:   2, 4, 6, 8, 10, 12, 14, 16, 18, **20**

$\frac{1}{4}$ 4:   4, 8, 12, 16, **20**

The LCM of 5, 2, and 4 is 20.

Step 2. Write equivalent fractions with the LCM. The LCM is now the least common denominator (LCD).

$\frac{1}{5} \times \frac{4}{4} = \frac{4}{20} \qquad \frac{1}{2} \times \frac{10}{10} = \frac{10}{20} \qquad \frac{1}{4} \times \frac{5}{5} = \frac{5}{20}$

Step 3. Compare numerators, then order.

$4 < 5 < 10$, so $\frac{1}{5} < \frac{1}{4} < \frac{1}{2}$

- In pairs, have students write a fraction on each of 20 small squares, fold them, and place them in a pile. The fractions should be less than 1.

- Partners each choose a square. The partner with the greater fraction keeps the slips. When the pile is gone the partner with the most slips wins.

Basic Skills Workshop 8

Fractions: Greatest Common Factors and Simplifying

Number Sense

20 minutes

Simplifying Fractions

Management whole class or small group
Materials number line (Just the Facts Support Master 17)

- Provide an estimation example to show that fractions can be simplified using mental math.

- Draw a number line on the board with marks and labels at 0, 1, and 2 as shown. Have students copy. Model how to label the points for $\frac{1}{2}$ and $1\frac{1}{2}$. Next write examples of fractions that are not in simplest form and ask students to label these points on their number lines: $\frac{2}{4}$, $\frac{8}{8}$, $\frac{20}{10}$, $\frac{3}{6}$, $\frac{6}{3}$ and $\frac{4}{4}$.

0          $\frac{1}{2}$ 1 $1\frac{1}{2}$ 2

- Ask small groups to create a table of fractions which are not in simplest form. Have students label the rows in the table: "Names for $\frac{1}{2}$" (example: $\frac{2}{4}$, $\frac{4}{8}$, $\frac{3}{6}$), "Names for $\frac{1}{4}$" (example: $\frac{2}{8}$, $\frac{3}{12}$, $\frac{4}{16}$), "Names for $\frac{3}{4}$" (example: $\frac{6}{8}$, $\frac{9}{12}$, $\frac{12}{16}$) and so on.

- Point out that the simplest form in each row is the fraction that they started with. Discuss the fact that the denominator of the original fraction is a factor of the denominator of all the fractions in that row.

Skill Application

40 minutes

Using the GCF to Simplify

Management whole class, then pairs
Materials 10 index cards per student, Just the Facts Support Master 20

- The GCF of two numbers is the greatest factor they have in common. For numbers like 3 and 5, the GCF is 1.

- Model the steps for simplying the fraction $\frac{12}{18}$.

Step 1. List the factors of the numerator and denominator.

Factors of 12   Factors of 18
1, 2, 3, 4, 6, 12   1, 2, 3, 6, 18

Step 2. Find the greatest factor from both lists.

Factors of 12   Factors of 18
1, 2, 3, 4, **6**, 12   1, 2, 3, **6**, 18

Step 3. Divide numerator and denominator by the GCF.

$$\frac{12}{18} = \frac{2}{3}$$

÷6

÷6

> Explain that 12 and 18 have other factors in common, but the greatest is 6.

Step 4. Check for simplest form. The fraction $\frac{2}{3}$ is simplified because the numerator and denominator have no common factors greater than 1.

- Have students work in pairs to create GCF flash cards. On the front of 10 index cards, students write pairs of numbers no greater than 50. One partner flashes a card, while the other lists factors for both numbers and finds the GCF. Then they switch roles.

Basic Skills Workshop 9

Adding and Subtracting Fractions with Like Denominators

Number Sense

20 minutes

Finding Close Whole Numbers

Management whole class, or small group
Materials paper fraction models (Just the Facts Support Master 18)

- Point out that when adding or subtracting fractions or mixed numbers, estimation can help in finding close whole numbers.

- For example, use $\frac{5}{8}$ and $\frac{7}{8}$. Ask students:

  Between which two whole numbers is the sum? Have students use the eighths fraction model and fold it to show $\frac{5}{8}$ then $\frac{7}{8}$.

- Students should see that $\frac{5}{8} + \frac{7}{8}$ is between 1 and 2. Explain that both fractions are greater than $\frac{1}{2}$ so the answer is greater than $\frac{2}{2}$ or 1. The fractions are also both less than 1, so the sum is less than 2.

- Write these exercises on the board. Ask students to name the closest pair of whole numbers that a sum or difference falls between. Remind them that zero is also a whole number.

  1. $\frac{1}{8} + \frac{3}{8}$ **2.** $2\frac{3}{4} + \frac{3}{4}$ **3.** $3\frac{4}{5} - 1\frac{2}{5}$

  4. $5\frac{5}{8} - 2\frac{5}{8}$ **5.** $\frac{7}{10} + \frac{9}{10}$ **6.** $\frac{5}{6} - \frac{3}{6}$

- Discuss students' estimates. Ask how students arrived at their estimates. Did they notice any patterns? For example, the sum of two fractions less than 1 is always between 0 and 2.

Skill Application

40 minutes

Getting a Simple Answer

Management whole class, then pairs
Materials 10 index cards per student, Just the Facts Support Master 20

- Find $\frac{5}{8} + \frac{7}{8}$. First, elicit that the sum is between 1 and 2.

Step 1. Add the fractions.

$$\begin{array}{r} \frac{5}{8} \\ + \frac{7}{8} \\ \hline \frac{12}{8} \end{array}$$

5 eighths + 7 eighths = 12 eighths

Step 2. Simplify. The GCF of 12 and 8 is 4.

$$\frac{12}{8} = \frac{\div 4}{\div 4} = \frac{3}{2} = 1\frac{1}{2}$$

- Next, model renaming a fraction in order to subtract. Find $6\frac{1}{3} - 1\frac{2}{3}$. First, elicit that the difference is between 5 and 4.

  Rename, then subtract.

$$\begin{array}{ccc} 6\frac{1}{3} & \rightarrow & 5\frac{4}{3} \\ -1\frac{2}{3} & & -1\frac{2}{3} \\ & & \overline{4\frac{2}{3}} \end{array}$$

- Assign student pairs a denominator. They should write fractions with that denominator on each of 10 cards. Partners use the cards to write 10 addition exercises for each other, and find answers using the steps above. Later partners may trade with another pair.

Basic Skills Workshop 10

Adding Fractions with Unlike Denominators

Number Sense

20 minutes

Finding Close Whole Numbers

Management whole class or small group

Materials number line for each student (Just the Facts Support Master 17)

- Tell students they need 1 can of blue paint. They have a can that is $\frac{3}{4}$ full and another that is $\frac{1}{3}$ full. Do they have enough?

- Ask how finding the closest whole number can help them. Distribute number lines, and have students label the numbers 0–9. Model estimating the sum.

- Explain that $\frac{3}{4}$ is close to but less than 1. Since $\frac{1}{3}$ is less than $\frac{1}{2}$, the sum will be less than $1\frac{1}{4}$. So, you will have about 1 can of paint.

- Encourage students to use the number line as a guide while estimating sums. Read the following exercises:

1. $\frac{1}{3} + \frac{3}{8}$ **2.** $2\frac{3}{4} + 2\frac{3}{8}$ **3.** $3\frac{2}{6} + 1\frac{4}{5}$

4. $7\frac{5}{8} + \frac{1}{4}$ **5.** $6\frac{3}{8} + \frac{4}{5}$

- Call on volunteers to show how they used the number line. Example: For $2\frac{3}{4} + 2\frac{3}{8}$, I found a point $\frac{3}{4}$ of the way from 2 to 3. I counted up 2, and I was almost to 5. I estimated $\frac{3}{8}$ of a space more. I was past 5, but still close to 5.

Skill Application

40 minutes

Using the LCD

Management whole class, then pairs

Materials 10 index cards per student, Just the Facts Support Master 20

- Model the steps for adding unlike fractions. Recall the paint example: $\frac{3}{4} + \frac{1}{3}$.

Step 1. When the denominators are different, find the LCD.

$\frac{3}{4}$ Multiples of 4: 4, 8, **12**, 16

$\frac{1}{3}$ Multiples of 3: 3, 6, 9, **12**

The LCD of 4 and 3 is 12.

Step 2. Use the LCD to write equivalent fractions.

$\frac{3}{4} = \frac{?}{12}$ $\frac{3}{4} = \frac{\times 3}{\times 3} = \frac{9}{12}$

$\frac{1}{3} = \frac{?}{12}$ $\frac{1}{3} = \frac{\times 4}{\times 4} = \frac{4}{12}$

Step 3. Add the new fractions.

$\frac{9}{12} + \frac{4}{12} = \frac{13}{12}$

Step 4. Simplify if possible.

In $\frac{13}{12}$ there is one whole. $\frac{12}{12} = 1$.

That leaves $\frac{1}{12}$. So, $\frac{13}{12} = 1\frac{1}{12}$.

- In pairs, have each student write a mixed number or fraction on 10 index cards. The denominator should be no greater than 16. Then, students should make a stack of 20 cards between them. Taking turns, one partner pulls 2 cards from the pile and creates an addition exercise. The other finds an estimate and the answer.

Basic Skills Workshop 11

Subtracting Fractions with Unlike Denominators

Number Sense

20 minutes

Finding the Closest Whole Number

Management whole class or small group
Materials 10 index cards per student

- Provide an example of subtracting fractions.
  For example, you have $2\frac{1}{8}$ yd of cloth. You use $\frac{1}{4}$ yd to make a pillow. How much will you have left?

- Ask, How can you estimate the closest whole number? Explain that rounding up or down can help:

Step 1. Round $2\frac{1}{8}$ down to 2.

Step 2. Round $\frac{1}{4}$ down to zero.

Step 3. Subtract with mental math: $2 - 0 = 2$.

- Interpret the answer. You have about 2 yd left.

- Next, ask students to estimate the following differences. Encourage them to use rounding to help them find the closest whole number.

1. $1\frac{1}{3} - \frac{7}{8}$ **2.** $6\frac{3}{4} - 2\frac{3}{8}$ **3.** $3\frac{2}{6} - 1\frac{4}{5}$

4. $7\frac{7}{8} - \frac{1}{6}$ **5.** $\frac{4}{5} - \frac{0}{5}$

- Call on student volunteers to demonstrate how they arrived at estimates.

- On 10 index cards, each student should write 5 mixed numbers and 5 fractions less than 1. Working in pairs, students pile their cards together. Taking turns, students draw 2 cards from the pile and partners estimate each difference aloud.

Skill Application

30 minutes

Renaming Fractions and Using LCDs

Management whole class, then pairs
Materials Just the Facts Support Master 20

- Model the steps for subtracting fractions with different denominators. Use the example $6\frac{1}{8} - \frac{5}{6}$.

Step 1. Notice that the denominators are different. Write equivalent fractions using the LCD.

$$
\begin{array}{ccc}
6\frac{1}{8} & \rightarrow & 6\frac{3}{24} \\
-\ \frac{5}{6} & \rightarrow & -\ \frac{20}{24}
\end{array}
$$

Step 2. Since $\frac{20}{24} > \frac{3}{24}$, you need to rename $6\frac{3}{24}$.

$$
\begin{array}{l}
6\frac{3}{24} \\
-\ \frac{20}{24}
\end{array}
\qquad
\boxed{\text{Think: } 6 = 5 + \frac{24}{24} \\
\text{So, } 6\frac{3}{24} = 5 + \frac{24}{24} + \frac{3}{24} = 5\frac{27}{24}}
$$

Step 3. Subtract the fractions and whole numbers.

$$
\begin{array}{l}
5\frac{27}{24} \\
-\ \frac{20}{24} \\
\hline
5\frac{7}{24}
\end{array}
$$

Step 4. Simplify if possible. $\frac{7}{24}$ is simplified because the GCF of the numerator and denominator is 1.

- Assign student pairs to find exact answers for Number Sense exercises 1–5. They should take turns writing each step in the exercise. They can use estimation to check that the answers are reasonable.

Basic Skills Workshop 12

Decimals: Comparing and Ordering

Number Sense

15 minutes

Decimals and Place Value

Management whole class or small group
Materials overhead projector, hundredths squares transparency (Just the Facts Support Master 19)

- On the transparency, highlight one small square, a rod with ten squares, then a hundredths square. Ask:

  1. How many squares are in the rod?
  2. How many rods make up the whole grid?
  3. How many tens are in a rod?
  4. How many tens are in the grid?
  5. How can you describe this pattern?

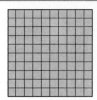

- Point out that the whole grid is one whole. Then 1 rod $= \frac{1}{10}$ or 0.1 and 1 square $= \frac{1}{100}$ or 0.01. Show these place values on a place value chart.

Step 1. Compare 1.5 to 1.05. Begin on the left.

1.5
1.05

Step 2. If the digits in the greatest place are equal, compare digits in the next place to the right.

1.**5**
1.**0**5

5 > than 0, so 1.5 > 1.05.

Skill Application

30 minutes

Decimal Number Lines

Management whole class, then pairs
Materials teacher-made transparency of number line, number lines (Just the Facts Support Master 17), Just the Facts Support Master 20

- Model an exercise for students in which five decimals are ordered on a number line. Write on the board or a transparency the numbers 1.02, 2.1, 1.2, 1.73, and 1.32. Ask students to predict the order of these numbers, from least to greatest. After they have written their predictions, mark the numbers in correct order on the number line transparency with the following sentence written below:
  1.02 < 1.2 < 1.32 < 1.73 < 2.1

- Now, have students work in pairs to compare and order decimals. Student pairs should create six number lines, each containing five numbers.

  Step 1. Have one student write a list of five random decimals. The numbers should all be between three consecutive whole numbers. At least two numbers should be to the thousandths place.

  Step 2. Have the other student order the five numbers by plotting them on the number line.

  Step 3. The student pairs should discuss their results and then write number sentences to describe how the numbers are related using > or <.

- Have students continue switching roles and working as described, until they complete six number lines.

Basic Skills Workshop 13

Adding and Subtracting Decimals

Number Sense

20 minutes

Estimation and Place Value

Management whole class or small group
Materials overhead projector, teacher-made transparency of place value chart

- Making rough estimates first can help students compute exact sums and differences with decimals. Give students a real-world situation for estimating a sum. For example, a videotape costs $14.95, a puzzle book costs $2.79, and a magazine costs $4.25. About how much money would you need to buy all 3 items?

- Point out that, in this case, rounding to the nearest whole number means rounding to the nearest dollar.

If students have trouble rounding as they estimate, distribute number lines to help them. Ask students to explain their reasoning. **$14.95 is closer to $15 than $14; $2.79 is closer to $3 than $2; $4.25 is closer to $4 than $5 So I add $14, $3, and $4. The total is $22.**

- Now, emphasize to students that adding and subtracting decimals is like adding and subtracting whole numbers. They need to think of place value. To help them do so, display the following place value chart on the overhead. Model the problem above.

		Ones		Tenths	
1		4	.	9	5
		2	.	7	9
		4	.	2	5

- Repeat the above exercises with the subtraction problem $20.25 − $15.89.

Skill Application

40 minutes

Stepping Out
Decimal Computation

Management whole class, then individuals
Materials Just the Facts Support Master 20

- Model the following problems.

Addition	Subtraction
Find 4.53 + 8 + 11.02.	Find 21.7 − 8.43.
Step 1. Line up the digits by place value. Write a decimal point and additional zeros if needed.	**Step 1.** Line up the digits by place value. Write a zero in any empty decimal places.

$$\begin{array}{r} 4.53 \\ 8.00 \leftarrow \boxed{\begin{array}{l}8= \\ 8.00\end{array}} \\ + 11.02 \\ \hline \end{array}$$

Step 2. Add. Regroup if necessary. Then write the decimal point.

$$\begin{array}{r} 4.53 \\ 8.00 \\ + 11.02 \\ \hline 23.55 \end{array}$$

$$\begin{array}{r} 21.70 \leftarrow \boxed{\begin{array}{l}21.7= \\ 21.70\end{array}} \\ - 8.43 \\ \hline \end{array}$$

Step 2. Subtract. Regroup if necessary. Then write the decimal point.

$$\begin{array}{r} 21.70 \\ - 8.43 \\ \hline 13.27 \end{array}$$

- Elicit 20 decimals from students. Have them say the decimal correctly. Write the decimals. Decimals should not exceed 100.0.

- Now, have students write and solve 15 addition and 15 subtraction equations using a combination of numbers from the board. Each number should be used at least once. Have students check each other's answers.

Name_____ Date _____

1A BASIC SKILLS

....

Addition and Subtraction: Mental Math Strategies

Find the sum.

1. $6 + 5 =$ _____   **2.** $1 + 9 =$ _____   **3.** $2 + 7 =$ _____   **4.** $8 + 1 =$ _____

5. $2 + 5 =$ _____   **6.** $4 + 3 =$ _____   **7.** $5 + 5 =$ _____   **8.** $5 + 6 =$ _____

9. $5 + 8 =$ _____   **10.** $4 + 7 =$ _____   **11.** $8 + 8 =$ _____   **12.** $6 + 3 =$ _____

13. $\begin{array}{r} 4 \\ +\,0 \\ \hline \end{array}$	**14.** $\begin{array}{r} 8 \\ +\,4 \\ \hline \end{array}$	**15.** $\begin{array}{r} 3 \\ +\,7 \\ \hline \end{array}$	**16.** $\begin{array}{r} 7 \\ +\,4 \\ \hline \end{array}$	**17.** $\begin{array}{r} 0 \\ +\,1 \\ \hline \end{array}$
18. $\begin{array}{r} 9 \\ +\,5 \\ \hline \end{array}$	**19.** $\begin{array}{r} 7 \\ +\,9 \\ \hline \end{array}$	**20.** $\begin{array}{r} 0 \\ +\,0 \\ \hline \end{array}$	**21.** $\begin{array}{r} 1 \\ +\,3 \\ \hline \end{array}$	**22.** $\begin{array}{r} 5 \\ +\,0 \\ \hline \end{array}$

Find the difference.

23. $15 - 7 =$ _____   **24.** $7 - 4 =$ _____   **25.** $9 - 2 =$ _____

26. $8 - 5 =$ _____   **27.** $5 - 0 =$ _____   **28.** $6 - 1 =$ _____

29. $\begin{array}{r} 11 \\ -\,6 \\ \hline \end{array}$	**30.** $\begin{array}{r} 13 \\ -\,9 \\ \hline \end{array}$	**31.** $\begin{array}{r} 14 \\ -\,7 \\ \hline \end{array}$	**32.** $\begin{array}{r} 17 \\ -\,9 \\ \hline \end{array}$	**33.** $\begin{array}{r} 12 \\ -\,3 \\ \hline \end{array}$
34. $\begin{array}{r} 11 \\ -\,8 \\ \hline \end{array}$	**35.** $\begin{array}{r} 12 \\ -\,4 \\ \hline \end{array}$	**36.** $\begin{array}{r} 10 \\ -\,7 \\ \hline \end{array}$	**37.** $\begin{array}{r} 11 \\ -\,2 \\ \hline \end{array}$	**38.** $\begin{array}{r} 15 \\ -\,6 \\ \hline \end{array}$

Name_____ Date _____

1B ▸ BASIC SKILLS
···
Addition and Subtraction: Mental Math Strategies

Use mental math to find the sum. Think of tens or doubles.

1. 3
   $+ 5$

2. 13
   $+ 5$

3. 23
   $+ 5$

4. 6
   $+ 3$

5. 5
   $+ 7$

6. 25
   $+ 7$

7. 45
   $+ 7$

8. 8
   $+ 9$

9. $5 + 2 + 3 =$ _____

10. $9 + 6 + 5 =$ _____

11. $7 + 2 + 3 + 5 =$ _____

Write the difference.

12. 72
   $- 15$

13. 56
   $- 9$

14. 81
   $- 23$

15. 47
   $- 23$

16. 45
   $- 7$

17. 61
   $- 8$

18. 19
   $- 12$

19. 91
   $- 21$

20. 33
   $- 18$

21. 77
   $- 39$

Add parentheses to make the answer correct.

22. $12 - 5 + 3 = 10$ _____

23. $9 + 8 - 9 = 8$ _____

24. $7 + 4 - 3 = 8$ _____

25. $8 - 3 + 5 = 10$ _____

Name_____ Date _____

2A BASIC SKILLS

Multiplication and Division: Mental Math Strategies

Write a multiplication fact.

1. 4 + 4 + 4 + 4 + 4 _____   **2.** 4 + 4 + 4 _____

3. 4 + 4 _____   **4.** 2 + 2 + 2 + 2 _____

5. 6 fours _____   **6.** 9 fours _____

7. 9 twos _____   **8.** 4 threes _____

9. 3 twos _____   **10.** 7 threes _____

Use skip-counting to find the answer. Write the product only.

11. 7×2 _____   **12.** 6×2 _____   **13.** 3×3 _____

14. 8×3 _____   **15.** 7×4 _____   **16.** 4×4 _____

17. 2×2 _____   **18.** 9×3 _____   **19.** 8×4 _____

Find the quotient. Use a related multiplication fact.

20. $21 \div 7 =$ _____   **21.** $6 \div 6 =$ _____   **22.** $30 \div 6 =$ _____

23. $49 \div 7 =$ _____   **24.** $18 \div 6 =$ _____   **25.** $28 \div 7 =$ _____

26. $7 \div 7 =$ _____   **27.** $24 \div 6 =$ _____   **28.** $24 \div 4 =$ _____

Name_____ Date _____

BASIC SKILLS

2B

Multiplication and Division: Mental Math Strategies

Think of a related multiplication or division fact to solve. Write only the missing number.

1. _____ ÷ 6 = 7

2. _____ × 7 = 35

3. _____ ÷ 7 = 7

4. _____ × 6 = 36

5. _____ × 4 = 24

6. _____ ÷ 3 = 7

7. _____ × 2 = 4

8. _____ ÷ 5 = 3

9. _____ × 7 = 42

Find the quotient. Think of multiplication.

10. $2\overline{)14}$

11. $6\overline{)36}$

12. $4\overline{)16}$

13. $6\overline{)42}$

14. $5\overline{)20}$

15. $5\overline{)15}$

16. $6\overline{)12}$

17. $5\overline{)35}$

18. $7\overline{)0}$

19. $3\overline{)27}$

20. $4\overline{)32}$

21. $3\overline{)21}$

22. $4\overline{)28}$

23. $7\overline{)42}$

24. $3\overline{)24}$

Use mental math. Write only the answer.

25. 4 × 16 = _____

26. 3 × 23 = _____

27. 6 × 14 = _____

28. 2 × 38 = _____

29. 3 × 28 = _____

30. 7 × 13 = _____

Name_____   Date _____

3A ▸ BASIC SKILLS

Adding 2- and 3-Digit Whole Numbers

Estimate the sum.

1. 74 + 87	2. 38 + 28	3. 62 + 31	4. 54 + 28	5. 12 + 35

6. 93 + 24	7. 48 + 48	8. 76 + 28	9. 29 + 46	10. 70 + 32

11. 35 23 + 36	12. 42 36 + 14	13. 65 61 + 11	14. 24 73 + 32	15. 18 17 + 21

16. 16 21 + 32	17. 25 26 + 31	18. 49 32 + 15	19. 31 42 + 10	20. 38 17 + 17

Find the sum.

21. $86 + 7 =$ _____

22. $75 + 8 =$ _____

23. $26 + 6 =$ _____

24. $55 + 9 =$ _____

25. $26 + 38 =$ _____

26. $57 + 23 =$ _____

27. $64 + 28 =$ _____

28. $39 + 12 =$ _____

29. $647 + 228 =$ _____

30. $696 + 135 =$ _____

31. $443 + 278 =$ _____

32. $285 + 127 =$ _____

3B BASIC SKILLS

....

Adding 2- and 3-Digit Whole Numbers

Find the sum.

1.　14
　　+ 29

2.　16
　　+ 35

3.　25
　　+ 35

4.　29
　　+ 24

5.　36
　　+ 14

6.　72
　　+ 19

7.　11
　　72
　　+ 18

8.　21
　　63
　　+ 18

9.　12
　　28
　　+ 26

10.　31
　　47
　　+ 23

11.　42
　　66
　　+ 14

12.　11
　　49
　　+ 27

13.　175
　　+ 226

14.　284
　　+ 176

15.　297
　　+ 244

16.　375
　　+ 268

17.　329
　　+ 186

18.　295
　　+ 124

19.　141
　　257
　　+ 338

20.　114
　　726
　　+ 175

21.　693
　　46
　　+ 241

22.　728
　　210
　　+ 146

23.　654
　　31
　　+ 206

24.　123
　　881
　　+ 27

25.　216
　　270
　　+ 9

26. 307 + 256 = _____

27. 198 + 198 = _____

28. 326 + 85 = _____

29. 458 + 271 = _____

30. 329 + 116 = _____

31. 458 + 67 = _____

Name_____ Date _____

4A ◣ BASIC SKILLS

··

Subtracting 2- and 3-Digit Whole Numbers

Find the difference. Use an estimate to check that your answer is reasonable.

1.	35 $-\ 6$	**2.**	43 $-\ 8$	**3.**	60 -28	**4.**	75 -26

5.	30 -15	**6.**	71 -26	**7.**	65 -19	**8.**	83 $-\ 7$

9. $88 - 46 = $ _____   **10.** $71 - 29 = $ _____   **11.** $90 - 25 = $ _____

12. $41 - 19 = $ _____   **13.** $74 - 26 = $ _____   **14.** $81 - 16 = $ _____

15. $57 - 29 = $ _____   **16.** $28 - 19 = $ _____   **17.** $71 - 32 = $ _____

18. $53 - 19 = $ _____   **19.** $20 - 12 = $ _____   **20.** $50 - 29 = $ _____

Estimate the difference. Decide whether the answer given is reasonable. Write *yes* or *no*.

21.	46 -19 27 _____	**22.**	82 -33 39 _____	**23.**	67 -28 49 _____	**24.**	86 -57 29 _____

25.	46 -11 25 _____	**26.**	70 -32 48 _____	**27.**	26 -12 38 _____	**28.**	65 -26 39 _____

Name_____ Date _____

4B BASIC SKILLS

Subtracting 2- and 3-Digit Whole Numbers

Find the difference.

1. 851
    − 297

2. 913
    − 256

3. 831
    − 452

4. 724
    − 106

5. 488
    − 183

6. 521
    − 342

7. 783
    − 405

8. 842
    − 296

Use mental math to subtract. Write the difference.

9. 45 − 31 = _____

10. 67 − 25 = _____

11. 98 − 34 = _____

12. 846 − 226 = _____

13. 325 − 114 = _____

14. 795 − 254 = _____

Subtract. Check by adding.

15. 83
     − 25

16. 263
     − 184

17. 620
     − 233

18. 492
     − 177

19. 55
     − 17

20. 82
     − 73

21. 488
     − 298

22. 611
     − 264

Name_____ Date _____

5A BASIC SKILLS

Multiplying 2-Digit Numbers

Round to the greatest place to estimate the product.

1.	92	2.	76	3.	89	4.	47
	× 34		× 65		× 28		× 52

5.	63	6.	53	7.	69	8.	79
	× 18		× 71		× 21		× 83

9.	406	10.	275	11.	850	12.	234
	× 52		× 39		× 25		× 38

13.	184	14.	342	15.	458	16.	839
	× 68		× 46		× 32		× 58

Find the product.

17. $40 \times 60 =$ _____　　**18.** $20 \times 80 =$ _____　　**19.** $90 \times 10 =$ _____

20. $59 \times 300 =$ _____　　**21.** $43 \times 500 =$ _____　　**22.** $41 \times 800 =$ _____

Circle the products that are about 6000.

23.	300	24.	100	25.	60	26.	83	27.	67
	× 20		× 55		× 100		× 10		× 80

Name_____ Date _____

5B BASIC SKILLS
....
Multiplying 2-Digit Numbers

Find the product. Use an estimate to check your answer.

1.　 85
　　× 60

2.　 72
　　× 43

3.　 82
　　× 56

4.　 36
　　× 72

5.　 71
　　× 62

6.　 58
　　× 56

7.　 93
　　× 66

8.　 51
　　× 25

9.　 38
　　× 56

10.　 93
　　× 44

11.　 84
　　× 82

12.　 82
　　× 49

13.　 542
　　×　 61

14.　 448
　　×　 73

15.　 618
　　×　 61

Find the product.

16. $84 \times 263 =$ _____

17. $91 \times 405 =$ _____

18. $23 \times 827 =$ _____

19.　 724
　　×　 48

20.　 981
　　×　 29

21.　 306
　　×　 35

22.　 475
　　×　 52

23.　 634
　　×　 25

24.　 854
　　×　 37

25.　 563
　　×　 38

26.　 724
　　×　 26

27.　 929
　　×　 41

28.　 409
　　×　 35

6A BASIC SKILLS

Dividing by 1-Digit Divisors

Decide whether the first number in the pair is divisible by the second. Write *divisible* or *not divisible*.

1. 17; 4

2. 35; 3

3. 200; 5

_____

_____

_____

4. 70; 10

5. 95; 5

6. 29; 3

_____

_____

_____

7. 65; 10

8. 12; 6

9. 120; 4

_____

_____

_____

Circle the best estimate.

10. 85 ÷ 9
  a. 7
  b. 8
  c. 9

11. 49 ÷ 5
  a. 8
  b. 9
  c. 10

12. 19 ÷ 5
  a. 3
  b. 4
  c. 5

Estimate. Decide if the quotient will be greater than 10. Write *yes* or *no*.

13. $2\overline{)35}$ _____

14. $5\overline{)62}$ _____

15. $9\overline{)75}$ _____

16. $6\overline{)52}$ _____

17. $8\overline{)84}$ _____

18. $7\overline{)52}$ _____

Name_____ Date _____

6B ◣ BASIC SKILLS
··

Dividing by 1-Digit Divisors

Divide. Check your answers by multiplying.

1. $3\overline{)67}$ 2. $4\overline{)46}$ 3. $2\overline{)85}$ 4. $5\overline{)58}$ 5. $2\overline{)49}$

6. $4\overline{)85}$ 7. $3\overline{)94}$ 8. $2\overline{)65}$ 9. $3\overline{)38}$ 10. $7\overline{)89}$

Divide.

11. $2\overline{)462}$ 12. $3\overline{)669}$ 13. $7\overline{)924}$ 14. $5\overline{)585}$

15. $4\overline{)952}$ 16. $3\overline{)474}$ 17. $6\overline{)426}$ 18. $4\overline{)732}$

19. $8\overline{)9842}$ 20. $9\overline{)5581}$ 21. $5\overline{)9250}$ 22. $7\overline{)8123}$

Find the divided or divisor.

23. $\square \div 5 = 7$ 24. $56 \div \square = 7$ 25. $46 \div \square = 5\ R1$

26. $26 \div \square = 4\ R2$ 27. $50 \div \square = 8\ R2$ 28. $66 \div \square = 8\ R2$

Name_____ Date _____

7A ◣ BASIC SKILLS

Fractions: Comparing and Ordering

Use the list. Write the common multiple(s) and the least common multiple.

Multiples of 3: 3, 6, 9, 12, 15, 18   **Multiples of 4:** 4, 8, 12, 16, 20, 24
Multiples of 5: 5, 10, 15, 20, 25, 30   **Multiples of 6:** 6, 12, 18, 24, 30, 36
Multiples of 10: 10, 20, 30, 40, 50, 60   **Multiples of 12:** 12, 24, 36, 48, 60, 72

1. 3 and 5

_____

_____

2. 3 and 6

_____

_____

3. 4 and 12

_____

_____

4. 5 and 6

_____

_____

5. 5 and 10

_____

_____

6. 6 and 10

_____

_____

Write the least common multiple.

7. 3 and 8 _____

8. 6 and 8 _____

9. 6 and 7 _____

10. 4 and 5 _____

11. 3 and 7 _____

12. 4 and 9 _____

Compare. Write whether the fraction is closer to 0, $\frac{1}{2}$, or 1.

13. $\frac{1}{12}$ _____

14. $\frac{2}{4}$ _____

15. $\frac{7}{8}$ _____

16. $\frac{1}{3}$ _____

17. $\frac{2}{5}$ _____

18. $\frac{1}{7}$ _____

Name_____ Date _____

7B BASIC SKILLS

Fractions: Comparing and Ordering

Compare. Write >, <, or =.

1. $\frac{1}{6}$ ◯ $\frac{5}{6}$ 2. $\frac{2}{3}$ ◯ $\frac{4}{6}$ 3. $\frac{3}{4}$ ◯ $\frac{2}{4}$

4. $\frac{5}{7}$ ◯ $\frac{2}{3}$ 5. $\frac{7}{8}$ ◯ $\frac{4}{5}$ 6. $\frac{5}{6}$ ◯ $\frac{7}{9}$

7. $\frac{1}{4}$ ◯ $\frac{3}{8}$ 8. $\frac{2}{3}$ ◯ $\frac{4}{5}$ 9. $\frac{3}{4}$ ◯ $\frac{7}{8}$

Order from least to greatest.

10. $\frac{7}{8}, \frac{4}{5}, \frac{6}{10}$ 11. $\frac{2}{3}, \frac{5}{6}, \frac{2}{9}$ 12. $\frac{3}{4}, \frac{2}{9}, \frac{10}{12}$

_____   _____   _____

Order from greatest to least.

13. $\frac{7}{10}, \frac{4}{5}, \frac{1}{2}$ 14. $\frac{3}{8}, \frac{1}{4}, \frac{13}{16}$ 15. $\frac{1}{2}, \frac{6}{8}, \frac{2}{3}$

_____   _____   _____

16. $\frac{1}{3}, \frac{1}{5}, \frac{1}{4}$ 17. $\frac{2}{3}, \frac{3}{4}, \frac{7}{8}$ 18. $\frac{5}{6}, \frac{9}{10}, \frac{4}{5}$

_____   _____   _____

19. $\frac{2}{3}, \frac{1}{12}, \frac{4}{9}$ 20. $\frac{3}{4}, \frac{1}{3}, \frac{11}{12}$ 21. $\frac{3}{5}, \frac{1}{2}, \frac{1}{3}, \frac{7}{10}$

_____   _____   _____

Name_____ Date _____

8A BASIC SKILLS
···
Fractions: GCF and Simplifying

Find an equivalent fraction. Divide the numerator and the denominator by 4.

1. $\frac{8}{12} = \frac{2}{}$

2. $\frac{16}{20} = \frac{}{5}$

3. $\frac{8}{28} = \frac{2}{}$

4. $\frac{12}{20} = \frac{}{5}$

Is the fraction in simplest form? Write *yes* or *no*.

5. $\frac{8}{16}$ _____

6. $\frac{9}{12}$ _____

7. $\frac{7}{8}$ _____

8. $\frac{6}{8}$ _____

9. $\frac{10}{20}$ _____

10. $\frac{5}{9}$ _____

Write the fraction in simplest form.

11. $\frac{8}{16}$ _____

12. $\frac{3}{12}$ _____

13. $\frac{4}{12}$ _____

14. $\frac{12}{15}$ _____

15. $\frac{6}{10}$ _____

16. $\frac{4}{16}$ _____

Write the fraction as a whole number.

17. $\frac{12}{6}$

18. $\frac{15}{3}$

19. $\frac{9}{3}$

20. $\frac{20}{2}$

21. $\frac{10}{5}$

22. $\frac{21}{3}$

Name_____ Date _____

◢8B◣ BASIC SKILLS

Fractions: GCF and Simplifying

List all factors.

1. 5 _____

2. 12 _____

3. 4 _____

4. 6 _____

5. 8 _____

6. 9 _____

List all factors. Circle the common factors.
Write the greatest common factor.

7. 16: _____
   18 : _____
   GCF: _____

8. 20: _____
   25: _____
   GCF: _____

9. 10: _____
   45: _____
   GCF: _____

10. 24: _____
    48: _____
    GCF: _____

11. 30: _____
    60: _____
    GCF: _____

Write the GCF of the numerator and denominator.
Then write the fraction in simplest form.

12. $\frac{4}{6}$ _____

13. $\frac{5}{15}$ _____

14. $\frac{6}{20}$ _____

15. $\frac{3}{18}$ _____

16. $\frac{4}{8}$ _____

17. $\frac{3}{12}$ _____

18. $\frac{15}{20}$ _____

19. $\frac{6}{15}$ _____

20. $\frac{6}{9}$ _____

Name_____   Date _____

◢9A◣ BASIC SKILLS

··

Adding and Subtracting Fractions with Like Denominators

Is the fraction less than, equal to, or greater than one half? Write >, <, or =.

1. $\frac{3}{6}$ _____

2. $\frac{5}{8}$ _____

3. $\frac{3}{10}$ _____

4. $\frac{9}{16}$ _____

5. $\frac{5}{12}$ _____

6. $\frac{7}{14}$ _____

7. $\frac{12}{20}$ _____

8. $\frac{6}{18}$ _____

9. $\frac{4}{8}$ _____

Round to the nearest whole number.

10. $3\frac{1}{2}$ _____

11. $4\frac{1}{4}$ _____

12. $8\frac{5}{8}$ _____

13. $13\frac{1}{3}$ _____

14. $7\frac{1}{6}$ _____

15. $9\frac{2}{3}$ _____

16. $11\frac{3}{4}$ _____

17. $10\frac{5}{6}$ _____

18. $5\frac{7}{8}$ _____

Write the closest pair of whole numbers that the sum or difference falls between.

19. $\frac{1}{9} + \frac{4}{9}$

20. $2\frac{1}{5} + \frac{1}{5}$

21. $3\frac{5}{8} - 2\frac{1}{8}$

22. $5\frac{4}{5} - 3\frac{2}{5}$

_____   _____   _____   _____

Name_____ Date _____

BASIC SKILLS

Adding and Subtracting Fractions with Like Denominators

Add or subtract. Write the answer in simplest form.

1.   2 sevenths
  + 3 sevenths

2.   5 ninths
  − 2 ninths

3.   6 tenths
  − 1 tenth

4.   7 twelfths
  − 3 twelfths

5.   2 fifths
  + 1 fifth

6.   10 fifteenths
  + 2 fifteenths

7. $\frac{5}{8}$
$-\frac{2}{8}$

8. $3\frac{3}{5}$
$+2\frac{1}{5}$

9. $5\frac{2}{7}$
$-2\frac{4}{7}$

10. $\frac{2}{3}$
$+\frac{1}{3}$

11. $6\frac{2}{6}$
$+3\frac{2}{6}$

12. $9\frac{1}{8}$
$-4\frac{3}{8}$

13. $\frac{2}{6}$
$+\frac{3}{6}$

14. $2\frac{7}{8}$
$+4\frac{2}{8}$

15. $7\frac{3}{9}$
$-2\frac{5}{9}$

16. $\frac{1}{2}$
$+\frac{1}{2}$

17. $6\frac{3}{4}$
$-2\frac{1}{4}$

18. $5\frac{1}{6}$
$-3\frac{5}{6}$

Name_____ Date _____

10A ◣ BASIC SKILLS

···
Adding Fractions with Unlike Denominators

Use the list. Write the first 3 common multiple(s) and
the least common multiple.

Multiples of 3: 3, 6, 9, 12, 15, 18   **Multiples of 4:** 4, 8, 12, 16, 20,24
Multiples of 5: 5, 10, 15, 20, 25, 30   **Multiples of 6:** 6, 12, 18, 24, 30, 36
Multiples of 10: 10, 20, 30, 40, 50, 60   **Multiples of 12:** 12, 24, 36, 48, 60, 72

1. 3 and 5   **2.** 4 and 12   **3.** 5 and 10   **4.** 3 and 6

_____   _____   _____   _____

_____   _____   _____   _____

Write the least common denominator of the two fractions.

5. $\frac{1}{2}$ and $\frac{5}{8}$ _____   **6.** $\frac{5}{6}$ and $\frac{5}{8}$ _____   **7.** $\frac{2}{3}$ and $\frac{1}{6}$ _____

8. $\frac{3}{4}$ and $\frac{2}{5}$ _____   **9.** $\frac{2}{7}$ and $\frac{8}{9}$ _____   **10.** $\frac{1}{4}$ and $\frac{7}{9}$ _____

11. $\frac{1}{6}$ and $\frac{7}{12}$ _____   **12.** $\frac{5}{6}$ and $\frac{5}{9}$ _____   **13.** $\frac{2}{3}$ and $\frac{5}{7}$ _____

14. $\frac{6}{7}$ and $\frac{1}{8}$ _____   **15.** $\frac{1}{3}$ and $\frac{2}{9}$ _____   **16.** $\frac{2}{3}$ and $\frac{7}{10}$ _____

17. $\frac{5}{12}$ and $\frac{1}{2}$ _____   **18.** $\frac{2}{5}$ and $\frac{2}{3}$ _____   **19.** $\frac{4}{9}$ and $\frac{7}{10}$ _____

20. $\frac{1}{2}$ and $\frac{2}{3}$ _____   **21.** $\frac{5}{6}$ and $\frac{1}{4}$ _____   **22.** $\frac{1}{5}$ and $\frac{3}{10}$ _____

Name_____ Date _____

10B BASIC SKILLS
···

Adding Fractions with Unlike Denominators

Estimate. Then write the sum in simplest form.

1. $\frac{1}{3}$
$+\frac{1}{6}$
_____

2. $\frac{1}{9}$
$+\frac{1}{3}$
_____

3. $\frac{1}{4}$
$+\frac{3}{8}$
_____

4. $\frac{1}{10}$
$+\frac{2}{5}$
_____

5. $\frac{2}{3}$
$+\frac{1}{9}$
_____

6. $\frac{2}{12}$
$+\frac{2}{4}$
_____

7. $\frac{6}{14}$
$+\frac{3}{7}$
_____

8. $\frac{1}{2}$
$+\frac{3}{8}$
_____

9. $\frac{6}{7}$
$+\frac{3}{14}$
_____

10. $\frac{4}{5}$
$+\frac{4}{15}$
_____

11. $\frac{5}{18}$
$+\frac{2}{9}$
_____

12. $\frac{3}{5}$
$+\frac{7}{20}$
_____

13. $\frac{7}{12}$
$+\frac{2}{3}$
_____

14. $\frac{4}{6}$
$+\frac{3}{18}$
_____

15. $\frac{7}{6}$
$+\frac{5}{12}$
_____

16. $\frac{2}{9}$
$+\frac{2}{3}$
_____

17. $\frac{2}{5} + \frac{7}{10} =$ _____

18. $\frac{1}{2} + \frac{7}{8} =$ _____

19. $\frac{5}{8} + \frac{3}{4} =$ _____

20. $\frac{3}{10} + \frac{9}{20} =$ _____

21. $\frac{2}{3} + \frac{4}{9} =$ _____

22. $\frac{5}{12} + \frac{2}{3} =$ _____

23. $\frac{9}{10} + \frac{4}{5} =$ _____

24. $\frac{1}{6} + \frac{11}{12} =$ _____

25. $\frac{7}{8} + \frac{3}{4} =$ _____

BASIC SKILLS

Subtracting Fractions with Unlike Denominators

Estimate the answer. Tell whether the difference is closer to 0, $\frac{1}{2}$, or 1.

1. $\frac{5}{6}$
$-\frac{1}{10}$

2. $\frac{8}{10}$
$-\frac{5}{7}$

3. $\frac{7}{8}$
$-\frac{2}{5}$

4. $\frac{12}{12}$
$-\frac{1}{13}$

5. $\frac{4}{5}$
$-\frac{7}{15}$

6. $\frac{6}{11}$
$-\frac{1}{9}$

7. $\frac{7}{9}$
$-\frac{2}{7}$

8. $\frac{7}{12}$
$-\frac{9}{16}$

Estimate. Then write the difference in simplest form.

9. $\frac{3}{4}$
$-\frac{1}{12}$

10. $\frac{5}{8}$
$-\frac{1}{2}$

11. $\frac{6}{9}$
$-\frac{1}{3}$

12. $\frac{4}{5}$
$-\frac{1}{10}$

13. $4\frac{7}{8}$
$-2\frac{1}{2}$

14. $3\frac{4}{7}$
$-2\frac{1}{3}$

15. $16\frac{3}{4}$
$-3\frac{2}{3}$

16. $9\frac{8}{10}$
$-2\frac{2}{5}$

17. $18\frac{4}{6}$
$-5\frac{1}{3}$

18. $12\frac{5}{6}$
$-3\frac{2}{4}$

19. $8\frac{3}{4}$
-4

20. $9\frac{9}{10}$
$-7\frac{1}{2}$

Name_____ Date _____

BASIC SKILLS

Subtracting Fractions with Unlike Denominators

Rewrite the fraction using the LCD. Then, order from least to greatest.

1. $\frac{2}{9}, \frac{1}{2}, \frac{1}{3}, \frac{1}{6}$

2. $\frac{2}{5}, \frac{1}{2}, \frac{3}{10}, \frac{3}{5}$

3. $\frac{2}{3}, \frac{1}{2}, \frac{1}{9}, \frac{2}{9}$

_____

_____

_____

4. $\frac{2}{3}, \frac{3}{4}, \frac{2}{8}, \frac{1}{2}$

5. $\frac{5}{6}, \frac{3}{8}, \frac{1}{2}, \frac{3}{4}$

6. $\frac{2}{3}, \frac{2}{9}, \frac{1}{2}, \frac{5}{6}$

_____

_____

_____

Subtract. Write the difference in simplest form.

7. $\begin{array}{r} 7 \\ -\ 2\frac{3}{5} \\ \hline \end{array}$

8. $\begin{array}{r} 6 \\ -\ \frac{5}{8} \\ \hline \end{array}$

9. $\begin{array}{r} 4 \\ -\ 1\frac{1}{4} \\ \hline \end{array}$

10. $\begin{array}{r} 9 \\ -\ 5\frac{4}{6} \\ \hline \end{array}$

11. $\begin{array}{r} 10 \\ -\ 5\frac{1}{3} \\ \hline \end{array}$

12. $\begin{array}{r} 14 \\ -\ 6\frac{4}{6} \\ \hline \end{array}$

13. $\begin{array}{r} 9 \\ -\ 2\frac{2}{5} \\ \hline \end{array}$

14. $\begin{array}{r} 8 \\ -\ 2\frac{6}{8} \\ \hline \end{array}$

15. $\begin{array}{r} 4\frac{2}{8} \\ -\ 1\frac{4}{5} \\ \hline \end{array}$

16. $\begin{array}{r} 7\frac{2}{4} \\ -\ 3\frac{5}{6} \\ \hline \end{array}$

17. $\begin{array}{r} 12\frac{1}{2} \\ -\ 6\frac{3}{5} \\ \hline \end{array}$

18. $\begin{array}{r} 9\frac{2}{8} \\ -\ 2\frac{1}{3} \\ \hline \end{array}$

Name_____ Date _____

12A BASIC SKILLS

Decimals: Comparing and Ordering

Write in short word form.

1. 0.9

_____

2. 3.6

_____

3. 9.3

_____

4. 12.8

_____
_____

5. 45.2

_____
_____

6. 173.4

_____
_____

Write the decimal.

7. 4 tenths _____

8. 5 tenths _____

9. 1 tenth _____

10. 6 and 3 tenths _____

11. 2 and 1 tenth _____

12. 7 and 5 tenths _____

13. 8 and 7 tenths _____

14. 6 and 4 tenths _____

15. 5 and 9 tenths _____

16. 23 and 5 tenths _____

17. 13 and 8 tenths _____

18. 34 and 6 tenths _____

19. 51 and 1 tenth _____

20. 45 and 7 tenths _____

21. 93 and 3 tenths _____

Write >, <, or =.

22. 29.06 ◯ 29.6

23. 0.54 ◯ 0.58

24. 63.211 ◯ 63.31

25. 80.09 ◯ 90.08

26. 75.43 ◯ 34.57

27. 6.07 ◯ 6.070

28. 98.71 ◯ 98.17

29. 2.002 ◯ 4.002

30. 9.357 ◯ 9.36

Name_____ Date _____

12B ▸ BASIC SKILLS
....
Decimals: Comparing and Ordering

Order from least to greatest.

1. 0.4, 0.38, 0.42 _____

2. 5.66, 6.56, 4.56, 6.66 _____

3. 0.12, 2.12, 1.20, 1.22 _____

4. 6.999, 9.996, 90.6 _____

5. 92.344, 92.4, 92.034 _____

6. 29.007, 29.70, 29.070 _____

7. 75.647, 75.65, 75.562 _____

8. 6.39, 3.96, 9.6, 9.36, 3.69 _____

9. 0.80, 0.7, 1.08, 0.9, 1.03, 1.2 _____

Write >, <, or =.

10. 6.37 ◯ 6.29   **11.** 25.07 ◯ 23.89   **12.** 426.76 ◯ 426.67

13. 39.2 ◯ 29.8   **14.** 148.386 ◯ 148.863   **15.** 9.4 ◯ 90.4

16. 2.047 ◯ 1.998   **17.** 761.502 ◯ 761.524   **18.** 3.86 ◯ 3.08

19. 17.006 ◯ 17.060   **20.** 83.563 ◯ 83.056   **21.** 70.5 ◯ 70.5

Name_____   Date _____

13A ▸ BASIC SKILLS

Adding and Subtracting Decimals

Write the value of the digits in the number 76.052.

Tens	Ones		Tenths	Hundredths	Thousandths
		.			

1. The value of the digit 6 is _____

2. The value of the digit 0 is _____

3. The value of the digit 5 is _____

4. The value of the digit 2 is _____

Write the value of the underlined digit.

5. 5.4̲48 _____

6. 4.78̲3 _____

7. 8.37̲5 _____

8. 9̲.431 _____

9. 6.40̲2 _____

10. 4.21̲2 _____

11. 31̲.296 _____

12. 27.5̲08 _____

13. 16.42̲8 _____

Round to the greatest place value. Then estimate.

14.   9.3
  + 3.9

15.   7.8
  − 6.4

16.   5.2
  − 3.7

17.   56.7
  + 9.13

18.   25.04
  + 25.19

19.   32.82
  + 9.10

Name_____   Date _____

13B BASIC SKILLS
Adding and Subtracting Decimals

Find the sum.

1. 0.6 + 0.2	**2.** 0.7 + 0.5	**3.** 7.4 + 0.1	**4.** 8.4 + 0.41	**5.** 6.7 + 1.45
6. 4.34 + 2.8	**7.** 0.312 + 0.82	**8.** .59 + 0.21	**9.** 12.45 + 2.16	**10.** 35.6 + 2.45
11. 15 + 2.45	**12.** 2.6 + 11.35	**13.** 3.95 + 0.246	**14.** 14.34 + 2.05	**15.** 12.04 + 3.02

Find the difference.

16. 4.33 − 1.96	**17.** 5.80 − 1.94	**18.** 4.394 − 2.4	**19.** 7.832 − 3.915	**20.** 4.763 − 3.913
21. 8.9 − 2.134	**22.** 7.02 − 3.199	**23.** 5 − 2.8	**24.** 7.8 − 1.9	**25.** 16 − 9.32
26. 58.37 − 16.292	**27.** 76.8 − 21.49	**28.** 92.134 − 21.982	**29.** 96.805 − 12.6	**30.** 79.1 − 15.32

Basic Skills Workshop 1

Adding and Subtracting 2- and 3-Digit Numbers

Number Sense

15 minutes

Parts of 100

Management whole class or small group

- Students can explore adding and subtracting 2- digit numbers using the number 100. Give students a number and have them use mental math to find the number they need to add to equal 100.

- Example: for the number 36, first skip-count by 10's: 36, 46, 56, 66, 76, 86, 96, which adds on 60. Then count up to 100: 96, 97, 98, 99, 100, which adds on 4 more. So, 6 tens + 4 ones = 64.

- Ask students how they can use basic facts to help them solve these problems using mental math. Example: use the basic facts for 10 because the ones of each pair of numbers always total 10; use the basic facts for 9 because the tens of each pair always total 9.

- This activity can be used with other totals besides 100. When students become comfortable with the activity using 100, have them match numbers that add up to 150 or 200.

Skill Application

30 minutes

Finding Sums and Differences

Management whole class, then pairs
Materials Just the Facts Support Master 20

- Model how to find the sum 172 + 219. Remind students to check answers using an inverse operation.

Step 1. Add the ones.
Regroup a ten if necessary.

```
  172
+ 219
────
    1
```

Step 2. Add the tens.
Regroup a hundred if necessary.

```
  172
+ 219
────
   91
```

Step 3. Add the hundreds.

```
  172
+ 219
────
  391
```

- Also model the subtraction problem 436 − 277.

Step 1. Subtract the ones.
Regroup a ten if necessary.

```
  436
− 277
────
    9
```

Step 2. Subtract the tens.
Regroup a hundred if necessary.

```
  436
− 277
────
   59
```

Step 3. Subtract the hundreds.

```
  436
− 277
────
  159
```

- Students can practice these exercises with a partner: 48 + 24, 238 + 195, 339 − 182, 73 − 17. For each exercise, one partner completes the first step, then the other completes the next step, and so on.

Basic Skills Workshop 2

Multiplying 2- and 3-Digit Numbers

 Number Sense 🕐

15 minutes

Estimating Products

Management whole class or small group

- Ask students when they might estimate products of 2- and 3-digit numbers. Give a real-world example: An in-line skate shop installs 16 bearings on a pair of skates. In one week, the shop replaces bearings on 168 pairs. About how many bearings do they use?

- Ask students to give a multiplication expression for the problem. **168 × 16**

- Now, ask students to describe how to estimate the product. Responses should include rounding to the nearest ten or hundred. Have students apply their strategies. Then model one method.

  Step 1. Round both factors.

  $168 \times 16 \rightarrow 170 \times 20$

  Step 2. Multiply to find the estimate.

  $170 \times 20 = 3400$

  Step 3. Interpret the estimate. The shop uses about 3400 bearings.

- Ask students whether the actual product will be less than or greater than the estimated product and why they think so. **The actual product is less than the estimate because the factors were rounded up.**

 Skill Application 🕐

15 minutes

Finding Exact Products

Management whole class, then pairs
Materials Just the Facts Support Master 20

- Ask students to help you describe the steps for finding 168 × 16. Model the steps and label them, using student language whenever possible.

  Step 1. Multiply by the ones and regroup.

$$\begin{array}{r} {\scriptstyle 4} \\ 168 \\ \times\ \ 16 \\ \hline 1008 \end{array}$$

Step 2. Multiply the tens. Add in the regrouped tens. Regroup any hundreds.

$$\begin{array}{r} {\scriptstyle 4\,4} \\ 168 \\ \times\ \ 16 \\ \hline 1008 \\ 168 \end{array}$$

Step 3. Add the products from Step 1 and Step 2 to find the total product.

$$\begin{array}{r} {\scriptstyle 4\,4} \\ 168 \\ \times\ \ 16 \\ \hline 1008 \\ 168 \\ \hline 2688 \end{array}$$

- Compare the product to the estimate. Point out that the answer is reasonable.

- Have students write ten 2- and 3-digit multiplication exercises, and then trade exercises with a partner.

Basic Skills Workshop 3

Dividing by 1-Digit Divisors

Number Sense

20 minutes

Estimation

Management whole class or small group

- Give students a real-world example using division. A high school stadium seats 1580 people. There are 8 sections and each section has the same number of seats. How many people sit in each section? Elicit other real-world examples from students.

- Have students find the division expression for the stadium problem. **1580 ÷ 8** Elicit how to estimate the answer. Accept strategies such as rounding or using compatible numbers. Have students apply the strategy to the problem.

- Estimate 1580 ÷ 8.

- Show students how to use compatible numbers to estimate the quotient: Think of basic facts. Replace 1580 with a close number that is easily divide by 8.

- Ask students what number is close to 1580 that is evenly divisible by 8. **1600** Elicit from students how to find the estimated quotient. **200**

- Students should be encouraged to use number sense to interpret their answer. Have them justify 200 as a reasonable estimate of 1580 ÷ 8.

Skill Application

30 minutes

Dividing to Find the Exact Quotient

Management whole class, then pairs
Materials Just the Facts Support Master 20

- Find 1580 ÷ 8. Elicit student input for each step.

Step 1. Divide the hundreds. Multiply and subtract.

$$\boxed{8 \times 1 \text{ hundred}} \quad \begin{array}{r} 1 \\ 8\overline{)1580} \\ -\,8 \\ \hline 7 \end{array}$$

Step 2. Next, divide the tens. Multiply and subtract.

$$\boxed{8 \times 9 \text{ tens}} \quad \begin{array}{r} 19 \\ 8\overline{)1580} \\ -\,8 \\ \hline 78 \\ -\,72 \end{array}$$

Step 3. Finally, divide the ones. Write the remainder as part of the answer.

$$\boxed{8 \times 7 \text{ ones}} \quad \begin{array}{r} 197 \text{ R4} \\ 8\overline{)1580} \\ -\,8 \\ \hline 78 \\ -\,72 \\ \hline 60 \\ -\,56 \\ \hline 4 \end{array}$$

- Ask students to create a sheet of 10 division exercises. Then, have students trade sheets with a partner, find the answers, and check each other's work.

Basic Skills Workshop 4

Dividing by 2-Digit Divisors

Number Sense

20 minutes

Estimation

Management whole class or small group

- Give students a real-world example using division. A town orders 1248 park benches for its 24 neighborhoods. If each neighborhood gets the same number of benches, how many benches will each get? Elicit other real-world examples from students.

- Elicit how to estimate the answer. Accept strategies such as rounding or using compatible numbers. Have students apply the strategy to the problem.

- Estimate 1248 ÷ 24.

- Use compatible numbers to estimate the quotient. Think of basic facts. Replace 1248 with a number close to it that you can easily divide by a number close to 24.

- Ask, In what place can you begin to divide? **The tens place.** What number times 20 is close to 120? **6** Elicit from students that a 6 in the tens place would mean the estimated quotient is 60.

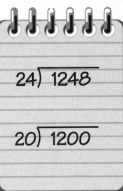

- Use number sense to interpret the answer: Do 60 park benches for 24 neighborhoods total approximately 1200 park benches?

Skill Application

30 minutes

Dividing to Find the Exact Quotient

Management whole class, then pairs
Materials Just the Facts Support Master 20

- Write: 1248 ÷ 24. Elicit student input for each step as you model the division.

  Step 1. Divide the tens. Multiply and subtract.

$$
\begin{array}{r}
5 \\
24)\overline{1248} \\
-120 \\
\hline
4
\end{array}
$$

 24×5 tens

Step 2. Next, divide the ones. Multiply and subtract.

$$
\begin{array}{r}
52 \\
24)\overline{1248} \\
-120 \\
\hline
48 \\
-48 \\
\hline
0
\end{array}
$$

24×2 ones

Step 3. Compare the exact quotient to the estimate quotient for reasonableness. Since the estimated quotient was 60, does 52 seem a reasonable quotient for 1248 ÷ 24? Have students justify their reasoning.

- Ask students to create a sheet of 10 division exercises with 2-digit divisors. Then, students should trade sheets with a partner, find the answers, and finish by checking each other's work.

Basic Skills Workshop 5

Fractions: Greatest Common Factors and Simplifying

Number Sense

20 minutes

Simplifying Fractions

Management whole class or small group

- As a review, elicit from students a definition for the term Greatest Common Factor. Responses should mention that the GCF of two numbers is the greatest factor they both have in common.

- Have students connect finding the GCF to simplifying fractions. Responses should mention that one way to simplify a fraction is to divide the numerator and the denominator by the GCF. Model simplifying $\frac{4}{12}$.

- Model finding the simplest form of a fraction. Write:

$$\frac{12}{30} \rightarrow \frac{12 \div 2}{30 \div 2} \rightarrow \frac{6}{15}$$

This is not simplest form because 6 and 15 can both be divided by 3.

$$\frac{12}{30} \rightarrow \frac{12 \div 3}{30 \div 3} \rightarrow \frac{4}{10}$$

This is not simplest form because 4 and 10 can both be divided by 2.

$$\frac{12}{30} \rightarrow \frac{12 \div 6}{30 \div 6} \rightarrow \frac{2}{5}$$

This is simplest form.

- Ask students how they know that $\frac{2}{5}$ is in simplest form. Responses should mention that the numerator and the denominator have no common factors other than 1. Then elicit a list of fractions that are in simplest form. Ask what these fractions have in common with each other.

Skill Application

30 minutes

Using the GCF to Simplify

Management whole class, then pairs
Materials Just the Facts Support Master 20

- Simplify $\frac{24}{40}$.
  Demonstrate finding the GCF of 24 and 40.

  Step 1. List the factors of each number.

  Factors of 24: 1, 2, 3, 4, 6, 8, 12, 24

  Factors of 40: 1, 2, 4, 5, 8, 10, 20, 40

  Step 2. Compare lists to find the GCF.

Factors of 24: 1, 2, 3, 4, 6, **8**, 12, 24

Factors of 40: 1, 2, 4, 5, **8**, 10, 20, 40

The GCF of 24 and 40 is 8.

Step 3. Divide the numerator and the denominator by the GCF, 8.

$$\frac{24}{40} = \frac{24 \div 8}{40 \div 8} \text{ or } \frac{3}{5}$$

- Ask students how they know that $\frac{3}{5}$ is in its simplest form.

- Have students simplify the fractions from the compiled list of unsimplified fractions from Number Sense. Then, on a separate sheet of paper, have pairs of students write 15 new fractions that need to be simplified. Have partners trade papers and simplify the other's fractions. Partners should check each other's work to see that fractions are simplified correctly.

Basic Skills Workshop 6
Adding and Subtracting Fractions

Number Sense

20 minutes

Fraction Estimation

Management whole class or small group
Materials overhead projector, number line transparency
(Just the Facts Support Master 17)

- Point out that determining whether a fraction is closer to 0, $\frac{1}{2}$, or 1 is helpful in estimating the sum or difference of two fractions.

- Label the number line as shown below.

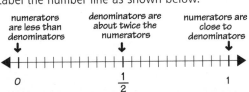

numerators are less than denominators

denominators are about twice the numerators

numerators are close to denominators

$0 \qquad \frac{1}{2} \qquad 1$

- Ask for an example of a fraction that matches each description on the number line. Have students justify the examples they give.

- List these fractions: $\frac{3}{7}, \frac{8}{9}, \frac{1}{32}, \frac{12}{25}, \frac{7}{8}, \frac{4}{5}, \frac{5}{11}, \frac{1}{9}, \frac{3}{100}, \frac{3}{7}, 6\frac{2}{3},$
$1\frac{3}{16}, \frac{12}{14}, \frac{1}{4}, 2\frac{4}{10}.$

- Name $\frac{3}{7}, \frac{8}{9},$ and $\frac{1}{32}$. Ask students to tell you whether the fraction is closer to 0, $\frac{1}{2}$, or 1. As they respond, mark the number line as indicated below.

$$\frac{1}{32} \qquad\qquad \frac{3}{7} \qquad\qquad\qquad \frac{8}{9}$$

$0 \qquad\qquad\qquad \frac{1}{2} \qquad\qquad\qquad 1$

- Now have students choose pairs of fractions from the list to estimate the sum or difference. Have students estimate by naming the closest benchmark (0, $\frac{1}{2}$, or 1).

Skill Application

30 minutes

Finding Fraction Sums and Differences

Management whole class, then pairs
Materials fraction models, paper, Just the Facts Support Master 20

- Find $2\frac{3}{4} + 1\frac{1}{3}$. Elicit that the sum is about 4 or 5.

Step 1. When the denominators are different, find the least common denominator (LCD).

The multiples of 4 are 4, 8, 12, 16...

The multiples of 3 are 3, 6, 9, 12...

The LCD of 4 and 3 is 12.

Step 2. Use the LCD to write $\frac{3}{4}$ as $\frac{9}{12}$ and $\frac{1}{3}$ as $\frac{4}{12}$.

Step 3. Add the equivalent fractions. Add the whole numbers. Simplify.

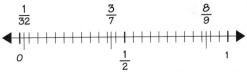

$$2\frac{3}{4} = 2\frac{9}{12}$$
$$+ 1\frac{1}{3} = 1\frac{4}{12}$$
$$\overline{\phantom{+ 1\frac{1}{3} =}\; 3\frac{13}{12} \text{ or } 4\frac{1}{12}}$$

- Next, find $7\frac{2}{3} - 5\frac{4}{5}$. First elicit that the difference is almost 2 and the LCD is 15.

- Rename $7\frac{10}{15}$ since $\frac{12}{15}$ cannot be subtracted from $\frac{10}{15}$.
$$7\frac{10}{15} = 6\frac{15}{15} + \frac{10}{15} = 6\frac{25}{15}$$

- Subtract.

$$7\frac{2}{3} = 7\frac{10}{15} = 6\frac{25}{15}$$
$$- 5\frac{4}{5} = 5\frac{12}{15} = 5\frac{12}{15}$$
$$\overline{\phantom{- 5\frac{4}{5} = 5\frac{12}{15} =}\; 1\frac{13}{15}}$$

- Have students find sums and differences from the list in Number Sense. Have partners check their work.

Basic Skills Workshop 7

Multiplying Fractions

 Number Sense

20 minutes

Shade to Find Fraction Products

Management whole class or small group
Materials overhead projector, blank transparencies, markers

- Review the meaning of multiplication. For example, 4×1 means 4 groups of 1. Ask, About how much is $4 \times \frac{5}{6}$? **The product will be less than 4 because there are 4 groups and each group contains a bit less than one.**

- Discuss other examples, keeping the first factor a whole number. Discuss other ways of thinking about the product of two fractions, and of finding estimates.

Use these examples: $3 \times \frac{1}{2}$, $9 \times \frac{1}{12}$, and $6 \times 2\frac{4}{5}$.

- Model finding $7 \times \frac{3}{5}$. Draw 7 vertical rectangles. Point out that in order to find 7 groups with $\frac{3}{5}$ in each group, think of each rectangle divided into fifths.

- Divide the 7 vertical rectangles evenly into fifths by drawing horizontal lines. Shade $\frac{3}{5}$ of each of the 7 rectangles. Ask how many regions are shaded.

- Explain that the model depicts the product, $\frac{21}{5}$.

- Elicit from students how to simplify $\frac{21}{5}$. Have students explain how they simplified the product. **The numerator is divided by the denominator to get $4\frac{1}{5}$.**

 Skill Application

25 minutes

Teaching the Algorithm

Management whole class, then pairs
Materials Just the Facts Support Master 20

- Model multiplying a fraction by a fraction. Find $\frac{2}{3} \times \frac{6}{7}$.

Step 1. If possible, simplify first.

Divide both 3 and 6 by 3, the common factor.

$$\frac{2}{\underset{1}{3}} \times \frac{\overset{2}{6}}{7}$$

Step 2. Multiply the numerators and denominators.

$$\frac{2}{1} \times \frac{2}{7} = \frac{4}{7}$$

- Model multiplying mixed numbers. Find $1\frac{3}{4} \times 2\frac{2}{3}$.

Step 1. Rewrite the numbers as fractions.

$$1\frac{3}{4} \times 2\frac{2}{3} \ \rightarrow \ \frac{7}{4} \times \frac{8}{3}$$

Step 2. Simplify. Then, multiply.

Divide both 4 and 8 by 4, the common factor.

$$\frac{7}{\underset{1}{4}} \times \frac{\overset{2}{8}}{3} = \frac{14}{3}$$

Step 3. Simplify again if possible.

$$\frac{14}{3} = 4\frac{2}{3}$$

- Have student pairs write and solve 15 exercises: 5 whole numbers times a fraction, 5 fractions times a fraction, and 5 mixed numbers times a mixed number. They should draw fraction models for the first five exercises, and use estimation to check that their partners' answers are reasonable.

Basic Skills Workshop 8

Dividing Fractions

 Number Sense

15 minutes

Understanding Fraction Division

Management whole class or small group

- Provide a context in which to think about fraction division. First, use a fraction divided by a whole number. A bag of cherries weighs $1\frac{3}{4}$ lb. You want to give each of your 3 friends the same amount of cherries. How much should each get? Have students complete the sentence ___ ÷ ___ = ___. For this problem, have them explain how they arrived at each number. $\frac{7}{4} \div 3 = \frac{7}{12}$. **Each friend gets $\frac{7}{12}$ lb of cherries.**

- Now use a mixed number divided by a fraction. A camper makes $4\frac{1}{2}$ gallons of punch for a picnic. Water coolers hold $\frac{3}{4}$-gal of liquid. How many water coolers will she need? Elicit the division equation $4\frac{1}{2} \div \frac{3}{4}$. Use a number line to demonstrate the quotient. **6 $\frac{3}{4}$-gallon water coolers will hold $4\frac{1}{2}$ gallons of punch.**

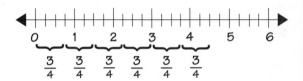

 Skill Application

25 minutes

Teaching the Algorithm

Management whole class, then pairs
Materials Just the Facts Support Master 20

- Model dividing a fraction divided by a fraction.

  Find $\frac{2}{3} \div \frac{1}{2}$.

  Step 1. Rewrite as a product using the reciprocal of the divisor. Explain the meaning of "reciprocal".

  $$\frac{2}{3} \times \frac{1}{2} = \frac{2}{3} \times \frac{2}{1}$$

  Step 2. Multiply. Simplify if possible.

  $$\frac{2}{3} \times \frac{2}{1} = \frac{4}{3} \text{ or } 1\frac{1}{3}$$

- Model dividing a mixed number by a whole number. Find $2\frac{5}{8} \div 3$.

  Step 1. Write the factors in fraction form.

  $$2\frac{5}{8} \div \frac{3}{1} = \frac{21}{8} \div \frac{3}{1}$$

  Step 2. Write as a product. Use the reciprocal of the divisor. Simplify if possible.

  $$\frac{21}{8} \div \frac{1}{3} = \frac{21}{8} \times \frac{1}{3} \rightarrow \frac{\overset{7}{\cancel{21}}}{8} \times \frac{1}{\underset{1}{\cancel{3}}}$$

  Step 3. Multiply.

  $$\frac{7}{8} \times \frac{1}{1} = \frac{7}{8}$$

- In pairs, have students write and solve 15 exercises: 5 fraction divided by a fraction, 5 whole number divided by a fraction, and 5 mixed number divided by a mixed number. Have students use estimation to check that answers are reasonable.

Basic Skills Workshop 9
Decimals: Comparing and Ordering

Number Sense

20 minutes

From Fractions to Decimals

Management whole class or small group
Materials overhead projector, hundredths square transparency (Just the Facts Support Master 7), teacher-made chart transparency

- Introduce a discussion of decimals by relating them to fractions. Students should be familiar with fractions now and can use this familiarity to help them with decimal number sense. In this activity, students use a base-ten model to translate familiar fractions to less familiar decimals.

- Model a base-ten fraction, such as $\frac{20}{100}$. Ask students which portion to shade to represent the fraction. Then shade the hundredths square on the transparency. Display next to it a three-column chart labeled Ones, Tenths, and Hundredths. Draw two tens rods in the appropriate column. Ask students how many hundredths equal two tenths. As they respond, write the decimal form, 0.20, on the transparency. Emphasize that decimals and fractions are two different ways to show the same information.

- Continue the modeling activity, eliciting from students other fractions with denominators of 10, 100, and 1000. If time permits, do a variation of the activity in which you elicit decimals from students and rewrite these as fractions.

Skill Application

30 minutes

Who Bought More?

Management whole class, then pairs
Materials newspapers, magazines, Just the Facts Support Master 20

- Provide students with a real-world example: Many gasoline pumps show the amount of gasoline dispensed to the nearest thousandth of a gallon. Who bought more gasoline, Shana who got 6.605 gal, or Lewis who got 6.655 gal?

Step 1. Line up the digits by place value. Keep the decimal points aligned.

  6.605
  6.655

Step 2. Compare digits. Begin with the digit in the greatest place on the left.

  6.605
  6.655

Step 3. If the digits in the greatest place are equal, compare digits in the next place to the right. Compare until you find a place with different digits.

  6.**6**05 ➔ 6.6**0**5
  6.**6**55 ➔ 6.6**5**5

Lewis bought more, 6.655 gal.

- Have students look for decimals on packaging and in newspaper and magazine advertisements. Student pairs should list 10 decimals that they find. Have them write number sentences using > and < to compare the decimals.

Basic Skills Workshop 10
Adding and Subtracting Decimals

Number Sense

20 minutes

About How Much?

Management whole class or small group

- Present students with the following situation: the class needs ten loaves of bread to make sandwiches for a field trip. They know that each loaf costs $1.90. How much money do they need to buy the ten loaves?

- Ask students if they need an exact answer or an estimate. Elicit that in such situations, it makes more sense to find an estimate. Then, ask students how they would estimate this answer. **$1.90 is close to $2; $2 times 10 is $20; the ten loaves will cost about $20.**

- Now write five different prices on the board and have students estimate their sum explaining how they made their estimates. As they do so, point out and discuss different strategies such as rounding to the nearest ten, rounding to the closest dollar, and grouping two or more numbers together.

- Do a similar exercise with a simple subtraction problem. For example, give students an item originally priced at $28.94 which is now on sale for $15.95. Ask them to estimate the difference. **Estimates and estimation strategies may vary. One way to estimate: $28.94 is close to $30.00; $15.95 is close to $16.00; $30.00 − $16.00 = $14.00.**

Skill Application

30 minutes

Finding Exact Sums

Management whole class, then pairs
Materials Just the Facts Support Master 20

- Model these addition and subtraction problems.

Addition	**Subtraction**
Find 12.5 + 8.95.	Find 12.5 − 8.95.
Step 1. Estimate.	**Step 1.** Estimate.
The sum should be about 13 + 9 or 22.	The difference should be about 13 − 9 or 4.
Step 2. Line up the digits by place value.	**Step 2.** Line up the digits by place value.

Write zeros in empty decimal places.

$$\begin{array}{r} 12.50 \\ +\ \ 8.95 \end{array} \leftarrow \boxed{\begin{array}{l} 12.5 = \\ 12.50 \end{array}}$$

Write zeros in empty decimal places.

$$\begin{array}{r} 12.50 \\ -\ \ 8.95 \end{array}$$

Step 3. Add. Regroup if necessary. Then, place the decimal point in the answer.

$$\begin{array}{r} 12.50 \\ +\ \ 8.95 \\ \hline 21.45 \end{array}$$

The answer is reasonable. It is close to the estimate of 22.

Step 3. Subtract. Regroup if necessary. Then, place the decimal point in the answer.

$$\begin{array}{r} 12.50 \\ -\ \ 8.95 \\ \hline 3.55 \end{array}$$

The answer is reasonable. It is close to the estimate of 4.

- Now, have students write ten pairs of decimal numbers and add them, checking the sums by using subtraction.

Basic Skills Workshop **11**

Multiplying Decimals

Number Sense

20 minutes

Estimating to Place Decimals

Management whole class or small group
Materials pencil and paper

- Discuss with students the strategy of using estimation to place the decimal point when multiplying decimals. To help illustrate this strategy, give students several examples of decimal multiplication problems using the same digits, but with the decimal point in a different place for each problem.

- For example, ask students where the decimal point belongs in each product.

2.89	28.9	289	2.89
× 4.3	× 4.3	× 4.3	× 0.43
12427	12427	12427	12427

- Have the students round each factor to the greatest digit to estimate the product. Then use the estimate to place the decimal point. Example: In the first problem 2.89 is close to 3, and 4.3 is close to 4, so $3 \times 4 = 12$. Since the product should be around 12, the decimal point should come after the first two digits.

- After placing the decimal point in the above examples, have students try these: 19.4×6.1, 19.4×0.61, and 19.4×0.061.

- Have students look at these examples and try to find a rule for placing the decimal point in a product.

Skill Application

30 minutes

Predicting and Computing Products

Management whole class, then pairs
Materials Just the Facts Support Master 20

- Review the estimation strategy with this problem: A serving of frozen yogurt is 0.35 cup. A cup is 0.25 quart. How many quarts is a serving of frozen yogurt?

Step 1. Estimate the product.

$0.25 \times 0.35 \rightarrow \frac{1}{4} \times \frac{1}{3} \approx \frac{1}{12}$

When both factors are less than 1, use benchmarks.

Step 2. Multiply as with whole numbers.

```
   0.25
 × 0.35
    125   ← 5 × 0.25
    75    ← 3 × 0.25
    875   ← final product
```

Step 3. Count decimal places to place the decimal point in the product.

```
   0.25   ← 2 decimal places
 × 0.35   ← 2 decimal places
    125
    75      Need to have 2 + 2 or
  .0875   ← 4 decimal places
```

A serving of frozen yogurt is 0.0875 qt. This answer is slightly less than $\frac{1}{10}$, so it is reasonable.

- Now have students write down ten similar problems. Have them exchange papers with their partners, who will estimate, and then multiply.

Basic Skills Workshop 12

Dividing Decimals

Number Sense

20 minutes

Quotient Estimation

Management whole class or small group

- Making estimates first can help students compute exact decimal quotients. Give students a real-world situation for estimating a quotient by dividing a decimal by a whole number. For example, 8 game club members will share the $42.80 cost for board games. How much will each member spend?

- Assist students in using compatible numbers to arrive at an estimate. Using this strategy, elicit that the actual cost can be rounded down to $40.00. Point out that $40.00 is compatible because it is close to

$42.80 and is evenly divided by 8.

- Have students arrive at a reasonable cost per person estimate. **$5.00**

- Now, give students an example of dividing a decimal by a decimal. Use 2.107 ÷ 7.3 as an example. Assist students in using rounding to find an estimate. 2.107 can be rounded down to 2; 7.3 can be rounded down to 7. $2 \div 7$ is less than $\frac{1}{2}$ and greater than $\frac{2}{10}$. Ask students to explain why each relationship is true. $\frac{2}{7} < \frac{1}{2}$ because $3\frac{1}{2}$ sevenths $= \frac{1}{2}$. **Since sevenths are greater than tenths, $\frac{2}{10} < \frac{2}{7}$.**

- Emphasize that using rounding in decimal division helps to understand the quotient. When students find exact quotients they will know how to find a close number based on their estimates.

Skill Application

30 minutes

Finding the Exact Quotient

Management whole class, then pairs
Materials Just the Facts Support Master 20

Step 1. Model 26.70 ÷ 5. First, estimate the quotient. Elicit that 25 is a compatible number evenly divided by 5. Assist students in finding that the estimated quotient of 26.70 ÷ 5 is 5. Use the estimate to place the decimal point in the actual quotient.

Step 2. Divide as you would with whole numbers. Divide the hundreds. Multiply and subtract.

Step 3. Next, divide the tens. Multiply and subtract.

Step 4. Finally, divide the ones. Use the estimate to place the decimal point in the actual quotient.

- Ask students to create and solve 10 division exercises with decimals in the dividend. Then have students check their partners' papers.

Basic Skills Workshop 13

Ratio and Percent

Number Sense

20 minutes

Expressing a Ratio

Management whole class or small group
Materials hundredths squares transparency (Just the Facts Support Master 19), crayons or markers

- Begin with this scenario: You have a notebook with 100 tiny stars. Out of 100 stars, 25 are purple. You can express this amount as a ratio and as a percent.

- You can write the ratio 25 to 100 in the form of a fraction.

$$\frac{\text{number of purple stars}}{\text{number of stars total}} = \frac{25}{100} \quad \frac{\text{first term}}{\text{second term}}$$

- A ratio can be written as a percent when the second term is 100.

$$\frac{25}{100} = 25\%$$

- It can also be written as a decimal.

$$\frac{25}{100} = .25 = 25\%$$

- Ask, Imagine that two corners of the 100-square paper are shaded. Elicit ratio, percent and decimal responses to this picture. **2% or $\frac{2}{100}$ or 0.02**

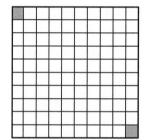

2% or $\frac{2}{100}$ or 0.02

Skill Application

20 minutes

Ratio by Color

Management pairs
Materials hundredths squares transparency (Just the Facts Support Master 19), crayons or markers, Just the Facts Support Master 20

Step 1. Ask each student to choose a color and shade parts of each of the nine hundredths squares on the master. Encourage them to create interesting patterns. Within each hundredth square, a different amount of squares should be shaded.

Step 2. Students will exchange their completed squares with partners. The partner will record beside

each square the ratio and percent that the square illustrates.

Step 3. Students will exchange their papers once again, receiving their drawings and checking their partners' answers. They can then write the fraction in simplest form, and a decimal that corresponds to the percent. Remind students that a percent can be written as a ratio whose second term is 100. When this ratio is expressed in fraction form, it may be simplified so that 50% is $\frac{1}{2}$ or 1 out of 2.

Step 4. Have students discuss with their partners any discrepancies in answers, and try to reach an agreement.

Name_____ Date _____

BASIC SKILLS

··

Adding and Subtracting 2- and 3-Digit Numbers

Estimate.

1. 32 + 79 = _____

2. 28 + 11 = _____

3. 43 + 121 = _____

4. 81 − 14 = _____

5. 76 + 223 = _____

6. 974 + 173 = _____

7. 87 + 12	**8.** 628 177 + 39	**9.** 490 − 71	**10.** 278 129 + 92	**11.** 485 − 199

Estimate to determine whether the sum or difference is reasonable. Write *yes* or *no*.

12. 92 + 36 128 _____	**13.** 504 − 175 329 _____	**14.** 55 98 + 34 287 _____	**15.** 216 − 109 207 _____

16. 872 − 325 447 _____	**17.** 527 175 + 69 671 _____	**18.** 617 + 68 685 _____	**19.** 892 − 264 628 _____

Find the sum or difference.

20. 62 + 13	**21.** 105 + 171	**22.** 86 − 42	**23.** 567 + 221	**24.** 543 − 420

Name_____ Date _____

BASIC SKILLS

Adding and Subtracting 2- and 3-Digit Numbers

Find the sum.

1. 37 $\underline{+\ 20}$	2. 790 $\underline{+\ 56}$	3. 47 $\underline{+\ 22}$	4. 650 $\underline{+\ 278}$	5. 184 $\underline{+\ 15}$
6. 325 $\underline{+\ 57}$	7. 344 $\underline{+\ 17}$	8. 776 $\underline{+\ 4}$	9. 399 $\underline{+\ 405}$	10. 64 $\underline{+\ 79}$
11. 591 $\underline{+\ 19}$	12. 834 418 $\underline{+\ 521}$	13. 487 $\underline{+\ 534}$	14. 29 $\underline{+\ 77}$	15. 531 154 $\underline{+\ 217}$

Find the difference.

16. 19 $\underline{-\ 13}$	17. 85 $\underline{-\ 24}$	18. 80 $\underline{-\ 9}$	19. 302 $\underline{-\ 101}$	20. 364 $\underline{-\ 140}$
21. 73 $\underline{-\ 49}$	22. 543 $\underline{-\ 17}$	23. 532 $\underline{-\ 74}$	24. 642 $\underline{-\ 82}$	25. 503 $\underline{-\ 86}$
26. 561 $\underline{-\ 43}$	27. 64 $\underline{-\ 58}$	28. 457 $\underline{-\ 19}$	29. 778 $\underline{-\ 409}$	30. 890 $\underline{-\ 229}$

Name_____ Date _____

2A | BASIC SKILLS

Multiplying 2- and 3-Digit Numbers

Find the product. Look for a pattern.

1. $45 \times 10 =$ _____   **2.** $45 \times 100 =$ _____   **3.** $45 \times 1000 =$ _____

4. $234 \times 20 =$ _____   **5.** $234 \times 200 =$ _____   **6.** $234 \times 2000 =$ _____

Estimate the product.

7. 37	**8.** 81	**9.** 721	**10.** 58	**11.** 289
$\times\ 2$	$\times\ 6$	$\times\ 9$	$\times 22$	$\times\ 4$

Is the product reasonable? Write *yes* or *no*.

12. 43	**13.** 500	**14.** 60	**15.** 200
$\times 20$	$\times\ 70$	$\times 70$	$\times\ 14$
960 _____	350 _____	350 _____	280 _____

Find the product.

16. $100 \times 219 =$ _____   **17.** $775 \times 10 =$ _____   **18.** $4100 \times 2 =$ _____

19. 76	**20.** 300	**21.** 47	**22.** 314	**23.** 190
$\times 10$	$\times\ 5$	$\times 200$	$\times 600$	$\times 100$

Name_____   Date _____

2B ◥ BASIC SKILLS

Multiplying 2- and 3-Digit Numbers

Find the product. Use mental math.

1. $10 \times 20 =$ _____

2. $50 \times 100 =$ _____

3. $41 \times 10 =$ _____

4. $100 \times 43 =$ _____

5. $6 \times 10 =$ _____

6. $200 \times 30 =$ _____

7. $39 \times 10 =$ _____

8. $100 \times 77 =$ _____

9. $400 \times 2 =$ _____

Estimate the product.

10. $22 \times 79 =$ _____

11. $15 \times 12 =$ _____

12. $27 \times 31 =$ _____

13. $\begin{array}{r} 32 \\ \times\ 12 \\ \hline \end{array}$

14. $\begin{array}{r} 49 \\ \times\ 27 \\ \hline \end{array}$

15. $\begin{array}{r} 662 \\ \times\ 11 \\ \hline \end{array}$

16. $\begin{array}{r} 61 \\ \times\ 57 \\ \hline \end{array}$

17. $\begin{array}{r} 544 \\ \times\ 8 \\ \hline \end{array}$

Find the product.

18. $\begin{array}{r} 10 \\ \times\ 91 \\ \hline \end{array}$

19. $\begin{array}{r} 200 \\ \times\ 4 \\ \hline \end{array}$

20. $\begin{array}{r} 32 \\ \times\ 100 \\ \hline \end{array}$

21. $\begin{array}{r} 701 \\ \times\ 10 \\ \hline \end{array}$

22. $\begin{array}{r} 543 \\ \times\ 100 \\ \hline \end{array}$

23. $\begin{array}{r} 62 \\ \times\ 7 \\ \hline \end{array}$

24. $\begin{array}{r} 104 \\ \times\ 9 \\ \hline \end{array}$

25. $\begin{array}{r} 80 \\ \times\ 33 \\ \hline \end{array}$

26. $\begin{array}{r} 31 \\ \times\ 62 \\ \hline \end{array}$

27. $\begin{array}{r} 17 \\ \times\ 19 \\ \hline \end{array}$

Name_____ Date _____

▶ BASIC SKILLS

3A

··

Dividing by 1-Digit Divisors

Estimate the quotient.

1. 29 ÷ 3 = _____   **2.** 37 ÷ 5 = _____   **3.** 178 ÷ 8 = _____

4. 161 ÷ 5 = _____   **5.** 430 ÷ 8 = _____   **6.** 770 ÷ 9 = _____

7. 89 ÷ 3 = _____   **8.** 276 ÷ 4 = _____   **9.** 111 ÷ 3 = _____

10. 6)174   **11.** 2)157   **12.** 7)190   **13.** 4)162   **14.** 8)243

15. 2)109   **16.** 4)354   **17.** 9)33   **18.** 5)391   **19.** 2)232

Is the estimated quotient reasonable? Write *yes* or *no*.

     20   72   60   70

20. 2)392 _____   **21.** 6)462 _____   **22.** 5)3233 _____   **23.** 4)372 _____

Find the quotient.

24. 8)912   **25.** 9)1642   **26.** 5)868   **27.** 3)545   **28.** 4)170

29. 7)665   **30.** 3)926   **31.** 5)1534   **32.** 9)7605   **33.** 7)802

Name_____ Date _____

3B BASIC SKILLS

Dividing by 1-Digit Divisors

Estimate the quotient.

1. $2\overline{)109}$ 2. $4\overline{)354}$ 3. $9\overline{)33}$ 4. $5\overline{)391}$ 5. $2\overline{)232}$

6. 29 ÷ 3 = _____   7. 37 ÷ 5 = _____   8. 178 ÷ 8 = _____

9. 161 ÷ 5 = _____   10. 430 ÷ 8 = _____   11. 770 ÷ 9 = _____

Match the problem with the correct quotient.

12. $8\overline{)310}$

| 53R6 |

13. $6\overline{)278}$

| 68R6 |

| 38R6 |

14. $9\overline{)419}$

| 59R2 |

15. $4\overline{)238}$

| 46R5 |

16. $7\overline{)482}$

| 46R2 |

17. $7\overline{)377}$

Find the quotient.

18. $4\overline{)821}$ 19. $3\overline{)504}$ 20. $4\overline{)648}$ 21. $8\overline{)289}$ 22. $3\overline{)807}$

23. $5\overline{)473}$ 24. $3\overline{)519}$ 25. $3\overline{)186}$ 26. $5\overline{)801}$ 27. $3\overline{)474}$

Name_____   Date _____

BASIC SKILLS

Dividing by 2-Digit Divisors

Find the quotient. Look for a pattern.

1. $10\overline{)90}$ **2.** $10\overline{)900}$ **3.** $10\overline{)9000}$ **4.** $10\overline{)90,000}$

5. $20\overline{)400}$ **6.** $20\overline{)4000}$ **7.** $70\overline{)1400}$ **8.** $70\overline{)14,000}$

Estimate the quotient.

9. $292 \div 10 =$ _____ **10.** $400 \div 22 =$ _____ **11.** $178 \div 41 =$ _____

12. $211 \div 35 =$ _____ **13.** $542 \div 81 =$ _____ **14.** $166 \div 62 =$ _____

Is the estimated quotient reasonable? Write *yes* or *no*.

15. $39\overline{)392}$ 10 _____   **16.** $63\overline{)3621}$ 60 _____   **17.** $15\overline{)2763}$ 45 _____

Find the quotient.

18. $32\overline{)294}$ **19.** $12\overline{)152}$ **20.** $24\overline{)215}$ **21.** $39\overline{)4305}$ **22.** $32\overline{)902}$

23. $18\overline{)151}$ **24.** $14\overline{)138}$ **25.** $23\overline{)193}$ **26.** $31\overline{)165}$ **27.** $26\overline{)215}$

Name_____ Date _____

4B ▸ BASIC SKILLS
···
Dividing by 2-Digit Divisors

Find the quotient. Look for a pattern.

1. 30)$\overline{120}$ **2.** 30)$\overline{1200}$ **3.** 10)$\overline{5000}$ **4.** 10)$\overline{50,000}$

Estimate the quotient.

5. 32)$\overline{251}$ **6.** 44)$\overline{133}$ **7.** 12)$\overline{50}$ **8.** 32)$\overline{233}$ **9.** 18)$\overline{137}$

10. 114 ÷ 18 = _____ **11.** 194 ÷ 24 = _____ **12.** 100 ÷ 12 = _____

Find the quotient.

13. 4998 ÷ 45 = _____ **14.** 8160 ÷ 31 = _____ **15.** 2067 ÷ 12 = _____

16. 17)$\overline{1956}$ **17.** 32)$\overline{6219}$ **18.** 50)$\overline{903}$ **19.** 29)$\overline{7165}$ **20.** 12)$\overline{3215}$

21. 19)$\overline{4259}$ **22.** 38)$\overline{9249}$ **23.** 64)$\overline{1299}$ **24.** 36)$\overline{408}$ **25.** 47)$\overline{4948}$

26. 67)$\overline{7658}$ **27.** 37)$\overline{7886}$ **28.** 31)$\overline{8160}$ **29.** 36)$\overline{10,350}$ **30.** 78)$\overline{1800}$

Name_____ Date _____

5A BASIC SKILLS

Fractions: GCF and Simplifying

Write the factors of 12: _____

Write the factors of 18: _____

The common factors of 12 and 18 are: _____

The GCF of 12 and 18 is _____

Complete the chart.

Numbers	Factors	Common Factors	Greatest Common Factor
1. 6 and 16			
2. 15 and 24			
3. 10 and 20			
4. 12 and 15			

Simplify the fraction.

5. $\frac{8}{12}$ = _____

6. $\frac{6}{18}$ = _____

7. $\frac{20}{30}$ = _____

8. $\frac{8}{24}$ = _____

9. $\frac{18}{24}$ = _____

10. $\frac{16}{20}$ = _____

11. $\frac{2}{6}$ = _____

12. $\frac{3}{12}$ = _____

13. $\frac{9}{27}$ = _____

14. $\frac{6}{18}$ = _____

15. $\frac{7}{21}$ = _____

16. $\frac{10}{20}$ = _____

Name_____ Date _____

5B ▸ BASIC SKILLS

Fractions: GCF and Simplifying

Complete the chart. Find the Greatest Common
Factor (GCF) of the two numbers.

Numbers		Factors	Common Factors	GCF
1. 15 and 9	15:			
	9:			
2. 9 and 6	9:			
	6:			
3. 8 and 4	8:			
	4:			
4. 6 and 12	6:			
	12:			

Write the greatest common factor.

5. 21 and 24 _____   **6.** 15 and 25 _____   **7.** 7 and 28 _____

8. 14 and 21 _____   **9.** 18 and 9 _____   **10.** 12 and 11 _____

11. 6 and 36 _____   **12.** 20 and 25 _____   **13.** 2 and 10 _____

Write in simplest form.

14. $\frac{3}{15} =$ ___   **15.** $\frac{2}{8} =$ ___   **16.** $\frac{6}{12} =$ ___   **17.** $\frac{14}{35} =$ ___

18. $\frac{20}{30} =$ ___   **19.** $\frac{8}{16} =$ ___   **20.** $\frac{2}{4} =$ ___   **21.** $\frac{3}{21} =$ ___

Name_____ Date _____

BASIC SKILLS

Adding and Subtracting Fractions

Find the sum or difference.

1. $\frac{1}{3} + \frac{1}{3} =$ ___

2. $\frac{2}{5} + \frac{1}{5} =$ ___

3. $\frac{6}{12} - \frac{5}{12} =$ ___

4. $\frac{6}{7} - \frac{4}{7} =$ ___

5. $\frac{8}{11} - \frac{1}{11} =$ ___

6. $\frac{4}{14} + \frac{5}{14} =$ ___

Find the sum or difference. Write in simplest form.

7.
$$\begin{array}{r} \frac{9}{10} \\ -\frac{7}{10} \\ \hline \end{array}$$

8.
$$\begin{array}{r} \frac{5}{9} \\ -\frac{2}{9} \\ \hline \end{array}$$

9.
$$\begin{array}{r} \frac{3}{8} \\ +\frac{3}{8} \\ \hline \end{array}$$

10.
$$\begin{array}{r} \frac{2}{3} \\ +\frac{2}{3} \\ \hline \end{array}$$

11.
$$\begin{array}{r} \frac{1}{3} \\ +\frac{1}{6} \\ \hline \end{array}$$

12.
$$\begin{array}{r} \frac{1}{4} \\ +\frac{3}{8} \\ \hline \end{array}$$

13.
$$\begin{array}{r} \frac{3}{4} \\ -\frac{1}{12} \\ \hline \end{array}$$

14.
$$\begin{array}{r} \frac{4}{5} \\ -\frac{1}{10} \\ \hline \end{array}$$

15.
$$\begin{array}{r} \frac{1}{9} \\ +\frac{1}{3} \\ \hline \end{array}$$

16.
$$\begin{array}{r} \frac{1}{10} \\ +\frac{2}{5} \\ \hline \end{array}$$

17.
$$\begin{array}{r} \frac{2}{3} \\ +\frac{1}{9} \\ \hline \end{array}$$

18.
$$\begin{array}{r} \frac{5}{8} \\ -\frac{1}{2} \\ \hline \end{array}$$

19.
$$\begin{array}{r} 3\frac{3}{6} \\ +1\frac{2}{3} \\ \hline \end{array}$$

20.
$$\begin{array}{r} 3\frac{7}{10} \\ +4\frac{4}{5} \\ \hline \end{array}$$

21.
$$\begin{array}{r} 4\frac{7}{8} \\ -2\frac{1}{2} \\ \hline \end{array}$$

22.
$$\begin{array}{r} 2\frac{5}{8} \\ +2\frac{3}{4} \\ \hline \end{array}$$

Name_____ Date _____

6B ▸ BASIC SKILLS

Adding and Subtracting Fractions

Find the sum or difference. Write in simplest form.

1. $\frac{13}{25}$
   $-\frac{1}{5}$

2. $\frac{5}{8}$
   $-\frac{1}{4}$

3. $\frac{4}{9}$
   $-\frac{1}{3}$

4. $\frac{11}{12}$
   $-\frac{3}{4}$

5. $3\frac{4}{7}$
   $-2\frac{1}{3}$

6. $5\frac{1}{3}$
   $+4\frac{3}{4}$

7. $7\frac{2}{3}$
   $+1\frac{4}{8}$

8. $4\frac{3}{5}$
   $+1\frac{2}{6}$

9. $9\frac{8}{10}$
   $-2\frac{2}{5}$

10. $\frac{1}{3}$
    $+\frac{3}{5}$

11. $18\frac{4}{6}$
    $-5\frac{1}{3}$

12. $9\frac{9}{10}$
    $-7\frac{1}{2}$

Rename before subtracting. Write the answer in simplest form.

13. $4\frac{1}{8}$
    $-2\frac{3}{8}$

14. $9\frac{2}{8}$
    $-2\frac{5}{8}$

15. $7\frac{3}{5}$
    $-1\frac{4}{5}$

16. $9\frac{2}{8}$
    $-2\frac{5}{8}$

17. $4\frac{2}{8}$
    $-1\frac{3}{5}$

18. $12\frac{1}{2}$
    $-6\frac{4}{5}$

19. $7\frac{2}{4}$
    $-3\frac{4}{6}$

20. $35\frac{1}{5}$
    $-31\frac{1}{2}$

Name_____ Date _____

BASIC SKILLS

Multiplying Fractions

Draw a model to find the product.

1. $2 \times \frac{3}{4}$

2. $8 \times \frac{3}{4}$

3. $10 \times \frac{5}{6}$

4. $3 \times \frac{4}{5}$

5. $6 \times \frac{3}{5}$

6. $5 \times \frac{2}{3}$

Write the product in simplest form.

7. $\frac{3}{7} \times \frac{4}{5} =$ _____

8. $\frac{3}{10} \times \frac{3}{10} =$ _____

9. $10 \times \frac{2}{5} =$ _____

10. $3 \times \frac{4}{5} =$ _____

11. $5 \times \frac{1}{3} =$ _____

12. $\frac{3}{5} \times \frac{2}{7} =$ _____

13. $1\frac{2}{3} \times 2\frac{1}{2} =$ _____

14. $\frac{3}{8} \times 1\frac{3}{4} =$ _____

15. $2\frac{3}{4} \times 3 =$ _____

16. $2\frac{3}{7} \times 2 =$ _____

17. $\frac{2}{9} \times \frac{5}{9} =$ _____

18. $\frac{1}{2} \times 6 =$ _____

19. $9 \times \frac{1}{6} =$ _____

20. $2\frac{1}{2} \times 3 =$ _____

21. $6\frac{1}{4} \times 10 =$ _____

22. $4\frac{1}{2} \times 1\frac{1}{4} =$ _____

23. $1\frac{2}{3} \times 1\frac{2}{5} =$ _____

24. $\frac{6}{7} \times 2\frac{1}{2} =$ _____

Name_____ Date _____

7B ◣ BASIC SKILLS

Multiplying Fractions

Write the product in simplest form.

1. $3 \times \frac{4}{5} =$ _____

2. $5 \times \frac{1}{3} =$ _____

3. $\frac{3}{5} \times \frac{2}{7} =$ _____

4. $\frac{2}{3} \times 8 =$ _____

5. $\frac{4}{9} \times \frac{3}{8} =$ _____

6. $3 \times \frac{2}{3} =$ _____

7. $\frac{7}{8} \times \frac{3}{4} =$ _____

8. $\frac{5}{6} \times \frac{5}{7} =$ _____

9. $\frac{3}{10} \times \frac{4}{5} =$ _____

10. $\frac{4}{5} \times \frac{4}{5} =$ _____

11. $\frac{4}{9} \times \frac{3}{8} =$ _____

12. $\frac{2}{9} \times \frac{2}{5} =$ _____

13. $\frac{3}{8} \times \frac{6}{7} =$ _____

14. $3 \times \frac{2}{7} =$ _____

15. $\frac{1}{4} \times 2 =$ _____

16. $6 \times \frac{1}{5} =$ _____

17. $\frac{5}{12} \times \frac{3}{4} =$ _____

18. $\frac{5}{7} \times \frac{5}{6} =$ _____

19. $\frac{3}{4} \times \frac{7}{10} =$ _____

20. $\frac{3}{7} \times \frac{3}{7} =$ _____

21. $\frac{5}{6} \times \frac{3}{10} =$ _____

22. $3\frac{1}{5} \times 2 =$ _____

23. $5 \times 2\frac{1}{4} =$ _____

24. $2 \times 4\frac{1}{3} =$ _____

25. $2\frac{1}{5} \times 4 =$ _____

26. $1\frac{1}{9} \times 6 =$ _____

27. $6 \times 1\frac{3}{7} =$ _____

28. $\frac{3}{5} \times 2\frac{3}{4} =$ _____

29. $3\frac{1}{3} \times 1\frac{1}{4} =$ _____

30. $\frac{6}{7} \times 2\frac{1}{2} =$ _____

Name_____ Date _____

8A ◣ BASIC SKILLS

Dividing Fractions

1. How many fifths are in four?

$4 \div \frac{1}{5} =$ _____

Draw a model to find the quotient.

2. $5 \div \frac{1}{6}$

3. $3 \div \frac{1}{8}$

4. $5 \div \frac{1}{5}$

5. $2 \div \frac{1}{3}$

6. $4 \div \frac{1}{5}$

7. $4 \div \frac{1}{6}$

Write the quotient in simplest form.

8. $2 \div \frac{1}{6} =$ _____

9. $4 \div \frac{1}{2} =$ _____

10. $3 \div \frac{1}{6} =$ _____

11. $6 \div \frac{1}{4} =$ _____

12. $2 \div \frac{1}{2} =$ _____

13. $4 \div \frac{1}{5} =$ _____

14. $5 \div \frac{1}{2} =$ _____

15. $3 \div \frac{1}{3} =$ _____

16. $2 \div \frac{1}{6} =$ _____

17. $12 \div \frac{1}{3} =$ _____

18. $16 \div \frac{1}{3} =$ _____

19. $8 \div \frac{1}{4} =$ _____

Name_____ Date _____

8B ▸ BASIC SKILLS
....
Dividing Fractions

Write the quotient in simplest form.

1. $3 \div \frac{1}{3} =$ _____

2. $2 \div \frac{1}{2} =$ _____

3. $15 \div \frac{1}{5} =$ _____

4. $7 \div \frac{1}{3} =$ _____

5. $30 \div \frac{1}{2} =$ _____

6. $14 \div \frac{2}{3} =$ _____

7. $12 \div \frac{1}{3} =$ _____

8. $16 \div \frac{1}{3} =$ _____

9. $8 \div \frac{1}{4} =$ _____

10. $8 \div \frac{7}{10} =$ _____

11. $6 \div \frac{2}{9} =$ _____

12. $9 \div \frac{5}{6} =$ _____

13. $\frac{1}{2} \div \frac{2}{5} =$ _____

14. $\frac{1}{3} \div \frac{1}{3} =$ _____

15. $\frac{2}{5} \div \frac{1}{2} =$ _____

16. $\frac{4}{9} \div \frac{1}{3} =$ _____

17. $\frac{2}{7} \div \frac{1}{14} =$ _____

18. $\frac{3}{8} \div \frac{2}{5} =$ _____

19. $\frac{1}{2} \div \frac{4}{9} =$ _____

20. $\frac{8}{15} \div \frac{4}{5} =$ _____

21. $\frac{3}{11} \div \frac{1}{22} =$ _____

22. $7\frac{3}{5} \div 5 =$ _____

23. $2\frac{1}{2} \div 10 =$ _____

24. $4\frac{2}{3} \div 3 =$ _____

25. $6\frac{2}{3} \div \frac{5}{6} =$ _____

26. $3\frac{1}{4} \div \frac{1}{2} =$ _____

27. $5 \div 5\frac{2}{3} =$ _____

28. $6\frac{1}{8} \div 5\frac{1}{2} =$ _____

29. $5\frac{2}{3} \div 3\frac{5}{9} =$ _____

30. $10\frac{1}{4} \div 2\frac{1}{3} =$ _____

Name_____ Date _____

9A ◤ BASIC SKILLS:

Decimals: Comparing and Ordering

Write the decimal as a fraction. Then rewrite in simplest form.

1. 0.02 _____   **2.** 0.10 _____   **3.** 0.20 _____

4. 0.50 _____   **5.** 0.41 _____   **6.** 0.355 _____

Compare. Write >, <, or =.

7. 5.2 ◯ 4.6   **8.** 72.9 ◯ 72.1   **9.** 1.5 ◯ 1.511

10. 4.09 ◯ 4.1   **11.** 0.6 ◯ 0.65   **12.** 3.2 ◯ 3.09

13. 0.8 ◯ 0.78   **14.** 8.19 ◯ 8.912   **15.** 1.1 ◯ 1.10

16. 0.324 ◯ 0.21   **17.** 12.3 ◯ 12.29   **18.** 2.7 ◯ 2.71

19. 0.87 ◯ 0.08   **20.** 1.43 ◯ 1.5   **21.** 5.2 ◯ 5.09

22. 5.06 ◯ 5.60   **23.** 1.12 ◯ 2.12   **24.** 4.2 ◯ 2.361

25. 36.02 ◯ 63.01   **26.** 8.02 ◯ 0.81   **27.** 51.0 ◯ 1.50

28. 3.35 ◯ 3.453   **29.** 0.31 ◯ 3.01   **30.** 4.17 ◯ 7.04

31. 66.7 ◯ 66.29   **32.** 9.06 ◯ 9.6   **33.** 3.03 ◯ 0.303

34. 14.40 ◯ 14.4   **35.** 5.12 ◯ 5.01   **36.** 0.07 ◯ 0.70

Name_____ Date _____

9B ▶ BASIC SKILLS:

Decimals: Comparing and Ordering

Compare. Write >, <, or =.

1. 3.03 ◯ 0.30

2. 7.08 ◯ 0.87

3. 1.11 ◯ 1.10

4. 2.97 ◯ 29.7

5. 14.14 ◯ 4.14

6. 9.8 ◯ 98.1

7. 19.83 ◯ 198.3

8. 52.20 ◯ 52.02

9. 8.06 ◯ 8.060

10. 38.83 ◯ 83.38

11. 5.55 ◯ 5.50

12. 7.9 ◯ 9.72

13. 5.12 ◯ 2.98

14. 32.95 ◯ 3.295

15. 0.063 ◯ 0.603

16. 91 ◯ 19.91

17. 0.4 ◯ 0.40

18. 8.872 ◯ 8.827

Order from least to greatest.

19. 0.77, 1.70, 0.70, 7.07 _____

20. 0.8, 1.08, 0.81, 0.081 _____

21. 3.5, 0.35, 30.5, 0.035 _____

22. 2.05, 1.15, 0.5, 0.55 _____

23. 14.06, 0.36, 6.86, 0.8 _____

24. 39.5, 9.5, 3.09, 5.93 _____

25. 3.20, 4.32, 2.04, 3.22 _____

Name_____ Date _____

BASIC SKILLS

Adding and Subtracting Decimals

Estimate the sum or difference.

1. $3.2 + 4.3 =$ _____   **2.** $9.1 - 1.9 =$ _____   **3.** $16.3 + 2.8 =$ _____

4.	**5.**	**6.**	**7.**
6.2	15.08	0.78	2.18
+ 4.9	+ 5.70	+ 66.51	+ 62.62

Estimate to determine whether the sum or difference is reasonable. Write *yes* or *no*.

8.	**9.**	**10.**
7.5	14.9	13.8
+ 9.0	− 10.2	− 8.1
25.5 _____	14.7 _____	0.7 _____

11.	**12.**	**13.**
8.62	14.8	239.9
− 7.24	+ 6.3	− 103.5
1.08 _____	20.1 _____	10.4 _____

Find the sum or difference. Estimate to check that your answer is reasonable.

14.	**15.**	**16.**	**17.**	**18.**
7.3	6.5	0.8	5.39	4.32
+ 0.2	+ 1.65	+ 0.4	− 2.30	− 1.97

19.	**20.**	**21.**	**22.**	**23.**
5.8	7.8	14.01	0.535	15
− 1.92	− 3.91	+ 0.35	+ 2.16	+ 2.45

Name _____ Date _____

◤10B◢ BASIC SKILLS

Adding and Subtracting Decimals

Estimate. Then find the sum.

1.	0.5	2.	8.5	3.	4.34	4.	3.95	5.	12.45
	+ 0.3		+ 0.31		+ 2.8		+ 0.21		+ 2.16

6.	0.312	7.	35.6	8.	4.34	9.	14.34	10.	3.95
	+ 0.82		+ 2.45		+ 2.8		+ 2.05		+ 0.246

11. $0.31 + 36.513 =$ _____   **12.** $5.16 + 2.043 =$ _____   **13.** $5 + 0.6 + 1.89 =$ _____

14. $98 + 8.01 + 0.62 =$ _____   **15.** $0.5 + 15.05 =$ _____   **16.** $3 + 0.2 =$ _____

Estimate. Then find the difference.

17.	5.4	18.	76.8	19.	16	20.	86.12
	− 1.3		− 21.9		− 9.32		− 5.984

21.	95	22.	86.3	23.	7	24.	5
	− 10.2		− 5.921		− 1.9		− 2.8

25. $5.6 − 1.92 =$ _____   **26.** $7.321 − 5 =$ _____   **27.** $5.38 − 0.9 =$ _____

28. $86 − 4.93 =$ _____   **29.** $76.8 − 21.49 =$ _____   **30.** $7.02 − 3.199 =$ _____

Name_____ Date _____

BASIC SKILLS

Multiplying Decimals

Use an estimate to write the decimal point in the product.

1. 6.27	**2.** 5.8	**3.** 27.8	**4.** 432.3
× 4.9	× 3.7	× 3.81	× 7.6
30723	2146	105918	328548

Estimate the product.

5. 5.72	**6.** 1.5	**7.** 16.2	**8.** 20.8
× 3.8	× 8.6	× 9.2	× 6.2

9. 25.9	**10.** 87.2	**11.** 14.9	**12.** 97.2
× 4.7	× 8.3	× 6.7	× 6.8

13. 36.6	**14.** 79.2	**15.** 69.8	**16.** 29.7
× 1.2	× 2.5	× 2.4	× 6.3

17. 8.91	**18.** 6.5	**19.** 37.0	**20.** 97.3
× 3.1	× 4.9	× 9	× 4.2

21. $26.6 \times 1.3 =$ _____   **22.** $0.79 \times 80.7 =$ _____

23. $0.66 \times 0.4 =$ _____   **24.** $27.3 \times 0.09 =$ _____

Name_____ Date _____

◢11B BASIC SKILLS
....
Multiplying Decimals

Write the factors as fractions. Then multiply the fractions. Rewrite the product as a decimal.

1. 0.2×0.4

$$\frac{}{10} \times \frac{}{10} = \frac{8}{100} = 0.08$$

2. 0.31×0.7

_____ × _____ = _____ = _____

3. 0.27×0.05

_____ × _____ = _____ = _____

4.	8.6	**5.**	0.7	**6.**	3.4	**7.**	5.8	**8.**	1.9
	$\times\,6.2$		$\times\,.002$		$\times\,5.8$		$\times\,2.9$		$\times\,7.3$

9.	.17	**10.**	7.15	**11.**	69.2	**12.**	80.3	**13.**	7.0
	$\times\,.005$		$\times\,\;3.8$		$\times\,\;4.3$		$\times\,\;9.1$		$\times\,5.9$

Estimate. Then find the product.

14. $2.9 \times .003 =$ _____   **15.** $8.6 \times 9.8 =$ _____

16. $9.2 \times 1.6 =$ _____   **17.** $6.1 \times 2.4 =$ _____

Name_____ Date _____

12A BASIC SKILLS

Dividing Decimals

Use compatible numbers to estimate the quotient.

1. $8\overline{)58.3}$ **2.** $5\overline{)2.04}$ **3.** $7\overline{)50.34}$ **4.** $6\overline{)7.35}$

5. $12\overline{).492}$ **6.** $4\overline{)1.73}$ **7.** $4\overline{)1.283}$ **8.** $31\overline{)62.9}$

Find the quotient.

9. $6\overline{)19.44}$ **10.** $5\overline{)21.8}$ **11.** $3\overline{)12.45}$ **12.** $4\overline{)94.4}$

13. $5\overline{)31.9}$ **14.** $7\overline{)25.06}$ **15.** $8\overline{).096}$ **16.** $5\overline{)39.3}$

17. $5\overline{)26.5}$ **18.** $2\overline{)4.298}$ **19.** $3\overline{)1.023}$ **20.** $9\overline{)19.89}$

21. $16.5 \div 10 =$ _____ **22.** $3.294 \div 1000 =$ _____ **23.** $29.85 \div 100 =$ _____

24. $73.4 \div 10 =$ _____ **25.** $0.43 \div 10 =$ _____ **26.** $27.14 \div 10 =$ _____

Name_____ Date _____

12B ▶ BASIC SKILLS

··

Dividing Decimals

Find the quotient.

1. $5\overline{)71.7}$ **2.** $2\overline{)9.15}$ **3.** $4\overline{)1.4}$ **4.** $6\overline{)3.3}$

5. $8\overline{)83.6}$ **6.** $5\overline{)13.7}$ **7.** $2\overline{)7.9}$ **8.** $6\overline{)5.82}$

9. $9\overline{)20.25}$ **10.** $11\overline{)3.41}$ **11.** $15\overline{)71.25}$ **12.** $32\overline{)81.6}$

Find the quotient. Remember to place the dollar sign in your answer.

13. $6\overline{)\$.42}$ **14.** $5\overline{)\$.65}$ **15.** $9\overline{)\$7.02}$ **16.** $4\overline{)\$2.56}$

17. $12\overline{)\$24.12}$ **18.** $9\overline{)\$123.30}$ **19.** $3\overline{)\$45.06}$ **20.** $7\overline{)\$620.20}$

21. $38\overline{)\$22.42}$ **22.** $5\overline{)\$62.15}$ **23.** $4\overline{)\$34.56}$ **24.** $25\overline{)\$23.75}$

Name_____ Date _____

13A ◢ BASIC SKILLS

Ratio and Percent

Model the percent by shading the number of squares.

1. 30%

2. 3%

3. 46%

4. 9%

5. 90%

6. 19%

Write as a percent.

7. $\frac{55}{100}$

8. $\frac{4}{100}$

9. $\frac{98}{100}$

10. $\frac{29}{100}$

_____

11. $\frac{5}{100}$

12. $\frac{35}{100}$

13. $\frac{10}{100}$

14. $\frac{84}{100}$

_____

Write as a percent.

15. 0.12

16. 0.8

17. 0.96

18. 0.42

_____

19. 0.77

20. 0.21

21. 0.51

22. 0.1

_____

Name_____ Date _____

13B ◢ BASIC SKILLS

Ratio and Percent

Write the decimal or fraction as a percent.

1. $\frac{3}{4}$

2. $\frac{35}{100}$

3. $\frac{15}{25}$

4. 0.06

_____ _____ _____ _____

5. 0.58

6. 0.8

7. $\frac{20}{50}$

8. 0.10

_____ _____ _____ _____

Write as a decimal.

9. 4%

10. 82%

11. 21%

12. 45%

_____ _____ _____ _____

13. 56%

14. 1%

15. 83%

16. 6%

_____ _____ _____ _____

Write as a fraction in simplest form.

17. 30%

18. 18%

19. 25%

20. 2%

_____ _____ _____ _____

21. 70%

22. 17%

23. 42%

24. 31%

_____ _____ _____ _____

Name_____ Date _____

BASIC FACTS: ADDITION

Find the sum. Use strategies to help you.

1.	4	2.	2	3.	0	4.	6	5.	8	6.	1
	+ 5		+ 4		+ 7		+ 1		+ 2		+ 4

7.	5	8.	8	9.	6	10.	9	11.	7	12.	5
	+ 4		+ 9		+ 5		+ 2		+ 8		+ 3

13.	9	14.	1	15.	3	16.	6	17.	5	18.	6
	+ 9		+ 0		+ 5		+ 4		+ 9		+ 7

19.	1	20.	8	21.	1	22.	3	23.	8	24.	6
	+ 9		+ 4		+ 5		+ 3		+ 8		+ 2

25.	5	26.	3	27.	3	28.	5	29.	7	30.	2
	+ 7		+ 7		+ 9		+ 8		+ 5		+ 8

I need more practice with these facts:

Name_____ Date _____

BASIC FACTS: ADDITION

Find the sum. Use strategies to help you.

1. 0 + 4	**2.** 9 + 6	**3.** 7 + 3	**4.** 4 + 5	**5.** 1 + 8	**6.** 3 + 6
7. 5 + 0	**8.** 2 + 1	**9.** 9 + 8	**10.** 7 + 6	**11.** 7 + 4	**12.** 4 + 9
13. 4 + 1	**14.** 8 + 5	**15.** 5 + 6	**16.** 4 + 7	**17.** 1 + 3	**18.** 7 + 9
19. 3 + 4	**20.** 2 + 2	**21.** 8 + 7	**22.** 9 + 3	**23.** 9 + 2	**24.** 7 + 0
25. 1 + 1	**26.** 6 + 8	**27.** 5 + 2	**28.** 0 + 6	**29.** 3 + 2	**30.** 0 + 0

I need more practice with these facts:

Name_____ Date _____

BASIC FACTS: ADDITION

Find the sum. Use strategies to help you.

1. 4
 + 3

2. 6
 + 1

3. 8
 + 9

4. 2
 + 5

5. 2
 + 0

6. 2
 + 7

7. 0
 + 3

8. 7
 + 2

9. 5
 + 5

10. 9
 + 4

11. 8
 + 0

12. 3
 + 1

13. 6
 + 6

14. 2
 + 3

15. 8
 + 3

16. 4
 + 2

17. 6
 + 9

18. 0
 + 5

19. 4
 + 8

20. 4
 + 6

21. 2
 + 9

22. 0
 + 1

23. 9
 + 1

24. 1
 + 2

25. 5
 + 1

26. 9
 + 5

27. 7
 + 7

28. 4
 + 0

29. 9
 + 7

30. 8
 + 1

I need more practice with these facts:

Name_____ Date _____

BASIC FACTS: SUBTRACTION

Find the difference. Use strategies to help you.

1. 9 − 3	**2.** 16 − 8	**3.** 3 − 1	**4.** 7 − 6	**5.** 12 − 5	**6.** 14 − 9
7. 8 − 5	**8.** 4 − 0	**9.** 10 − 7	**10.** 11 − 2	**11.** 6 − 3	**12.** 1 − 1
13. 7 − 1	**14.** 8 − 8	**15.** 9 − 4	**16.** 5 − 5	**17.** 16 − 7	**18.** 10 − 6
19. 11 − 2	**20.** 9 − 2	**21.** 14 − 5	**22.** 13 − 6	**23.** 7 − 2	**24.** 1 − 0
25. 9 − 8	**26.** 5 − 4	**27.** 18 − 9	**28.** 12 − 8	**29.** 6 − 2	**30.** 15 − 8

I need more practice with these facts:

Name_____ Date _____

BASIC FACTS: SUBTRACTION

Find the difference. Use strategies to help you.

1. 5 − 1	**2.** 3 − 3	**3.** 9 − 0	**4.** 15 − 7	**5.** 11 − 3	**6.** 8 − 2
7. 9 − 7	**8.** 3 − 2	**9.** 14 − 8	**10.** 2 − 1	**11.** 6 − 4	**12.** 7 − 7
13. 10 − 5	**14.** 13 − 5	**15.** 8 − 0	**16.** 13 − 4	**17.** 8 − 4	**18.** 17 − 8
19. 2 − 0	**20.** 11 − 4	**21.** 16 − 9	**22.** 10 − 2	**23.** 7 − 3	**24.** 2 − 1
25. 9 − 9	**26.** 5 − 3	**27.** 12 − 7	**28.** 7 − 5	**29.** 12 − 6	**30.** 15 − 6

I need more practice with these facts:

Name_____ Date _____

BASIC FACTS: SUBTRACTION

Find the difference. Use strategies to help you.

1. 7 − 0	**2.** 4 − 3	**3.** 13 − 8	**4.** 17 − 9	**5.** 4 − 4	**6.** 11 − 7
7. 8 − 3	**8.** 14 − 6	**9.** 10 − 1	**10.** 0 − 0	**11.** 13 − 7	**12.** 9 − 5
13. 6 − 1	**14.** 11 − 5	**15.** 4 − 1	**16.** 10 − 9	**17.** 12 − 4	**18.** 3 − 0
19. 7 − 4	**20.** 12 − 9	**21.** 6 − 5	**22.** 8 − 1	**23.** 14 − 7	**24.** 10 − 4
25. 5 − 0	**26.** 12 − 3	**27.** 8 − 6	**28.** 4 − 2	**29.** 15 − 9	**30.** 8 − 7

I need more practice with these facts:

Name_____ Date _____

BASIC FACTS: MULTIPLICATION

Find the product. Use strategies to help you.

1. 2 × 5	**2.** 4 × 1	**3.** 8 × 7	**4.** 2 × 0	**5.** 4 × 3	**6.** 6 × 3
7. 6 × 9	**8.** 6 × 6	**9.** 0 × 6	**10.** 2 × 7	**11.** 6 × 8	**12.** 6 × 5
13. 5 × 7	**14.** 3 × 5	**15.** 4 × 7	**16.** 2 × 9	**17.** 2 × 8	**18.** 3 × 3
19. 6 × 2	**20.** 0 × 4	**21.** 7 × 9	**22.** 7 × 5	**23.** 3 × 4	**24.** 7 × 6
25. 3 × 7	**26.** 4 × 6	**27.** 8 × 5	**28.** 4 × 8	**29.** 9 × 1	**30.** 9 × 5

I need more practice with these facts:

Name_____ Date _____

BASIC FACTS: MULTIPLICATION

Find the product. Use strategies to help you.

1. 0 × 8	2. 9 × 7	3. 5 × 5	4. 3 × 6	5. 2 × 1	6. 8 × 3
7. 4 × 3	8. 7 × 0	9. 1 × 7	10. 6 × 1	11. 8 × 8	12. 5 × 9
13. 9 × 2	14. 9 × 3	15. 1 × 9	16. 2 × 3	17. 0 × 0	18. 4 × 1
19. 7 × 7	20. 5 × 4	21. 5 × 1	22. 7 × 3	23. 9 × 6	24. 3 × 0
25. 3 × 6	26. 3 × 1	27. 6 × 7	28. 9 × 8	29. 2 × 6	30. 9 × 4

I need more practice with these facts:

Name_____ Date _____

BASIC FACTS: MULTIPLICATION

Find the product. Use strategies to help you.

1. 1 $\times$ 1	**2.** 7 $\times$ 8	**3.** 4 $\times$ 5	**4.** 9 $\times$ 2	**5.** 0 $\times$ 7	**6.** 2 $\times$ 4
7. 8 $\times$ 9	**8.** 8 $\times$ 1	**9.** 1 $\times$ 6	**10.** 5 $\times$ 2	**11.** 7 $\times$ 4	**12.** 9 $\times$ 0
13. 5 $\times$ 6	**14.** 7 $\times$ 3	**15.** 8 $\times$ 6	**16.** 3 $\times$ 4	**17.** 5 $\times$ 8	**18.** 8 $\times$ 4
19. 9 $\times$ 9	**20.** 0 $\times$ 1	**21.** 4 $\times$ 4	**22.** 0 $\times$ 5	**23.** 3 $\times$ 8	**24.** 6 $\times$ 2
25. 2 $\times$ 2	**26.** 5 $\times$ 3	**27.** 8 $\times$ 0	**28.** 3 $\times$ 9	**29.** 9 $\times$ 6	**30.** 4 $\times$ 9

I need more practice with these facts:

Name_____ Date _____

BASIC FACTS: DIVISION

Find the quotient. Use strategies to help you.

1. 1)6 **2.** 7)28 **3.** 4)12 **4.** 5)45 **5.** 3)0 **6.** 6)36

7. 3)27 **8.** 2)10 **9.** 8)8 **10.** 9)63 **11.** 3)21 **12.** 6)12

13. 5)25 **14.** 7)56 **15.** 2)2 **16.** 4)36 **17.** 5)15 **18.** 1)3

19. 5)35 **20.** 3)9 **21.** 1)9 **22.** 2)4 **23.** 6)0 **24.** 8)48

25. 9)27 **26.** 4)24 **27.** 2)14 **28.** 6)24 **29.** 4)20 **30.** 2)18

I need more practice with these facts:

Name_____ Date _____

BASIC FACTS: DIVISION

Find the quotient. Use strategies to help you.

1. $6\overline{)42}$ **2.** $4\overline{)32}$ **3.** $5\overline{)0}$ **4.** $1\overline{)2}$ **5.** $3\overline{)15}$ **6.** $8\overline{)64}$

7. $3\overline{)3}$ **8.** $6\overline{)18}$ **9.** $7\overline{)49}$ **10.** $3\overline{)6}$ **11.** $1\overline{)5}$ **12.** $8\overline{)40}$

13. $9\overline{)72}$ **14.** $5\overline{)30}$ **15.** $9\overline{)0}$ **16.** $4\overline{)16}$ **17.** $5\overline{)10}$ **18.** $7\overline{)21}$

19. $3\overline{)18}$ **20.** $6\overline{)6}$ **21.** $6\overline{)54}$ **22.** $2\overline{)16}$ **23.** $9\overline{)45}$ **24.** $7\overline{)14}$

25. $5\overline{)20}$ **26.** $1\overline{)0}$ **27.** $6\overline{)48}$ **28.** $4\overline{)28}$ **29.** $5\overline{)5}$ **30.** $7\overline{)35}$

I need more practice with these facts:

Name_____ Date _____

BASIC FACTS: DIVISION

Find the quotient. Use strategies to help you.

1. $1\overline{)4}$ **2.** $7\overline{)42}$ **3.** $8\overline{)24}$ **4.** $7\overline{)7}$ **5.** $2\overline{)12}$ **6.** $8\overline{)32}$

7. $6\overline{)30}$ **8.** $4\overline{)8}$ **9.** $2\overline{)0}$ **10.** $5\overline{)40}$ **11.** $7\overline{)0}$ **12.** $3\overline{)24}$

13. $1\overline{)7}$ **14.** $8\overline{)72}$ **15.** $2\overline{)16}$ **16.** $9\overline{)9}$ **17.** $9\overline{)54}$ **18.** $2\overline{)6}$

19. $7\overline{)63}$ **20.** $4\overline{)0}$ **21.** $9\overline{)81}$ **22.** $1\overline{)1}$ **23.** $9\overline{)36}$ **24.** $8\overline{)0}$

25. $5\overline{)45}$ **26.** $3\overline{)12}$ **27.** $9\overline{)18}$ **28.** $2\overline{)8}$ **29.** $8\overline{)56}$ **30.** $4\overline{)4}$

I need more practice with these facts:

Answers

Level 1 Worksheet 1A: 2. 4 3. 8 4. 10 5. 6 6. 7 7. 3
8. 5 Worksheet 1B: Drawings will vary. 2. 6 dots 3. 7
dots 4. 9 dots 5. 4 dots 6. 5 dots 7. 2 dots 8. 3 dots
Worksheet 2A: 2. 7 3. 9 4. 5 5. 10 6. 4 7. 6 8. 8
Worksheet 2B: 2. 4 3. 7 4. 8 5. 5 6. 9 7. 6 8. 3
Worksheet 3A: Drawings will vary. Possible answers
include: 5 + 2; 1 + 6; 7 + 0. Worksheet 3B: 2. 2 + 2
= 4 3. 3 + 2 = 5 4. 3 + 0 = 3 Worksheet 4A: 2. 9; 5 +
4 = 9 3. 9; 7 + 2 = 9 4. 9; 6 + 3 = 9 Worksheet 4B: 2.
6 + 4 = 10 3. 10 + 0 = 10 4. 7 + 3 = 10 Worksheet
5A: Drawings will vary. 2. 7 dots; 7 3. 9 dots; 9 4. 6
dots; 6 5. 4 dots; 4 6. 8 dots; 8 Worksheet 5B: 2.5 3. 0
4. 1 5. 0 6. 9 7. 0 8. 7 9. 4 10. 7 11. 0 12. 0 13. 3 14. 0
15. 8 16. 0 17. 0 18. 0 19. 9 20. 1 21. 2 Worksheet 6A:
2. 17 3. 11 4. 13 Worksheet 6B: 2. 10 + 2 = 12 3. 10
+ 6 = 16 4. 10 + 8 = 18 Worksheet 7A: 2. 5 + 3 = 8
3. 2 + 4 = 6 4. 4 + 2 = 6 5. 6 + 3 = 9 6. 3 + 6 = 9
Worksheet 7B: 2. 5,5 3. 6,6 4. 5,5 5. 9,9 6. 6,6 7. 7,7
8. 10,10 9. 8,8 10. 8,8 11. 7,7 12. 9,9 Worksheet 8A:
2. 8 3. 7 4. 2 5. 8 6. 9 7. 11 8. 6 9. 5 10. 4 11. 9 12. 10
13. 4 14. 7 15. 6 16. 10 17. 7 18. 8 19. 3 20. 9
Worksheet 8B: 2. 8 3. 11 4. 9 5. 7 6. 10 7. 8 8. 9 9. 11
10. 4 11. 10 12. 9 13. 12 14. 9 15. 7 16. 6 17. 8 18. 8
19. 10 20. 5 21. 6 Worksheet 9A: 2. 3 3. 7 4. 4 5. 7 6.
2 7. 9 8. 4 9. 2 10. 5 11. 6 12. 3 13. 1 14. 9 15. 1 16. 5
17. 2 18. 6 19. 7 20. 1 Worksheet 9B: 2. 6 3. 4 4. 3 5.
4 6. 7 7. 8 8. 5 9. 5 10. 3 11. 7 12. 4 13. 6 14. 2 15. 2
16. 1 17. 5 18. 6 19. 4 20. 3 21. 5 22. 2 23. 2
Worksheet 10A: 2. 1 3. 1 4. 1 5. 3 6. 2 7. 1 8. 2 9. 2
10. 2 11. 3 12. 1 13. 1 14. 3 15. 2 16. 2 17. 1 18. 2 19.
1 20. 3 Worksheet 10B: 2. 5 3. 1 4. 3 5. 4 6. 1 7. 5 8. 3
9. 7 10. 3 11. 2 12. 1 13. 2 14. 1 15. 2 16. 3 17. 1 18. 2
19. 2 20. 3 21. 4 Worksheet 11A: 2. 6 dots; 6 + 6 =
12 3. 5 dots; 5 + 5 = 10 4. 8 dots; 8 + 8 = 16 5. 14 6.
18 7. 16 8. 12 Worksheet 11B: 2. 10, 11, 11 3. 12, 13,
13 4. 14, 15, 15 5. 16, 17, 17 Worksheet 12A: 2. 5 3. 4
4. 6 5. 6 6. 5 7. 6 8. 7 9. 8 10. 7 11. 9 12. 9 13. 6 14. 9
15. 8 16. 5 17. 8 18. 6 19. 8 20. 7 21. 7 22. 4
Worksheet 12B: 2. 5 3. 6 4. 6 5. 7 6. 8 7. 8 8. 6 9. 9
10. 5 11. 4 12. 7 13. 6 14. 6 15. 3 16. 7 17. 9 18. 5 19.
8 20. 4 21. 9

Level 2 Worksheet 1A: 2. 2 3. 3 4. 2 5. 1 6. 9 7. 4 8.
6 9. 8 10. 8 11. 5 12. 1 13. 1 14. 5 15. 8 16. 1 17. 2 18.
6 19. 5 20. 2 21. 6 22. 7 23. 9 24. 3 25. 7 26. 4 27. 4
Worksheet 1B: 2. 0 3. 8 4. 3 5. 4 6. 1 7. 0 8. 6 9. 0 10.
4 11. 0 12. 0 13. 0 14. 7 15. 0 16. 0 17. 0 18. 5 19. 0

20. 0 21. 4 22. 8 23. 0 24. 9 25. 0 Worksheet 2A: 2. 9
3. 9 4. 10 5. 7 6. 7 7. 7 8. 9 9. 10 10. 10 11. 3 12. 11
13. 11 14. 4 15. 6 16. 12 17. 5 18. 10 19. 8 20. 10 21.
9 22. 8 23. 5 24. 4 Worksheet 2B: 2. 11 3. 4 4. 8 5. 9
6. 4 7. 10 8. 9 9. 12 10. 7 11. 9 12. 10 13. 5 14. 9 15.
10 16. 6 17. 5 18. 7 19. 8 20. 10 21. 12 22. 11 23. 7
24. 11 25. 6 Worksheet 3A: 2. 5 3. 5 4. 5 5. 4 6. 4 7. 7
8. 3 9. 3 10. 6 11. 2 12. 3 13. 6 14. 1 15. 1 16. 7 17. 3
18. 1 19. 3 20. 6 21. 2 22. 0 23. 8 24. 6 25. 3 26. 2 27.
4 Worksheet 3B: 2. 7 3. 6 4. 6 5. 4 6. 3 7. 2 8. 3 9. 4
10. 8 11. 2 12. 1 13. 5 14. 5 15. 3 16. 5 17. 1 18. 3 19.
4 20. 6 21. 2 22. 4 23. 2 24. 7 25. 2 26. 7 27. 1
Worksheet 4A: 2. 3; 5 + 3 = 8 3. 3; 4 + 3 = 7 4. 3; 9
+ 3 = 12 Worksheet 4B: 2. 1 3. 2 4. 3 5. 2 6. 3 7. 1 8.
1 9. 3 10. 3 11. 3 12. 3 13. 1 14. 2 15. 2 16. 1 17. 2 18.
2 19. 3 20. 2 21. 1 22. 3 23. 2 24. 3 25. 2 Worksheet
5A: 2. 9; 9 3. 11; 2 4. 9; 1 5. 5; 1 6. 6; 2 7. 11; 3 8. 8; 1
9. 10; 2 10. 10; 2 11. 8; 1 12. 9; 1 13. 10; 9 14. 4; 4 15.
10; 3 Worksheet 5B: 2. 10 3. 3 4. 5 5. 10 6. 8 7. 11 8.
2 9. 4 10. 9 11. 2 12. 6 13. 7 14. 9 15. 8 16. 2 17. 8 18.
7 19. 11 20. 7 21. 7 22. 3 23. 6 24. 2 25. 3 Worksheet
6A: 2. 8, 9, 10 3. 10, 11, 12 4. 12, 13, 14 5. 10 6. 11 7.
12 8. 16 9. 17 10. 14 11. 15 12. 15 13. 8 14. 9
Worksheet 6B: 2. 12, 13, 14 3. 8 4. 9 5. 10 6. 15 7. 15
8. 16 9. 10 10. 10 11. 11 12. 12 13. 10 14. 11 15. 12
16. 13 17. 14 18. 12 19. 13 20. 14 21. 16 22. 17
Worksheet 7A: 2. 7; 12 − 5 = 7 3. 6; 11 − 5 = 6 4. 7;
14 − 7 = 7 Worksheet 7B: 2. 5, 6, 7 3. 6, 7, 8 4. 4 5. 5
6. 4 7. 5 8. 6 9. 7 10. 5 11. 6 12. 6 13. 8 14. 8 15. 7 16.
6 17. 9 18. 9 Worksheet 8A: 2. 10 3. 3 4. 7 5. 7 6. 10
7. 11 8. 11 9. 10 10. 11 11. 8 12. 7 13. 1 14. 3 15. 12
16. 6 17. 9 18. 9 19. 1 20. 2 21. 3 22. 8 23. 9 24. 7 25.
8 Worksheet 8B: 2. 5 3. 17 4. 5 5. 12 6. 8 7. 8 8. 4 9. 6
10. 7 11. 7 12. 15 13. 8 14. 5 15. 8 16. 14 17. 16 18.
19. 7 20. 6 21. 16 22. 11 23. 14 24. 9 25. 15
Worksheet 9A: 2. 4,14 3. 6,16 4. 3,13 5. 5,15 6. 4,14
7. 3,13 8. 5,15 9. 1,11 10. 2,12 Worksheet 9B: 2. 3,13
3. 6,16 4. 6,16 5. 4,14 6. 3,13 7. 5,15 8. 2,12 9. 2,12
10. 3,13 Worksheet 10A: 2. 3 3. 7 4. 8 5. 8 6. 4 7. 9 8.
8 9. 5 10. 2 11. 5 12. 4 13. 7 14. 7 15. 9 16. 6 17. 8 18.
5 19. 4 20. 5 21. 6 22. 7 23. 6 24. 9 25. 2 Worksheet
10B: 2. 8 3. 8 4. 7 5. 8 6. 9 7. 3 8. 7 9. 9 10. 4 11. 9 12.
6 13. 4 14. 5 15. 7 16. 8 17. 4 18. 9 19. 6 20. 3 21. 8
22. 9 23. 6 24. 2 25. 4 Worksheet 11A: 2. 8 3. 7 4. 9 5.
5 6. 8 7. 6 8. 5 9. 8 10. 8 11. 4 2. 5 13. 9 14. 8 15. 7
16. 8 17. 9 18. 7 19. 4 20. 7 21. 9 22. 5 23. 4 24. 9 25.
6 Worksheet 11B: 2. 4 3. 4 4. 13 5. 9 6. 5 7. 8 8. 4 9.
14 10. 7 11. 12 12. 15 13. 9 14. 12 15. 6 16. 6 17. 9
18. 16 19. 15 20. 6 21. 9 22. 16 23. 16 24. 14 25. 7
Worksheet 12A: 2. 9 3. 10 4. 16 5. 11 6. 13 7. 17 8. 11
9. 18 10. 13 11. 7 12. 10 13. 15 14. 9 15. 13 16. 10 17.
14 18. 2 19. 7 20. 16 21. 12 22. 12 23. 16 24. 9 25. 17

Worksheet 12B: 2. 7 **3.** 7 **4.** 4 **5.** 6 **6.** 2 **7.** 5 **8.** 6 **9.** 8 **10.** 8 **11.** 6 **12.** 6 **13.** 9 **14.** 6 **15.** 9 **16.** 5 **17.** 4 **18.** 6 **19.** 5 **20.** 3 **21.** 3 **22.** 9 **23.** 9 **24.** 6 **25.** 2

Level 3 **Worksheet 1A: 1.** 6 **2.** 8 **3.** 9 **4.** 7 **5.** 9 **6.** 1 **7.** 8 **8.** 10 **9.** 8 **10.** 6 **11.** 7, 8, 9, 4 + 6 = 10 **12.** 6, 7, 8, 6 + 3 = 9 **13.** 5, 6, 7, 10 − 2 = 8 **14.** 4, 3, 2, 9 − 8 = 1 **Worksheet 1B: 1.** 7 **2.** 7 **3.** 7 **4.** 10 **5.** 8 **6.** 9 **7.** 11 **8.** 8 **9.** 6 **10.** 2 **11.** 3 **12.** 2 **13.** 3 **14.** 4 **15.** 1 **16.** 2 **17.** 3 **18.** 2 **19.** 1 **20.** 3 **21.** 3 **22.** 3 **23.** 4 **24.** 6 **25.** 6 **26.** 6 **27.** 4 **28.** 1 **29.** 2 **Worksheet 2A:** Answers will vary for doubles. **1.** 11 **2.** 17 **3.** 13 **4.** 11 **5.** 17 **6.** 13 **7.** 2 **8.** 3 **9.** 2 **10.** 5 **11.** 4 **12.** 8 **13.** 2 **14.** 6 **15.** 4 **16.** 1 **17.** 9 **18.** 11 **19.** 14 **20.** 12 **Worksheet 2B: 1.** 8 **2.** 13 **3.** 10 **4.** 9 **5.** 9 **6.** 18 **7.** 10 **8.** 6 **9.** 11 **10.** 15 **11.** 16 **12.** 3 **13.** 12 **14.** 14 **15.** 10 **16.** B; 8 **17.** C; 4 **18.** A; 9 **Worksheet 3A: 1.** 14 **2.** 11 **3.** 13 **4.** 14 **5.** 13 **6.** 16 **7.** 17 **8.** 12 **9.** 15 **10.** 7 **11.** 2 **12.** 2 **13.** 3 **14.** 5 **15.** 4 **16.** 8 **17.** 10 **18.** 2 **19.** 2 **20.** 3 **21.** 3 **22.** 1 **23.** 6 **24.** 2 **25.** 8 **26.** 3 **27.** 2 **28.** 6 **29.** 4 **Worksheet 3B: 1.** 5 **2.** 6 **3.** 8 **4.** 3 **5.** 6 **6.** 9 **7.** 15 **8.** 8 **9.** 13 **10.** 9 **11.** 8 **12.** 14 **13.** 5 **14.** 6 **15.** 15 **16.** 5 **17.** 12 **18.** 4 **19.** 8 **20.** 16 **21.** 5 **22.** 7 **23.** 11 **24.** 16 **25.** 9 **26.** 7 **27.** 2 **28.** 9 **29.** 8 **30.** 5 **Worksheet 4A:** Answers will vary. Possible answers are given. **1.** 10 + 5 = 15, 5 × 3 = 15 **2.** 7 + 7 = 14, 7 × 2 = 14 **3.** 4, 4 **4.** 6, 6 **5.** 8, 8 **6.** 10, 10 **7.** 18 **8.** 16 Drawings will vary. **9.** 14 **10.** 12 **11.** 8 **Worksheet 4B:** Drawings will vary. **1.** 18 **2.** 24 **3.** 15 **4.** 14 **5.** 12 **6.** 18 **7.** 8 **8.** 16 **9.** 10 **10.** 6 **11.** 18 **12.** 4 **13.** 15 **14.** 12 **15.** 21 **16.** < **17.** > **18.** > **19.** > **20.** > **21.** > **Worksheet 5A: 1.** 2 **2.** 6 **3.** 4 **4.** 7 **5.** 12 **6.** 1 **7.** 7 **8.** 18 **9.** 8 **10.** 5 **11.** 8 **12.** 6 **13.** 4 **14.** 4 **15.** 3 **16.** 10 **17.** 14 **18.** 6 **19.** 8 **20.** 9 **21.** 10 **22.** 0 **23.** 16 **24.** 6 **25.** 8 **26.** 4 **Worksheet 5B: 1.** 6 **2.** 10 **3.** 8 **4.** 18 **5.** 4 **6.** 16 **7.** 4 **8.** 8 **9.** 12 **10.** 9 **11.** 3 **12.** 4 **13.** 5 **14.** 14 **15.** 18 **16.** 2 **17.** 7 **18.** 10 **19.** 9 **20.** 2 **21.** 1 **22.** 6 **23.** 16 **24.** 4 **25.** 12 **26.** 8 **27.** 3 **28.** 6 **29.** 14 **30.** 8 **Worksheet 6A:** Answers will vary. Possible answers are given. **1.** 4 + 4 = 8, 4 × 2 = 8 **2.** 4 + 4 + 4 = 12, 4 × 3 = 12 **3.** 12 **4.** 32 **5.** 28 **6.** 20 **7.** 8 **8.** 16 **9.** 28 **10.** 16 **11.** 12 **12.** 36 **13.** 20 **14.** 24 **15.** 12 **16.** 28 **17.** 32 **18.** 8 **Worksheet 6B: 1.** 14 **2.** 12 **3.** 18 **4.** 8 **5.** 16 **6.** 10 **7.** 6 **8.** 18 **9.** 4 **10.** 12 **11.** 32 **12.** 28 **13.** 20 **14.** 8 **15.** 16 **16.** 36 **17.** 24 **18.** 32 **19.** 4 **20.** 8 **21.** 24 **22.** 28 **23.** 4 **24.** 36 **25.** 12 **26.** 20 **27.** 24 **28.** 32 **29.** 8 **30.** 28 **Worksheet 7A: 1.** 6 **2.** 15 **3.** 18 **4.** 12 **5.** 27 **6.** 24 **7.** 21 **8.** 9 **9.** 27 **10.** 15 **11.** 18 **12.** 6 **13.** Answer given. **14.** 14 **15.** 6 **16.** 8 **17.** 10 **18.** 9 **19.** 18 **20.** 4 **21.** 8 **22.** 5 **Worksheet 7B: 1.** c. **2.** d. **3.** b. **4.** f. **5.** g. **6.** a. **7.** e. Answers will vary. Possible answers are given. **8.** 2 × 2 **9.** 4 × 2 **10.** 3 × 1 **11.** 1 × 5 **12.** 2 × 3 **13.** 5 × 2 **14.** 1 × 7 **15.** 3 × 3 **16.** 6 × 2 **17.** 5 × 3 **Worksheet 8A: 1.** 18 **2.** 30 **3.** 12 **4.** 24 **5.** 0 **6.** 6 **7.** 24 **8.** 54 **9.** 48 **10.** 12 **11.** > **12.** = **13.** < **14.** = **15.** 18 **16.** 0 **17.** 54 **18.** 30 **19.** 6 **20.** 42 **21.** 12 **22.** 24

23. 36 **24.** 48 **25.** 18 **26.** 30 **Worksheet 8B:** Drawings will vary. **1.** 18 **2.** 12 **3.** 36 **4.** 24 **5.** 54 **6.** 18 **7.** 12 **8.** 42 **9.** 48 **10.** 24 **11.** 0 **12.** 48 **13.** 18 **14.** 30 **15.** 24 **16.** 6 **17.** 6 **Worksheet 9A: 1.** 15 **2.** 30 **3.** 35 **4.** 10 **5.** 40 **6.** 20 **7.** 45 **8.** 30 **9.** 40 **10.** 45 **11.** > **12.** < **13.** > **14.** > **15.** 36 **16.** 12 **17.** 48 **18.** 42 **19.** 54 **Worksheet 9B: 1.** 10, 10 **2.** 15, 15 **3.** 20, 20 **4.** 40, equal to **5.** 30, less than **6.** 10, less than **7.** 45, greater than **8.** 50, greater than **9.** 40 **10.** 15 **11.** 16 **12.** 45 **13.** 20 **14.** 30 **15.** 0 **16.** 35 **17.** 10 **Worksheet 10A: 1.** 9 **2.** 18 **3.** 27 **4.** 36 **5.** 45 **6.** 18 **7.** 36 **8.** 9 **9.** 4 **10.** 63 **11.** 36 **12.** 27 **13.** 18 **14.** 36 **15.** 72 **16.** 45 **17.** 81 **18.** 27 **19.** 18 **Worksheet 10B: 1.** 9 **2.** 18 **3.** 27 **4.** 36 **5.** 45 **6.** 54 **7.** 63 **8.** 72 **9.** 81 **10.** 36 **11.** 54 **12.** 20 **13.** 42 **14.** 63 **15.** 45 **16.** 9 **17.** 0 **18.** 9 **19.** 27 **20.** 1 **21.** 4 **22.** 1 **23.** 5 **Worksheet 11A: 1.** 21, less than **2.** 56, greater than **3.** 42, greater than **4.** 35, greater than **5.** 21 **6.** 28 **7.** 42 **8.** 35 **9.** 35 **10.** 56 **11.** 14 **12.** 7 **13.** 0 **14.** 63 **15.** > **16.** < **17.** < **18.** > **Worksheet 11B: 1.** 56 **2.** 21 **3.** 63 **4.** 42 **5.** 49 **6.** 49 **7.** 48 **8.** 7 **9.** 56 **10.** 28 **11.** 21 **12.** 28 **13.** 42 **14.** 63 **15.** 56 **16.** 27 **17.** 14 **18.** 59 **19.** 30 **20.** 18 **21.** 24 **Worksheet 12A: 1.** 48 **2.** 56 **3.** 24 **4.** 48 **5.** 40 **6.** 56 **7.** 32 **8.** 0 **9.** 64 **10.** 8 **11.** 16 **12.** 8 **13.** 56 **14.** 32 **15.** 5 **16.** 42 **17.** 12 **18.** 18 **19.** 25 **Worksheet 12B: 1.** 56 **2.** 40 **3.** 24 **4.** 8 **5.** 32 **6.** 16 **7.** 32 **8.** 8 **9.** 48 **10.** 4, 6, 10, 12, 14, 16, 18 **11.** 6, 9, 15, 18, 21, 24, 27 **12.** 8, 12, 20, 24, 28, 32, 36 **13.** 10, 15, 25, 30, 35, 40, 45 **14.** 12, 18, 30, 36, 42, 48, 54 **15.** 14, 21, 35, 42, 49, 56, 63 **16.** 16, 24, 40, 48, 56, 64, 72 **17.** 18, 27, 45, 54, 63, 72, 81 **18.** > **19.** < **20.** < **21.** = **22.** > **23.** <

Level 4 **Worksheet 1A: 1.** 3 × 4 = 12; 4 × 3 = 12 **2.** 3 × 6 = 18; 6 × 3 = 18 **3.** 3 × 5 = 15; 5 × 3 = 15 **4.** 5; 4 **5.** 6; 2 **6.** 3; 7 **7.** 2; 8 **8.** 3 × 7 = 21 **9.** 5 × 5 = 25 **10.** 12 ÷ 2 = 6 **11.** 15 ÷ 3 = 5 **Worksheet 1B:** Models will vary. **1.** 6 **2.** 16 **3.** 18 **4.** 16 **5.** 15 **6.** 8 **7.** 14 **8.** 12 **9.** 10 **10.** 12 **11.** 9 **12.** 20 Drawings will vary. **13.** 4 **14.** 5 **15.** 2 **16.** 6 **17.** 3 **18.** 9 **19.** 5 **20.** 4 **21.** 8 **Worksheet 2A: 1.** 4 ÷ 2 = 2 **2.** 10 ÷ 5 = 2 **3.** 12 ÷ 6 = 2 **4.** 2, 4, 6, 8, 10, 12, 14, 16, 18, 20 **5.** Drawings will vary. **6.** Drawings will vary. **7.** ÷ **8.** × **9.** + **10.** 2; 4 × 2 = 8 or 2 × 4 = 8 **11.** 1; 5 × 1 = 5 or 1 × 5 = 5 **12.** 2; 2 × 1 = 2 or 1 × 2 = 2 **13.** 2; 2 × 7 = 14 or 7 × 2 = 14 **Worksheet 2B: 1.** 14 **2.** 12 **3.** 18 **4.** 8 **5.** 16 **6.** 10 **7.** 6 **8.** 2 **9.** 4 **10.** 10 **11.** 6 **12.** 16 **13.** 18 **14.** 8 **15.** 12 **16.** 4 **17.** 3 **18.** 9 **19.** 5 **20.** 8 **21.** 6 **22.** 7 **23.** 2 **24.** 2 **25.** 14; 14 ÷ 7 = 2 or 14 ÷ 2 = 7 **26.** 6; 6 ÷ 3 = 2 or 6 ÷ 2 = 3 **27.** 8; 8 ÷ 4 = 2 or 8 ÷ 2 = 4 **28.** 16; 16 ÷ 8 = 2 or 16 ÷ 2 = 8 **Worksheet 3A: 1.** 4 **2.** 8 **3.** 3 **4.** 7 **5.** 4 **6.** 4 **7.** 4 **8.** 4 **9.** 6 **10.** 4, 8, 12, 16, 20, 24, 28, 32, 36, 40 **11.** 5; 5 × 2 = 10 or 2 × 5 = 10 **12.** 2; 2 × 4 = 8 or 4 × 2 = 8 **13.** 4; 4 × 4 = 16 **14.** 7; 7 × 2 = 14 or 2 × 7 = 14 **15.** 6; 6 × 4 = 24 or 4 × 6 = 24 **16.** 5; 5

× 4 = 20 or 4 × 5 = 20 **17.** 8; 8 × 4 = 32 or 4 × 8 = 32 **18.** 9; 9 × 2 = 18 or 2 × 9 = 18 **19.** 7; 7 × 4 = 28 or 4 × 7 = 28 **Worksheet 3B: 1.** 2; 2 × 4 = 8 **2.** 8; 8 × 4 = 32 **3.** 6; 6 × 4 = 24 **4.** 4; 4 × 4 = 16 **5.** 9; 9 × 4 = 36 **6.** 3; 4 × 3 = 12 **7.** 7; 7 × 4 = 28 **8.** 5; 5 × 4 = 20 **9.** 3; 3 × 4 = 12 **10.** 24 **11.** 20 **12.** 28 **13.** 32 **14.** 36 **15.** 12 **16.** 16 **17.** 36 **18.** 32 **19.** 20 **20.** 12 **21.** 14 **22.** 24 **Worksheet 4A: 1.** 40 **2.** 15 **3.** 10 **4.** 25 **5.** 40 **6.** 45 **7.** 30 **8.** 30 **9.** 5, 10, 15, 20, 25, 30, 35, 40, 45, 50 **10.** 8 **11.** 7 **12.** 5 **13.** 2 **14.** 4 **15.** 6 **16.** 3 **17.** 9 **18.** 5 **19.** 5 **20.** 5 **21.** 5 **Worksheet 4B: 1.** 5 **2.** 6 **3.** 9 **4.** 8 **5.** 7 **6.** 10 **7.** 3 **8.** 4 **9.** 4, 8, 12, 16, 20, 24, 28, 32, 36, 40, 44, 48 **10.** 9; 5 **11.** 5 **12.** 35 **13.** 40 **14.** 21 **15.** 9 **16.** 9; 6 **17.** 4; 5 **18.** 5 **19.** 5; 6 **20.** 5 **21.** 45 **22.** 3 **23.** 24 **24.** 3 **Worksheet 5A: 1.** 8 **2.** 12 **3.** 1 **4.** 10 **5.** 2 **6.** 7 **7.** 5 **8.** 9 **9.** 2 **10.** 1 **11.** 6 **12.** 8 **13.** 4 **14.** 6 **15.** 7 **16.** 3 **17.** 1; 1 × 5 = 5 **18.** 3; 1 × 3 = 3 **19.** 5 **20.** 1 **21.** 8 **22.** 3 **Worksheet 5B: 1.** 4 **2.** 8 **3.** 12 **4.** 9 **5.** 3 **6.** 8 **7.** 5 **8.** 7 **9.** 18 **10.** 4 **11.** 7 **12.** 20 **13.** 9 **14.** 2 **15.** 2 **16.** 6 **17.** 32 **18.** 4 **19.** 14 **20.** 4 **21.** 6 **22.** 2 **23.** 9 **24.** 12 **25.** 8 **26.** 5 **27.** 6 **28.** 8 **29.** 8 **30.** 11 **31.** 4 **Worksheet 6A: 1.** 6; 3; 6; 2 **2.** 18; 3; 18; 6 **3.** 24; 8; 24; 3 **4.** 27; 3; 27; 9 **5.** 15; 5; 15; 3 **6.** 3 × 4 = 12; 4 × 3 = 12; 12 ÷ 3 = 4; 12 ÷ 4 = 3 **7.** 3 × 7 = 21; 7 × 3 = 21; 21 ÷ 3 = 7; 21 ÷ 7 = 3 **Worksheet 6B: 1.** 2; 2, 3, 6 **2.** 7; 7, 3, 21 **3.** 4; 4, 3, 12 **4.** 1; 1, 3, 3 **5.** 3; 3, 3, 9 **6.** 8; 8, 3, 24 **7.** 5; 5, 3, 15 **8.** 0; 0,3,0 **9.** 6; 6, 3, 18 **10.** 9; 9, 3, 27 **11.** incorrect; corrections will vary. **12.** correct; 3 × 3 = 9 **13.** incorrect; corrections will vary. **Worksheet 7A: 1.** 0 **2.** 8 **3.** 0 **4.** 9 **5.** 0 **6.** 0 **7.** 5 **8.** 0 **9.** 0 **10.** 7 **11.** 25 **12.** 0 **13.** 2 **14.** 0 **15.** 0 **16.** 4 **17.** 3 **18.** 12 **19.** 14 **20.** 9 **21.** 21 **22.** 24 **23.** 15 **24.** 12 **25.** 10 **26.** 20 **27.** 8 **28.** 16 **29.** 0 **Worksheet 7B: 1.** 5 **2.** 0 **3.** 4 **4.** 0 **5.** 2 **6.** 0 **7.** 9 **8.** 1 **9.** 5 **10.** 8 **11.** 3 **12.** 0 **13.** 1 **14.** 0 **15.** 4 **16.** 7 **17.** 0, 0 × 4 = 0 **18.** 1, 1 × 5 = 5 **19.** 3, 3 × 1 = 3 **20.** 5, 5 × 2 = 10 **21.** 2, 2 × 3 = 6 **22.** 0, 0 × 3 = 0 **23.** 8, 8 × 1 = 8 **24.** 7, 7 × 2 = 14 **25.** 4, 4 × 1 = 4 **26.** 3, 3 × 3 = 9 **27.** 1, 1 × 3 = 3 **28.** 16, 16 × 1 = 16 **Worksheet 8A: 1.** 9 × 3 = 27; 3 × 9 = 27 **2.** 9 × 2 = 18; 2 × 9 = 18 **3.** 9 **4.** 8 **5.** 6 **6.** 6, 6 or 9, 4 **7.** 2, 9 or 3, 6 **8.** 9, 5 **9.** 45 **10.** 63 **11.** 27 **12.** 36 **13.** 81 **14.** 54 **15.** 40 **16.** 18 **17.** 9 **18.** 72 **Worksheet 8B: 1.** 0 **2.** 9 **3.** 5 **4.** 1 **5.** 9 **6.** 3 **7.** 3 **8.** 2 **9.** 5 **10.** 7 **11.** 4 **12.** 9 **13.** 8 **14.** 3 **15.** 6 **16.** > **17.** = **18.** < **19.** < **20.** 9 **21.** 9 **22.** 3 **23.** 1 **24.** 4 **25.** 9 **26.** 9 **27.** 9 **Worksheet 9A: 1.** 9; 18 **2.** 6; 12 **3.** 21; 42 **4.** 12; 24 **5.** 27; 54 **6.** 15; 30 **7.** 24; 48 **8.** 18; 36 **9.** 24 **10.** 18 **11.** 30 **12.** 42 **13.** 36 **14.** 6 **15.** 12 **16.** 0 **17.** 54 **18.** 48 **19.** 30 **20.** 42 **21.** 24 **22.** 18 **23.** 21 **24.** 12 **25.** 48 **26.** 54 **27.** 25 **28.** 16 **Worksheet 9B: 1.** 6, 7, 42; 7, 6, 42; 42, 7, 6; 42, 6, 7 **2.** 5, 6, 30; 6, 5, 30; 30, 6, 5; 30, 5, 6 **3.** 6, 8, 48; 8, 6, 48; 48, 8, 6; 48, 6, 8 **4.** 6, 9, 54; 9, 6, 54; 54, 9, 6; 54, 6, 9 **5.** 6, 4, 24; 4, 6, 24; 24, 4, 6; 24, 6, 4

Worksheet 10A: 1. 1; 1, 7, 7 **2.** 3; 3, 7, 21 **3.** 5; 5, 7, 35 **4.** 8; 8, 7, 56 **5.** 6; 6, 7, 42 **6.** 9; 9, 7, 63 **7.** 2; 2, 7, 14 **8.** 4; 4, 7, 28 **9.** 7; 7, 7, 49 **10.** 7, 9, 63; 9, 7, 63; 63, 9, 7; 63, 7, 9 **11.** 7, 8, 56; 8, 7, 56; 56, 8, 7; 56, 7, 8 **Worksheet 10B: 1.** 14 **2.** 35 **3.** 49 **4.** 28 **5.** 21 **6.** 56 **7.** 63 **8.** 42 **9.** 7 **10.** 0 **11.** 14 **12.** 42 **13.** 56 **14.** 28 **15.** 7 **16.** 63 **17.** 35 **18.** 49 **19.** 21 **20.** 0 **21.** 7 **22.** 9 **23.** 3 **24.** 1 **25.** 2 **26.** 8 **27.** 6 **28.** 4 **29.** 7 **30.** 5 **Worksheet 11A: 1.** 3 × 8 = 24; 8 × 3 = 24 **2.** 2 × 8 = 16; 8 × 2 = 16 **3.** 4 × 8 = 32; 8 × 4 = 32 **4.** 6 × 8 = 48 **5.** 5 × 8 = 40 **6.** 7 × 8 = 56 **7.** 9 × 8 = 72 **8.** 4 × 8 = 32 **9.** 8 × 8 = 64 **10.** Models will vary; 48 **11.** Models will vary; 24 **12.** 48 **13.** 40 **14.** 56 **15.** 32 **Worksheet 11B: 1.** 5 **2.** 7 **3.** 3 **4.** 8 **5.** 6 **6.** 9 **7.** 8, 9 **8.** 7, 8 **9.** 3, 8 **10.** 4 **11.** 2 **12.** 5 **13.** 3 **14.** 6 **15.** 1 **16.** 7 **17.** 8 **18.** - **23.** incorrect; corrections will vary. **Worksheet 12A: 1.** 32 **2.** 18 **3.** 40 **4.** 36 **5.** 64 **6.** 27 **7.** 63 **8.** 8 **9.** 45 **10.** 63 **11.** 81 **12.** 48 **13.** 72 **14.** 27 **15.** 56 **16.** 48 **17.** 45 **18.** 16 **19.** 49 **20.** 40 **21.** 56 **22.** 24 **23.** 36 **24.** 28 **25.** 54 **26.** 42 **27.** 27 **28.** 24 **29.** 36 **30.** 14 **Worksheet 12B: 1.** 4 **2.** 5 **3.** 1 **4.** 8 **5.** 4 **6.** 9 **7.** 6 **8.** 1 **9.** 7 **10.** 8 **11.** 3 **12.** 9 **13.** 5 **14.** 0 **15.** 2 **16.** 0 **17.** 6 **18.** 0 **19.** 7 **20.** 9 **21.** 6 **22.** 8 **23.** 5 **24.** 1 **25.** 4 **26.** 2 **27.** 2 **28.** 6 **29.** 4 **30.** 9 **31.** 3 **32.** 8 **33.** 6 **34.** 7 **35.** 3 **Worksheet 13A: 1.** 7, 4, 28; 4, 7, 28; 28, 4, 7; 28, 7, 4 **2.** 8, 3, 24; 3, 8, 24; 24, 3, 8; 24, 8, 3 **3.** 21; 63; 42; 49 **4.** 27; 7; 6; 5; 81 **5.** 27 **6.** 36 **7.** 72 **8.** 45 **9.** 81 **Worksheet 13B: 1.** 5 × 7 = 35; 7 × 5 = 35; 35 ÷ 7 = 5; 35 ÷ 5 = 7 **2.** 6 × 8 = 48; 8 × 6 = 48; 48 ÷ 8 = 6; 48 ÷ 6 = 8 **3.** 32; 4; 32; 8 **4.** 42; 6; 42; 7 **5.** 40; 8; 40; 5 **6.** 36; 4; 36; 9 **7.** 5 **8.** 8 **9.** 9 **10.** 4

Level 5 **Worksheet 1A: 1.** 11 **2.** 10 **3.** 9 **4.** 9 **5.** 7 **6.** 7 **7.** 10 **8.** 11 **9.** 13 **10.** 11 **11.** 16 **12.** 9 **13.** 4 **14.** 12 **15.** 10 **16.** 11 **17.** 1 **18.** 14 **19.** 16 **20.** 0 **21.** 4 **22.** 5 **23.** 8 **24.** 3 **25.** 7 **26.** 3 **27.** 5 **28.** 5 **29.** 5 **30.** 4 **31.** 7 **32.** 8 **33.** 9 **34.** 3 **35.** 8 **36.** 3 **37.** 9 **38.** 9 **Worksheet 1B: 1.** 8 **2.** 18 **3.** 28 **4.** 9 **5.** 12 **6.** 32 **7.** 52 **8.** 17 **9.** 10 **10.** 20 **11.** 17 **12.** 57 **13.** 47 **14.** 58 **15.** 24 **16.** 38 **17.** 53 **18.** 7 **19.** 70 **20.** 15 **21.** 38 **22.** (125) + 3 **23.** (9 + 8) − 9 **24.** (7 + 4) − 3 or 7 + (4 − 3) **25.** (8 − 3) + 5 **Worksheet 2A: 1.** 4 × 5 = 20 **2.** 4 × 3 = 12 **3.** 4 × 2 = 8 **4.** 2 × 4 = 8 **5.** 6 × 4 = 24 **6.** 9 × 4 = 36 **7.** 9 × 2 = 18 **8.** 4 × 3 = 12 **9.** 3 × 2 = 6 **10.** 7 × 3 = 21 **11.** 14 **12.** 12 **13.** 9 **14.** 24 **15.** 28 **16.** 16 **17.** 4 **18.** 27 **19.** 32 **20.** 3 **21.** 1 **22.** 5 **23.** 7 **24.** 3 **25.** 4 **26.** 1 **27.** 4 **28.** 6 **Worksheet 2B: 1.** 42 **2.** 5 **3.** 49 **4.** 6 **5.** 6 **6.** 21 **7.** 2 **8.** 15 **9.** 6 **10.** 7 **11.** 6 **12.** 4 **13.** 7 **14.** 4 **15.** 3 **16.** 2 **17.** 7 **18.** 0 **19.** 9 **20.** 8 **21.** 7 **22.** 7 **23.** 6 **24.** 8 **25.** 64 **26.** 69 **27.** 84 **28.** 76 **29.** 84 **30.** 91 **Worksheet 3A:** Estimates will vary. Possible estimates are given. **1.** about 160 **2.** about 70 **3.** about 90 **4.** about 80 **5.** about 50 **6.** about 110 **7.** about 100 **8.** about 110 **9.** about 80 **10.** about 100 **11.** about 100 **12.** about 90 **13.** about 140 **14.** about

120 **15.** about 60 **16.** about 70 **17.** about 90 **18.** about 100 **19.** about 80 **20.** about 80 **21.** 93 **22.** 83 **23.** 32 **24.** 64 **25.** 64 **26.** 80 **27.** 92 **28.** 51 **29.** 875 **30.** 831 **31.** 721 **32.** 412 **Worksheet 3B: 1.** 43 **2.** 51 **3.** 60 **4.** 53 **5.** 50 **6.** 91 **7.** 101 **8.** 102 **9.** 66 **10.** 101 **11.** 122 **12.** 87 **13.** 401 **14.** 460 **15.** 541 **16.** 643 **17.** 515 **18.** 419 **19.** 736 **20.** 1015 **21.** 980 **22.** 1084 **23.** 891 **24.** 1031 **25.** 495 **26.** 563 **27.** 396 **28.** 411 **29.** 729 **30.** 445 **31.** 525 **Worksheet 4A: 1.** 29 **2.** 35 **3.** 32 **4.** 49 **5.** 15 **6.** 45 **7.** 46 **8.** 76 **9.** 42 **10.** 42 **11.** 65 **12.** 22 **13.** 48 **14.** 65 **15.** 28 **16.** 9 **17.** 39 **18.** 34 **19.** 8 **20.** 21 **21.** yes **22.** no **23.** no **24.** yes **25.** no **26.** no **27.** no **28.** yes **Worksheet 4B: 1.** 554 **2.** 657 **3.** 379 **4.** 618 **5.** 305 **6.** 179 **7.** 378 **8.** 546 **9.** 14 **10.** 42 **11.** 64 **12.** 620 **13.** 211 **14.** 541 **15.** 58 **16.** 79 **17.** 387 **18.** 315 **19.** 38 **20.** 9 **21.** 190 **22.** 347 **Worksheet 5A: 1.** 2700 **2.** 5600 **3.** 2700 **4.** 2500 **5.** 1200 **6.** 3500 **7.** 1400 **8.** 6400 **9.** 20,000 **10.** 12,000 **11.** 27,000 **12.** 8000 **13.** 14,000 **14.** 15,000 **15.** 15,000 **16.** 48,000 **17.** 2400 **18.** 1600 **19.** 900 **20.** 17,700 **21.** 21,500 **22.** 32,800 **23.** 6000 **24.** 5500 **25.** 6000 **26.** 830 **27.** 5360 Exercises 23, 24, and 25 should be circled. **Worksheet 5B: 1.** 5100 **2.** 3096 **3.** 4592 **4.** 2592 **5.** 4402 **6.** 3248 **7.** 6138 **8.** 1275 **9.** 2128 **10.** 4092 **11.** 6888 **12.** 4018 **13.** 33,062 **14.** 32,704 **15.** 37,698 **16.** 22,092 **17.** 36,855 **18.** 19,021 **19.** 34,752 **20.** 28,449 **21.** 10,710 **22.** 24,700 **23.** 15,850 **24.** 31,598 **25.** 21,394 **26.** 18,824 **27.** 38,089 **28.** 14,315 **Worksheet 6A: 1.** not divisible **2.** not divisible **3.** divisible **4.** divisible **5.** divisible **6.** not divisible **7.** not divisible **8.** divisible **9.** divisible **10.** c **11.** c **12.** b **13.** yes **14.** yes **15.** no **16.** no **17.** no **18.** no **Worksheet 6B: 1.** 22 R1 **2.** 11 R2 **3.** 42 R1 **4.** 11 R3 **5.** 24 R1 **6.** 21 R1 **7.** 31 R1 **8.** 32 R1 **9.** 12 R2 **10.** 12 R5 **11.** 231 **12.** 223 **13.** 132 **14.** 117 **15.** 238 **16.** 158 **17.** 71 **18.** 183 **19.** 1230 R2 **20.** 620 R1 **21.** 1850 **22.** 1160 R3 **23.** 35 **24.** 8 **25.** 9 **26.** 6 **27.** 6 **28.** 8 **Worksheet 7A: 1.** 15;15 **2.** Multiples will vary. 6, 12, 18; 6 **3.** Multiples will vary. 12, 24; 12 **4.** 30; 30 **5.** Multiples will vary. 10, 20, 30; 10 **6.** 30; 30 **7.** 24 **8.** 24 **9.** 42 **10.** 20 **11.** 21 **12.** 36 **13.** 0 **14.** $\frac{1}{2}$ **15.** 1 **16.** $\frac{1}{2}$ **17.** $\frac{1}{2}$ **18.** 0 **Worksheet 7B: 1.** < **2.** = **3.** > **4.** > **5.** > **6.** > **7.** < **8.** < **9.** < **10.** $\frac{6}{10}, \frac{4}{5}, \frac{7}{8}$ **11.** $\frac{2}{9}, \frac{2}{3}, \frac{5}{6}$ **12.** $\frac{2}{9}, \frac{3}{4}, \frac{10}{12}$ **13.** $\frac{4}{5}, \frac{7}{10}, \frac{1}{2}$ **14.** $\frac{13}{16}, \frac{3}{8}, \frac{1}{4}$ **15.** $\frac{6}{8}, \frac{2}{3}, \frac{1}{2}$ **16.** $\frac{1}{3}, \frac{1}{4}, \frac{1}{5}$ **17.** $\frac{7}{8}, \frac{3}{4}, \frac{2}{3}$ **18.** $\frac{9}{10}, \frac{5}{6}, \frac{4}{5}$ **19.** $\frac{2}{3}, \frac{4}{9}, \frac{1}{12}$ **20.** $\frac{11}{12}, \frac{3}{4}, \frac{1}{3}$ **21.** $\frac{7}{10}, \frac{3}{5}, \frac{1}{2}, \frac{1}{3}$ **Worksheet 8A: 1.** 3 **2.** 4 **3.** 7 **4.** 3 **5.** no **6.** no **7.** yes **8.** no **9.** no **10.** yes **11.** $\frac{1}{2}$ **12.** $\frac{1}{4}$ **13.** $\frac{1}{3}$ **14.** $\frac{4}{5}$ **15.** $\frac{3}{5}$ **16.** $\frac{1}{4}$ **17.** 2 **18.** 5 **19.** 3 **20.** 10 **21.** 2 **22.** 7 **Worksheet 8B: 1.** 1, 5 **2.** 1, 2, 3, 4, 6, 12 **3.** 1, 2, 4 **4.**

1, 2, 3, 6 **5.** 1, 2, 4, 8 **6.** 1, 3, 9 **7.** factors of 16: 1, 2, 4, 8, 16; factors of 18: 1, 2, 3, 6, 9, 18; common factors: 1, 2; GCF: 2 **8.** factors of 20: 1, 2, 4, 5, 10, 20; factors of 25: 1, 5, 25; common factors: 1, 5; GCF: 5 **9.** factors of 10: 1, 2, 5, 10; factors of 45: 1, 3, 5, 9, 15, 45; common factors: 1, 5; GCF: 5 **10.** factors of 24: 1, 2, 3, 4, 6, 8, 12, 24; factors of 48: 1, 2, 3, 4, 6, 8, 12, 16, 24, 48; common factors: 1, 2, 3, 4, 6, 8, 12, 24; GCF: 24 **11.** factors of 30: 1, 2, 3, 5, 6, 10, 15, 30; factors of 60: 1, 2, 3, 4, 5, 6, 10, 12, 15, 20, 30, 60; common factors: 1, 2, 3, 5, 6, 10, 15, 30; GCF: 30 **12.** 2; $\frac{2}{3}$ **13.** 5; $\frac{1}{3}$ **14.** 2; $\frac{3}{10}$ **15.** 3; $\frac{1}{6}$ **16.** 4; $\frac{1}{2}$ **17.** 3; $\frac{1}{4}$ **18.** 5; $\frac{3}{4}$ **19.** 3; $\frac{2}{5}$ **20.** 3; $\frac{2}{3}$ **Worksheet 9A: 1.** = **2.** > **3.** < **4.** > **5.** < **6.** = **7.** > **8.** < **9.** = **10.** 4 **11.** 4 **12.** 9 **13.** 13 **14.** 7 **15.** 10 **16.** 12 **17.** 11 **18.** 6 **19.** 0, 1 **20.** 2, 3 **21.** 1, 2 **22.** 2, 3 **Worksheet 9B: 1.** 5 sevenths **2.** 3 ninths; $\frac{1}{3}$ **3.** 5 tenths; $\frac{1}{2}$ **4.** 4 twelfths; $\frac{1}{3}$ **5.** 3 fifths **6.** 12 fifteenths; $\frac{4}{5}$ **7.** $\frac{3}{8}$ **8.** $5\frac{4}{5}$ **9.** $2\frac{5}{7}$ **10.** 1 **11.** $9\frac{2}{3}$ **12.** $4\frac{3}{4}$ **13.** $\frac{5}{6}$ **14.** $7\frac{1}{8}$ **15.** $4\frac{7}{9}$ **16.** 1 **17.** $4\frac{1}{2}$ **18.** $1\frac{1}{3}$ **Worksheet 10A: 1.** common multiple: 15; LCM: 15 **2.** common multiples: 12, 24; LCM: 12 **3.** common multiples: 10, 20, 30; LCM: 10 **4.** common multiples: 6, 12, 18; LCM: 6 **5.** 8 **6.** 24 **7.** 6 **8.** 20 **9.** 63 **10.** 36 **11.** 12 **12.** 18 **13.** 21 **14.** 56 **15.** 9 **16.** 30 **17.** 12 **18.** 15 **19.** 90 **20.** 6 **21.** 12 **22.** 10 **Worksheet 10B: 1.** $\frac{1}{2}$ **2.** $\frac{4}{9}$ **3.** $\frac{5}{8}$ **4.** $\frac{1}{2}$ **5.** $\frac{7}{9}$ **6.** $\frac{2}{3}$ **7.** $\frac{6}{7}$ **8.** $\frac{7}{8}$ **9.** $1\frac{1}{14}$ **10.** $1\frac{1}{15}$ **11.** $\frac{1}{2}$ **12.** $\frac{19}{20}$ **13.** $1\frac{1}{4}$ **14.** $\frac{5}{6}$ **15.** $1\frac{7}{12}$ **16.** $\frac{8}{9}$ **17.** $1\frac{1}{10}$ **18.** $1\frac{3}{8}$ **19.** $1\frac{3}{8}$ **20.** $\frac{3}{4}$ **21.** $1\frac{1}{9}$ **22.** $1\frac{1}{12}$ **23.** $1\frac{7}{10}$ **24.** $1\frac{1}{12}$ **25.** $1\frac{5}{8}$ **Worksheet 11A: 1.** 1 **2.** 0 **3.** $\frac{1}{2}$ **4.** 1 **5.** $\frac{1}{2}$ **6.** $\frac{1}{2}$ **7.** $\frac{1}{2}$ **8.** 0 **9.** $\frac{2}{3}$ **10.** $\frac{1}{8}$ **11.** $\frac{1}{3}$ **12.** $\frac{7}{10}$ **13.** $2\frac{3}{8}$ **14.** $1\frac{5}{21}$ **15.** $13\frac{1}{12}$ **16.** $7\frac{2}{5}$ **17.** $13\frac{1}{3}$ **18.** $9\frac{1}{3}$ **19.** $4\frac{3}{8}$ **20.** $2\frac{2}{5}$ **Worksheet 11B: 1.** $\frac{1}{6}, \frac{2}{9}, \frac{1}{3}, \frac{1}{2}$ **2.** $\frac{3}{10}, \frac{2}{5}, \frac{1}{2}, \frac{2}{5}$ **3.** $\frac{1}{9}, \frac{2}{9}, \frac{1}{2}, \frac{2}{3}$ **4.** $\frac{2}{8}, \frac{1}{2}, \frac{2}{3}, \frac{3}{4}$ **5.** $\frac{3}{8}, \frac{1}{2}, \frac{3}{4}, \frac{5}{6}$ **6.** $\frac{2}{9}, \frac{1}{2}, \frac{2}{3}, \frac{5}{6}$ **7.** $4\frac{2}{5}$ **8.** $5\frac{3}{8}$ **9.** $2\frac{3}{4}$ **10.** $3\frac{1}{3}$ **11.** $4\frac{2}{3}$ **12.** $7\frac{1}{3}$ **13.** $6\frac{3}{5}$ **14.** $5\frac{1}{4}$ **15.** $2\frac{9}{20}$ **16.** $3\frac{2}{3}$ **17.** $5\frac{9}{10}$ **18.** $6\frac{11}{12}$ **Worksheet 12A: 1.** nine tenths **2.** three and six tenths **3.** nine and three tenths **4.** twelve and eight tenths **5.** forty-five and two tenths **6.** one hundred seventy-three and four tenths **7.** 0.4 **8.** 0.5 **9.** 0.1 **10.** 6.3 **11.** 2.1 **12.** 7.5 **13.** 8.7 **14.** 6.4 **15.** 5.9 **16.** 23.5 **17.** 13.8 **18.** 34.6 **19.** 51.1 **20.** 45.7 **21.** 93.3 **22.** < **23.** < **24.** < **25.** < **26.** > **27.** = **28.** > **29.** < **30.** < **Worksheet 12B: 1.** 0.38, 0.42, 0.4 **2.** 4.56, 5.66, 6.56,

6.66 **3.** 0.12, 1.20, 1.22, 2.12 **4.** 6.999, 9.996, 90.6 **5.** 92.034, 92.344, 92.4 **6.** 29.007, 29.070, 29.70 **7.** 75.562, 75.647, 75.65 **8.** 3.69, 3.96, 6.39, 9.36, 9.6 **9.** 0.7, 0.80, 0.9, 1.03, 1.08, 1.2 **10.** > **11.** > **12.** > **13.** > **14.** < **15.** < **16.** > **17.** < **18.** > **19.** < **20.** > **21.** =
Worksheet 13A: 1. 6 ones **2.** 0 tenths **3.** 5 hundredths **4.** 2 thousandths **5.** 4 tenths **6.** 3 thousandths **7.** 7 hundredths **8.** 9 ones **9.** 0 hundredths **10.** 2 thousandths **11.** 1 one **12.** 5 tenths **13.** 2 hundredths **14.** 13 **15.** 2 **16.** 1 **17.** 66 **18.** 50 **19.** 42
Worksheet 13B: 1. 0.8 **2.** 1.2 **3.** 7.5 **4.** 8.81 **5.** 8.15 **6.** 7.14 **7.** 1.132 **8.** 0.80 **9.** 14.61 **10.** 38.05 **11.** 17.45 **12.** 13.95 **13.** 4.196 **14.** 16.39 **15.** 15.06 **16.** 2.37 **17.** 3.86 **18.** 1.994 **19.** 3.917 **20.** 0.850 **21.** 6.766 **22.** 3.821 **23.** 2.2 **24.** 5.9 **25.** 6.68 **26.** 42.078 **27.** 55.31 **28.** 70.152 **29.** 84.205 **30.** 63.78

Level 6 **Worksheet 1A:** Estimates will vary Possible estimates are given. **1.** 110 **2.** 40 **3.** 160 **4.** 70 **5.** 300 **6.** 1200 **7.** 100 **8.** 840 **9.** 420 **10.** 500 **11.** 300 **12.** yes **13.** yes **14.** no **15.** no **16.** yes **17.** no **18.** yes **19.** yes **20.** 75 **21.** 276 **22.** 44 **23.** 788 **24.** 123
Worksheet 1B: 1. 57 **2.** 846 **3.** 69 **4.** 928 **5.** 199 **6.** 382 **7.** 361 **8.** 780 **9.** 804 **10.** 143 **11.** 610 **12.** 1773 **13.** 1021 **14.** 106 **15.** 902 **16.** 6 **17.** 61 **18.** 71 **19.** 201 **20.** 224 **21.** 24 **22.** 526 **23.** 458 **24.** 560 **25.** 417 **26.** 518 **27.** 6 **28.** 438 **29.** 369 **30.** 661 **Worksheet 2A: 1.** 450 **2.** 4500 **3.** 45, 000 **4.** 4680 **5.** 46,800 **6.** 468, 000 Estimates will vary. Possible estimates are given. **7.** 70 **8.** 480 **9.** 5700 **10.** 1200 **11.** 1200 **12.** yes **13.** no **14.** no **15.** no **16.** 21,900 **17.** 7750 **18.** 8200 **19.** 760 **20.** 1500 **21.** 9400 **22.** 188,400 **23.** 19,000 **Worksheet 2B: 1.** 200 **2.** 5000 **3.** 410 **4.** 4300 **5.** 60 **6.** 6000 **7.** 390 **8.** 7700 **9.** 800 Estimates will vary. Possible estimates are given. **10.** about 1600 **11.** about 200 **12.** about 900 **13.** about 360 **14.** about 1500 **15.** about 6620 **16.** about 3600 **17.** about 4000 **18.** 910 **19.** 800 **20.** 3200 **21.** 7010 **22.** 54,300 **23.** 434 **24.** 936 **25.** 2640 **26.** 1922 **27.** 323 **Worksheet 3A:** Estimates will vary. Possible answers are given. **1.** 10 **2.** 7 **3.** 20 **4.** 30 **5.** 50 **6.** 80 **7.** 30 **8.** 70 **9.** 40 **10.** 30 **11.** 80 **12.** 30 **13.** 40 **14.** 30 **15.** 50 **16.** 90 **17.** 4 **18.** 80 **19.** 120 **20.** no **21.** yes **22.** no **23.** no **24.** 114 **25.** 182 R4 **26.** 173 R3 **27.** 181 R2 **28.** 42 R2 **29.** 95 **30.** 308 R2 **31.** 306 R4 **32.** 845 **33.** 114 R4 **Worksheet 3B:** Estimates will vary. Possible estimates are given. **1.** about 50 **2.** about 90 **3.** about 4 **4.** about 80 **5.** about 120 **6.** about 10 **7.** about 7 **8.** about 20 **9.** about 30 **10.** about 50 **11.** about 80 **12.** 38 R6 **13.** 46 R2 **14.** 46 R5 **15.** 59 R2 **16.** 68 R6 **17.** 53 R6 **18.** 205 R1 **19.** 168 **20.** 162 **21.** 36 R1 **22.** 269 **23.** 94 R3 **24.** 173 **25.** 62 **26.** 160 R1 **27.** 158 **Worksheet 4A: 1.** 9 **2.** 90 **3.** 900 **4.** 9000 **5.** 20 **6.** 200 **7.** 20 **8.** 200 Estimates will vary. Possible estimates

are given. **9.** 30 **10.** 20 **11.** 4 **12.** 5 **13.** 6 **14.** 3 **15.** yes **16.** yes **17.** no **18.** 9 R6 **19.** 12 R8 **20.** 8 R23 **21.** 110 R15 **22.** 28 R6 **23.** 8 R7 **24.** 9 R12 **25.** 8 R9 **26.** 5 R10 **27.** 8 R7 **Worksheet 4B: 1.** 4 **2.** 40 **3.** 500 **4.** 5000 Estimates will vary. Possible estimates are given. **5.** about 8 **6.** about 3 **7.** about 4 **8.** about 8 **9.** about 6 **10.** about 6 **11.** about 10 **12.** about 8 **13.** 111 R3 **14.** 263 R7 **15.** 172 R3 **16.** 115 R1 **17.** 194 R11 **18.** 18 R3 **19.** 247 R2 **20.** 267 R11 **21.** 224 R3 **22.** 243 R15 **23.** 20 R19 **24.** 11 R12 **25.** 105 R13 **26.** 114 R20 **27.** 213 R5 **28.** 263 R7 **29.** 287 R18 **30.** 23 R6 **Worksheet 5A:** factors of 12: 1, 2, 3, 4, 6, 12; factors of 18: 1, 2, 3, 6, 9, 18; common factors of 12 and 18: 1, 2, 3, 6; GCF of 12 and 18: 6 **1.** factors: 1, 2, 3, 6; 1, 2, 4, 8, 16; common factors: 1, 2; GCF: 2 **2.** factors: 1, 3, 5, 15; 1, 2, 3, 4, 6, 8, 12, 24; common factors: 1, 3; GCF: 3 **3.** factors: 1, 2, 5, 10; 1, 2, 4, 5, 10, 20; common factors: 1, 2, 5, 10; GCF: 10 **4.** factors: 1, 2, 3, 4, 6, 12; 1, 3, 5, 15; common factors: 1, 3; GCF: 3 **5.** $\frac{2}{3}$ **6.** $\frac{1}{3}$ **7.** $\frac{2}{3}$ **8.** $\frac{1}{3}$ **9.** $\frac{3}{4}$ **10.** $\frac{4}{5}$ **11.** $\frac{1}{3}$ **12.** $\frac{1}{4}$ **13.** $\frac{1}{3}$ **14.** $\frac{1}{3}$ **15.** $\frac{1}{3}$ **16.** $\frac{1}{2}$ **Worksheet 5B: 1.** factors: 1, 3, 5, 15; 1, 3, 9; common factors: 1, 3; GCF: 3 **2.** factors: 1, 3, 9; 1, 2, 3, 6; common factors: 1, 3; GCF: 3 **3.** factors: 1, 2, 4, 8; 1, 2, 4; common factors: 1, 2, 4; GCF: 4 **4.** factors: 1, 2, 3, 6; 1, 2, 3, 4, 6, 12; common factors: 1, 2, 3, 6; GCF: 6 **5.** 3 **6.** 5 **7.** 7 **8.** 7 **9.** 9 **10.** 1 **11.** 6 **12.** 5 **13.** 2 **14.** $\frac{1}{5}$ **15.** $\frac{1}{4}$ **16.** $\frac{1}{2}$ **17.** $\frac{2}{5}$ **18.** $\frac{2}{3}$ **19.** $\frac{1}{2}$ **20.** $\frac{1}{2}$ **21.** $\frac{1}{7}$ **Worksheet 6A: 1.** $\frac{2}{3}$ **2.** $\frac{3}{5}$ **3.** $\frac{1}{12}$ **4.** $\frac{2}{7}$ **5.** $\frac{7}{11}$ **6.** $\frac{9}{14}$ **7.** $\frac{1}{5}$ **8.** $\frac{1}{3}$ **9.** $\frac{3}{4}$ **10.** $1\frac{1}{3}$ **11.** $\frac{1}{2}$ **12.** $\frac{5}{8}$ **13.** $\frac{2}{3}$ **14.** $\frac{7}{10}$ **15.** $\frac{4}{9}$ **16.** $\frac{1}{2}$ **17.** $\frac{7}{9}$ **18.** $\frac{1}{8}$ **19.** $5\frac{1}{6}$ **20.** $8\frac{1}{2}$ **21.** $2\frac{3}{8}$ **22.** $5\frac{3}{8}$ **Worksheet 6B: 1.** $\frac{8}{25}$ **2.** $\frac{3}{8}$ **3.** $\frac{1}{9}$ **4.** $\frac{1}{6}$ **5.** $1\frac{5}{21}$ **6.** $10\frac{1}{12}$ **7.** $9\frac{1}{6}$ **8.** $5\frac{14}{15}$ **9.** $7\frac{2}{5}$ **10.** $\frac{14}{15}$ **11.** $13\frac{1}{3}$ **12.** $2\frac{2}{5}$ **13.** $1\frac{3}{4}$ **14.** $6\frac{5}{8}$ **15.** $5\frac{4}{5}$ **16.** $6\frac{5}{8}$ **17.** $2\frac{13}{20}$ **18.** $5\frac{7}{10}$ **19.** $3\frac{5}{6}$ **20.** $3\frac{7}{10}$

Worksheet 7A: Models will vary **1.** $1\frac{1}{2}$ **2.** 6 **3.** $8\frac{1}{3}$ **4.** $2\frac{2}{5}$ **5.** $3\frac{3}{5}$ **6.** $3\frac{1}{3}$ **7.** $\frac{12}{35}$ **8.** $\frac{9}{100}$ **9.** 4 **10.** $2\frac{2}{5}$ **11.** $1\frac{2}{3}$ **12.** $\frac{6}{35}$ **13.** $4\frac{1}{6}$ **14.** $\frac{21}{32}$ **15.** $8\frac{1}{4}$ **16.** $4\frac{6}{7}$ **17.** $\frac{10}{81}$ **18.** 3 **19.** $1\frac{1}{2}$ **20.** $7\frac{1}{2}$ **21.** $62\frac{1}{2}$ **22.** $5\frac{5}{8}$ **23.** $2\frac{1}{3}$ **24.** $2\frac{1}{7}$ **Worksheet 7B: 1.** $2\frac{2}{5}$ **2.** $1\frac{2}{3}$ **3.** $\frac{6}{35}$ **4.** $5\frac{1}{3}$ **5.** $\frac{1}{6}$ **6.** 2 **7.** $\frac{21}{32}$ **8.** $\frac{25}{42}$ **9.** $\frac{6}{25}$ **10.** $\frac{16}{25}$ **11.** $\frac{1}{6}$ **12.** $\frac{4}{45}$ **13.** $\frac{9}{28}$ **14.** $\frac{6}{7}$ **15.** $\frac{1}{2}$ **16.** $1\frac{1}{5}$ **17.** $\frac{5}{16}$ **18.** $\frac{25}{42}$ **19.** $\frac{21}{40}$ **20.** $\frac{9}{49}$ **21.** $\frac{1}{4}$ **22.** $6\frac{2}{5}$ **23.** $11\frac{1}{4}$ **24.** $8\frac{2}{3}$ **25.** $8\frac{4}{5}$ **26.** $6\frac{2}{3}$ **27.** $8\frac{4}{7}$ **28.** $1\frac{13}{20}$ **29.** $4\frac{1}{6}$ **30.** $2\frac{1}{7}$ **Worksheet 8A: 1.** 20 Models will vary for 2-7. **2.** 30 **3.** 24 **4.** 25 **5.** 6 **6.** 20

7. 24 8. 12 9. 8 10. 18 11. 24 12. 4 13. 20 14. 10 15. 9 16. 12 17. 36 18. 48 19. 32 **Worksheet 8B: 1.** 9 **2.** 4 **3.** 75 **4.** 21 **5.** 60 **6.** 21 **7.** 36 **8.** 48 **9.** 32 **10.** $11\frac{3}{7}$ **11.** 27 **12.** $10\frac{4}{5}$ **13.** $1\frac{1}{4}$ **14.** 1 **15.** $\frac{4}{5}$ **16.** $1\frac{1}{3}$ **17.** 4 **18.** $\frac{15}{16}$ **19.** $1\frac{1}{8}$ **20.** $\frac{2}{3}$ **21.** 6 **22.** $1\frac{13}{25}$ **23.** $\frac{1}{4}$ **24.** $1\frac{5}{9}$ **25.** 8 **26.** $6\frac{1}{2}$ **27.** $\frac{15}{17}$ **28.** $1\frac{5}{44}$ **29.** $1\frac{19}{32}$ **30.** $4\frac{11}{28}$ **Worksheet 9A: 1.** $\frac{2}{100}$ or $\frac{1}{50}$ **2.** $\frac{10}{100}$ or $\frac{1}{10}$ **3.** $\frac{20}{100}$ or $\frac{1}{5}$ **4.** $\frac{50}{100}$ or $\frac{1}{2}$ **5.** $\frac{41}{100}$ **6.** $\frac{355}{1000}$ or $\frac{71}{200}$ **7.** > **8.** > **9.** < **10.** < **11.** < **12.** > **13.** > **14.** < **15.** = **16.** > **17.** > **18.** < **19.** > **20.** < **21.** > **22** < **23.** < **24.** > **25.** < **26.** > **27.** > **28.** < **29.** < **30.** < **31.** > **32.** < **33.** > **34.** = **35.** > **36.** < **Worksheet 9B: 1.** > **2** > **3.** > **4.** < **5.** > **6.** < **7.** < **8.** > **9.** = **10** < **11.** > **12.** > **13.** > **14.** > **15.** < **16.** > **17.** = **18.** > **19.** 0.70; 0.77; 1.70; 7.07 **20.** 0.081; 0.8; 0.81; 1.08 **21.** 0.035; 0.35; 3.5; 30.5 **22.** 0.5; 0.55; 1.15; 2.05 **23.** 0.36; 0.8; 6.86; 14.06 **24.** 3.09; 5.93; 9.5; 39.5 **25.** 2.04; 3.20; 3.22; 4.32 **Worksheet 10A:** Estimates will vary. Rounded answers are given. **1.** 7 **2.** 7.2 **3.** 19 **4.** 11 **5.** 21 **6.** 68 **7.** 65 **8.** no **9.** no **10.** no **11.** yes **12.** yes **13.** no **14.** 7.5 **15.** 8.15 **16.** 1.2 **17.** 3.09 **18.** 2.35 **19.** 3.88 **20** 3.89 **21.** 14.36 **22.** 2.695 **23.** 17.45 **Worksheet 10B: 1.** 0.8 **2.** 8.81 **3.** 7.14 **4.** 4.16 **5.** 14.61 **6.** 1.132 **7.** 38.05 **8.** 7.14 **9.** 16.39 **10.** 4.196 **11.** 36.823 **12.** 7.203 **13.** 7.49 **14.** 106.63 **15.** 15.55 **16.** 3.2 **17.** 4.1 **18.** 54.9 **19.** 6.68 **20.** 80.136 **21.** 84.8 **22.** 80.379 **23.** 5.1 **24.** 2.2 **25.** 3.68 **26.** 2.321 **27.** 4.48 **28.** 81.07 **29.** 55.31 **30.** 3.821 **Worksheet 11A: 1.** 30.723 **2.** 21.46 **3.** 105.918 **4.** 3285.48 Estimates will vary. Possible answers are given. **5.** 24 **6.** 9 **7.** 144 **8** 126 **9.** 130 **10.** 720 **11.** 105 **12.** 600 **13.** 37 **14.** 160 **15.** 140 **16.** 180 **17.** 27 **18.** 30 **19.** 360 **20.** 400 **21.** 27 **22.** 81 **23.** .5 **24.** 2 **Worksheet 11B: 1.** 2; 4 **2.** $\frac{31}{100} \times \frac{7}{10} = \frac{217}{1000} = 0.217$ **3.** $\frac{27}{100} \times \frac{5}{100} = \frac{135}{1000} = 0.135$ **4.** 53.32 **5.** 0.0014 **6.** 19.72 **7.** 16.82 **8.** 13.87 **9.** 0.00085 **10.** 27.17 **11.** 297.56 **12.** 730.73 **13.** 41.3 **14.** 0.0087 **15.** 84.28 **16.** 14.72 **17.** 14.64 **Worksheet 12A:** Estimates will vary. Possible answers are given. **1.** about 7 **2.** about 0.4 **3.** about 7 **4.** about 1.2 **5.** about .04 **6.** about 0.4 **7.** about 0.3 **8.** about 2 **9.** 3.24 **10.** 4.36 **11.** 4.15 **12.** 23.6 **13.** 6.38 **14.** 3.58 **15.** 0.012 **16.** 7.86 **17.** 5.3 **18.** 2.149 **19.** 0.341 **20.** 2.21 **21.** 1.65 **22.** 0.003294 **23.** 0.2985 **24.** 7.34 **25.** 0.043 **26.** 2.714 **Worksheet 12B: 1.** 14.34 **2.** 4.575 **3.** 0.35 **4.** 0.55 **5.** 10.45 **6.** 2.74 **7.** 3.95 **8.** 0.97 **9.** 2.25 **10.** 0.31 **11.** 4.75 **12.** 2.55 **13.** $0.07 **14.** $0.13 **15.** $0.78 **16.** $0.64 **17.** $2.01 **18.** $13.70 **19.** $15.02 **20** $88.60 **21.** $0.59 **22.** $12.43 **23.** $8.64 **24.** $0.95 **Worksheet 13A:** Models will vary for 1-6. **7.** 55% **8.** 4% **9.** 98% **10.** 29% **11.** 5% **12.** 35%

13. 10% 14. 84% 15. 12% 16. 8% or 80% 17. 96% 18. 42% 19. 77% 20. 21% 21. 51% 22. 1% or 10% **Worksheet 13B: 1.** 75% **2.** 35% **3.** 60% **4.** 6% **5.** 58% **6.** 8% or 80% **7.** 40% **8.** 1% or 10% **9.** 0.04 **10.** 0.82 **11.** 0.21 **12.** 0.45 **13.** 0.56 **14.** 0.01 **15.** 0.83 **16.** 0.06 **17.** $\frac{3}{10}$ **18.** $\frac{9}{50}$ **19.** $\frac{1}{4}$ **20** $\frac{1}{50}$ **21.** $\frac{7}{10}$ **22.** $\frac{17}{100}$ **23.** $\frac{21}{50}$ **24.** $\frac{31}{100}$

Cumulative Practice **Practice 1 : 1.** 9 **2.** 6 **3.** 7 **4.** 7 **5.** 10 **6.** 5 **7.** 9 **8.** 17 **9.** 11 **10.** 11 **11.** 15 **12.** 8 **13.** 18 **14.** 1 **15.** 8 **16.** 10 **17.** 14 **18.** 13 **19.** 10 **20.** 12 **21.** 6 **22.** 6 **23.** 16 **24.** 8 **25.** 12 **26.** 10 **27.** 12 **28.** 13 **29.** 12 **30.** 10 **Practice 2: 1.** 4 **2.** 15 **3.** 10 **4.** 9 **5.** 9 **6.** 9 **7.** 5 **8.** 3 **9.** 17 **10.** 13 **11.** 11 **12.** 13 **13.** 5 **14.** 13 **15.** 11 **16.** 11 **17.** 4 **18.** 16 **19.** 7 **20.** 4 **21.** 15 **22.** 12 **23.** 11 **24.** 7 **25.** 2 **26.** 14 **27.** 7 **28.** 6 **29.** 5 **30.** 0 **Practice 3: 1.** 7 **2.** 7 **3.** 17 **4.** 7 **5.** 2 **6.** 9 **7.** 3 **8.** 9 **9.** 10 **10.** 13 **11.** 8 **12.** 4 **13.** 12 **14.** 5 **15.** 11 **16.** 6 **17.** 15 **18.** 5 **19.** 12 **20.** 10 **21.** 11 **22.** 1 **23.** 10 **24.** 3 **25.** 6 **26.** 14 **27.** 14 **28.** 4 **29.** 16 **30.** 9 **Practice 4: 1.** 6 **2.** 8 **3.** 2 **4.** 1 **5.** 7 **6.** 5 **7.** 3 **8.** 4 **9.** 3 **10.** 9 **11.** 3 **12.** 0 **13.** 6 **14.** 0 **15.** 5 **16.** 0 **17.** 9 **18.** 4 **19.** 9 **20.** 7 **21.** 9 **22.** 7 **23.** 5 **24.** 1 **25.** 1 **26.** 1 **27.** 9 **28.** 4 **29.** 4 **30.** 7 **Practice 5: 1.** 4 **2.** 0 **3.** 9 **4.** 8 **5.** 8 **6.** 6 **7.** 2 **8.** 1 **9.** 6 **10.** 1 **11.** 2 **12.** 0 **13.** 5 **14.** 8 **15.** 8 **16.** 9 **17.** 4 **18.** 9 **19.** 2 **20.** 7 **21.** 7 **22.** 8 **23.** 4 **24.** 1 **25.** 0 **26.** 2 **27.** 5 **28.** 2 **29.** 6 **30.** 9 **Practice 6: 1.** 7 **2.** 1 **3.** 5 **4.** 8 **5.** 0 **6.** 4 **7.** 5 **8.** 9 **9.** 9 **10.** 0 **11.** 6 **12.** 4 **13.** 5 **14.** 6 **15.** 3 **16.** 1 **17.** 8 **18.** 3 **19.** 3 **20.** 3 **21.** 1 **22.** 7 **23.** 7 **24.** 6 **25.** 5 **26.** 9 **27.** 2 **28.** 2 **29.** 6 **30.** 1 **Practice 7: 1.** 10 **2.** 4 **3.** 56 **4.** 0 **5.** 12 **6.** 18 **7.** 54 **8.** 36 **9.** 0 **10.** 14 **11.** 48 **12.** 30 **13.** 35 **14.** 15 **15.** 28 **16.** 18 **17.** 16 **18.** 9 **19.** 12 **20.** 0 **21.** 63 **22.** 35 **23.** 12 **24.** 42 **25.** 21 **26.** 24 **27.** 40 **28.** 32 **29.** 9 **30.** 45 **Practice 8: 1.** 0 **2.** 63 **3.** 25 **4.** 18 **5.** 2 **6.** 24 **7.** 12 **8.** 0 **9.** 7 **10.** 6 **11.** 64 **12.** 45 **13.** 18 **14.** 27 **15.** 9 **16.** 6 **17.** 0 **18.** 4 **19.** 49 **20.** 20 **21.** 5 **22.** 21 **23.** 54 **24.** 0 **25.** 18 **26.** 3 **27.** 42 **28.** 72 **29.** 12 **30.** 36 **Practice 9: 1.** 1 **2.** 56 **3.** 20 **4.** 18 **5.** 0 **6.** 8 **7.** 72 **8.** 8 **9.** 6 **10.** 10 **11.** 28 **12.** 0 **13.** 30 **14.** 21 **15.** 48 **16.** 12 **17.** 40 **18.** 32 **19.** 81 **20.** 0 **21.** 16 **22.** 0 **23.** 24 **24.** 12 **25.** 4 **26.** 15 **27.** 0 **28.** 27 **29.** 54 **30.** 36 **Practice 10: 1.** 6 **2.** 4 **3.** 3 **4.** 9 **5.** 0 **6.** 6 **7.** 9 **8.** 5 **9.** 1 **10.** 7 **11.** 7 **12.** 2 **13.** 5 **14.** 8 **15.** 1 **16.** 9 **17.** 3 **18.** 3 **19.** 7 **20.** 3 **21.** 9 **22.** 2 **23.** 0 **24.** 6 **25.** 3 **26.** 6 **27.** 7 **28.** 4 **29.** 5 **30.** 9 **Practice 11: 1.** 7 **2.** 8 **3.** 0 **4.** 2 **5.** 5 **6.** 8 **7.** 1 **8.** 3 **9.** 7 **10.** 2 **11.** 5 **12.** 5 **13.** 8 **14.** 6 **15.** 0 **16.** 4 **17.** 2 **18.** 3 **19.** 6 **20.** 1 **21.** 9 **22.** 8 **23.** 5 **24.** 2 **25.** 4 **26.** 0 **27.** 8 **28.** 7 **29.** 1 **30.** 5 **Practice 12: 1.** 4 **2.** 6 **3.** 3 **4.** 1 **5.** 6 **6.** 4 **7.** 5 **8.** 2 **9.** 0 **10.** 8 **11.** 0 **12.** 8 **13.** 7 **14.** 9 **15.** 8 **16.** 1 **17.** 6 **18.** 3 **19.** 9 **20.** 0 **21.** 9 **22.** 1 **23.** 4 **24.** 0 **25.** 9 **26.** 4 **27.** 2 **28.** 4 **29.** 7 **30.** 1

Name

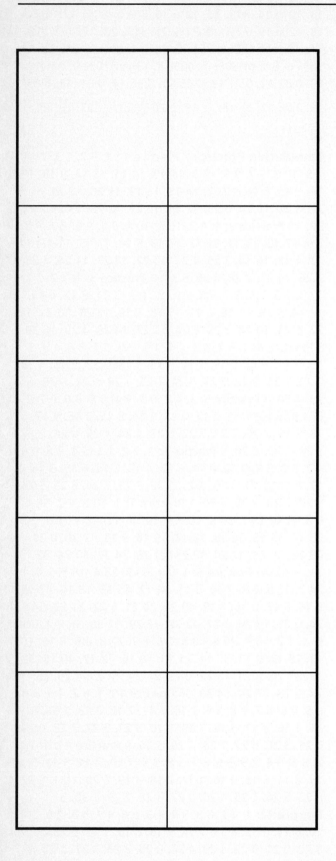

Just the Facts Support Master 1 **Ten-Frame**

Name

Name _____

Just the Facts Support Master 3   **Double Ten-Frames**

Name _____

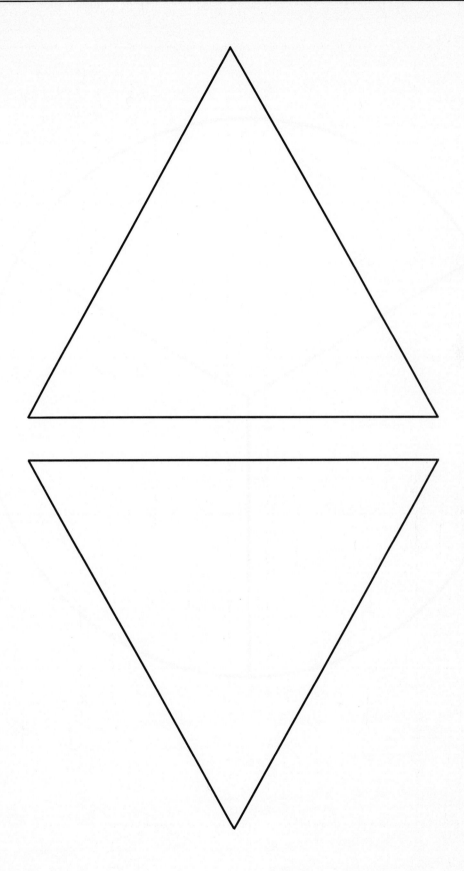

Name _____

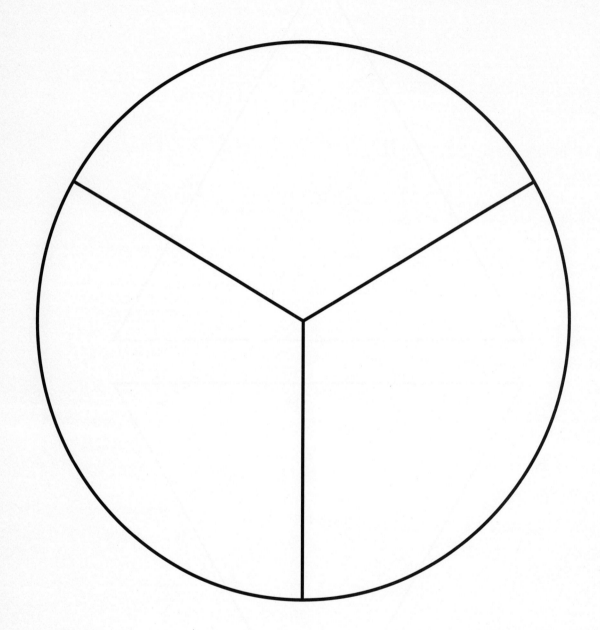

Just the Facts Support Master 5

3-Section Spinner

Name _____

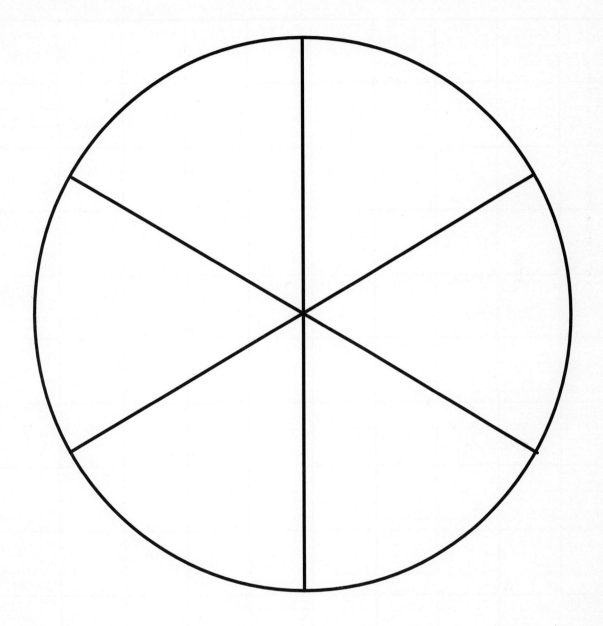

Name

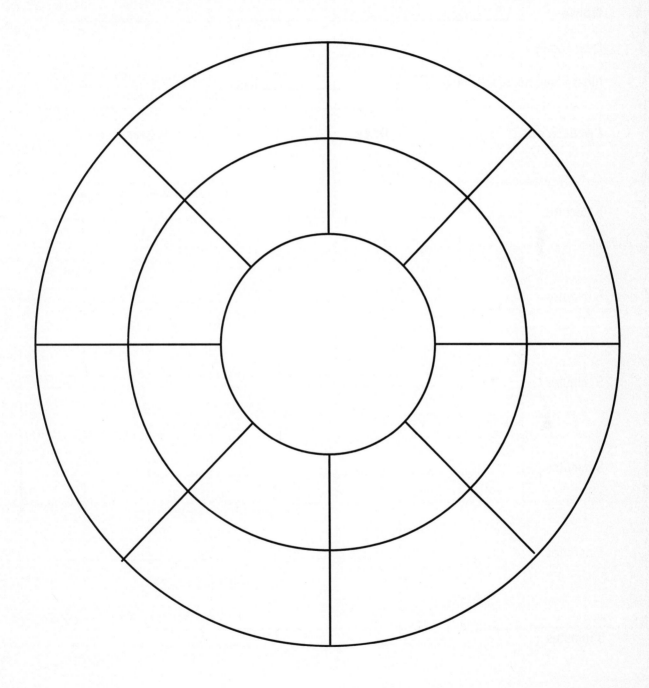

Practice Minutes Record

30 Minutes

Name _____

Dear Family,

Please help me practice my _____ facts.

....

I practiced: **Date**   **Helper**

5 minutes   _____   _____

5 minutes   _____   _____

5 minutes   _____   _____

5 minutes   _____   _____

5 minutes   _____   _____

5 minutes   _____   _____

Return completed record to your teacher.

Practice Minutes Record

60 Minutes

Name _____

Dear Family,

Please help me practice my _____ facts.

....

New Facts

I practiced:	Date	Helper
5 minutes	_____	_____
5 minutes	_____	_____
5 minutes	_____	_____
5 minutes	_____	_____
5 minutes	_____	_____
5 minutes	_____	_____

Review Facts

I practiced:	Date	Helper
5 minutes	_____	_____
5 minutes	_____	_____
5 minutes	_____	_____
5 minutes	_____	_____
5 minutes	_____	_____
5 minutes	_____	_____

Return completed record to your teacher.

Practice Minutes Record

100 Minutes

Name _____

Dear Family,

Please help me practice my _____ facts.

New Facts

I practiced:	Date	Helper
10 minutes	_____	_____
10 minutes	_____	_____
10 minutes	_____	_____
10 minutes	_____	_____
10 minutes	_____	_____

Review Facts

I practiced:	Date	Helper
10 minutes	_____	_____
10 minutes	_____	_____
10 minutes	_____	_____
10 minutes	_____	_____
10 minutes	_____	_____

Return completed record to your teacher.

Practice Minutes Record

120 Minutes

Name _____

Dear Family,

Please help me practice my _____ facts.

....

New Facts

I practiced:	Date	Helper
10 minutes	_____	_____
10 minutes	_____	_____
10 minutes	_____	_____
10 minutes	_____	_____
10 minutes	_____	_____
10 minutes	_____	_____

Review Facts

I practiced:	Date	Helper
10 minutes	_____	_____
10 minutes	_____	_____
10 minutes	_____	_____
10 minutes	_____	_____
10 minutes	_____	_____
10 minutes	_____	_____

Return completed record to your teacher.

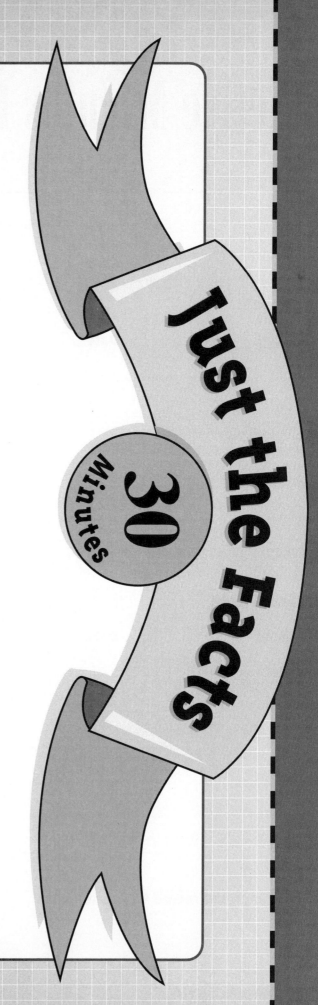

Practice Award

Just the Facts

30 Minutes

CONGRATULATIONS

on your hard work practicing your _____ facts.

_____
Student's Name

_____
Teacher's Signature

Just the Facts

60 Minutes

CONGRATULATIONS

_____
Student's Name

on your hard work practicing your _____ facts.

_____
Teacher's Signature

Practice Award

Practice Award

CONGRATULATIONS

on your hard work practicing your _____

_____
Student's Name

_____ facts.

_____
Teacher's Signature

Just the Facts

100 Minutes

Just the Facts

120 Minutes

CONGRATULATIONS

Student's Name

on your hard work practicing your _____ facts.

Teacher's Signature

Practice Award

Name _____

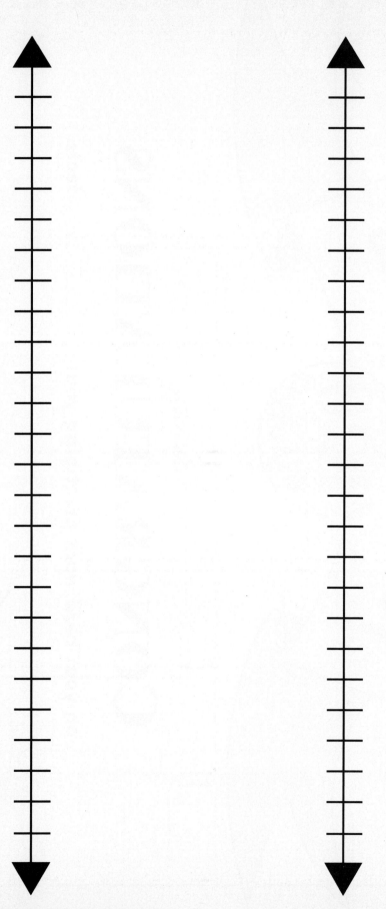

Name _____

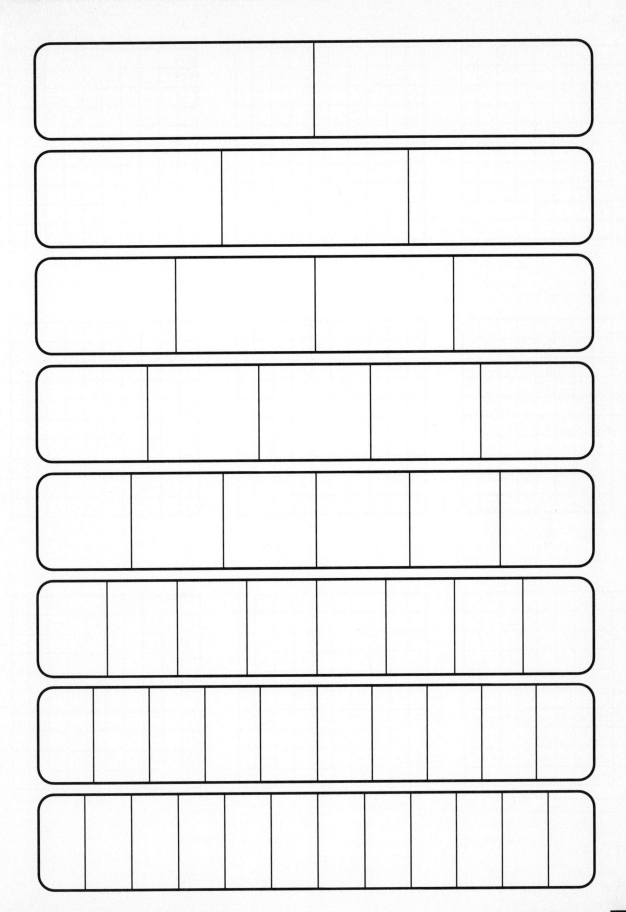

Name

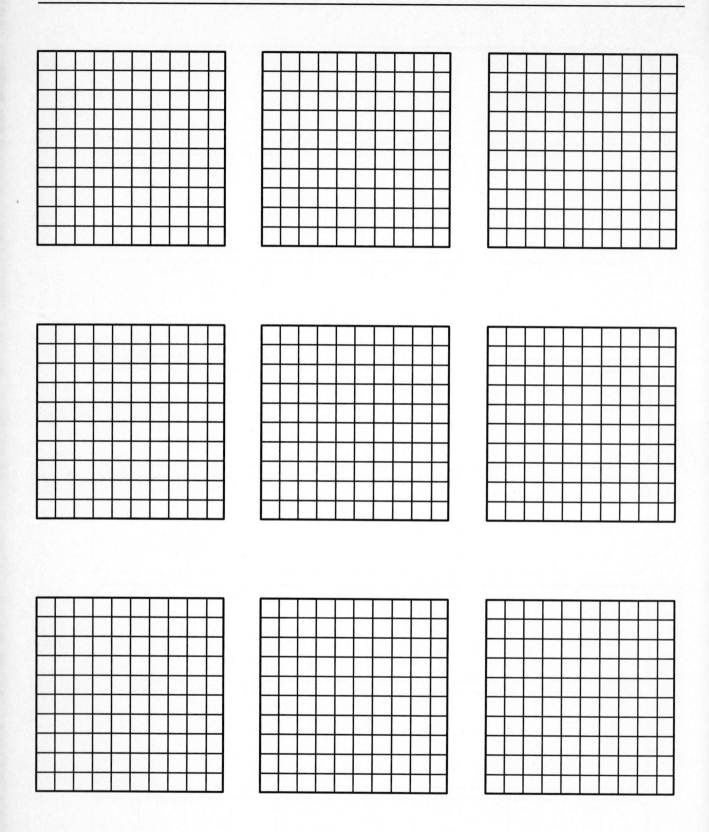

Just the Facts Support Master 19   **Hundredths Squares**

My Math Handbook

Name_____ Date _____

This is what I learned today.

_____

_____

_____

_____

_____

_____

_____

Here's an example of what I learned.

Level _____ Workshop _____